Cuba Transnational

Published in cooperation with the Cuban Research Institute
at Florida International University

Florida A&M University, Tallahassee
Florida Atlantic University, Boca Raton
Florida Gulf Coast University, Ft. Myers
Florida International University, Miami
Florida State University, Tallahassee
University of Central Florida, Orlando
University of Florida, Gainesville
University of North Florida, Jacksonville
University of South Florida, Tampa
University of West Florida, Pensacola

Cuba Transnational

Edited by Damián J. Fernández

University Press of Florida
Gainesville/Tallahassee/Tampa/Boca Raton
Pensacola/Orlando/Miami/Jacksonville/Ft. Myers

Copyright 2005 by Damián J. Fernández
Printed in the United States of America on acid-free paper
All rights reserved

10 09 08 07 06 05   6 5 4 3 2 1

Grateful acknowledgment is made to the following for permission to reprint previously published material:

"Cuando salí de La Habana" Copyright 1999 by Kelvis Ochoa Cruz. Peermusic Española, S.A./ Editorial Conspiradores, S.L./Sony ATV Music Publishing Holdings LLC for the world.

"Cubanita Descubanizada" by Gustavo Pérez-Firmat from *Bilingual Blues: Poems 1981–1994* (Bilingual Press, 1995). Reprinted by permission of Bilingual Press, Arizona State University, Tempe, AZ.

"Échate esto" by Luis Alberto Barbería-Díaz. Copyright 1997 PEERMUSIC ESPAÑOLA.

Figures 2.1 and 2.2., Tables 2.1–2.4 from "State Policy, Economic Crisis, Gender, and Family Ties: Determinants of Family Remittances to Cuba" in *Economic Geography* 80, no. 1: 63–82 (2004). Reprinted by permission of Clark University.

"Rap's Diasporic Dialogues: Cuba's Redefinition of Blackness" by Alan West-Durán in *Journal of Popular Music Studies* 16, no. 1: 4–39 (2004).

A record of cataloging-in-publication information is available from the Library of Congress.

ISBN 0-8130-2851-5

The University Press of Florida is the scholarly publishing agency for the State University System of Florida, comprising Florida A&M University, Florida Atlantic University, Florida Gulf Coast University, Florida International University, Florida State University, University of Central Florida, University of Florida, University of North Florida, University of South Florida, and University of West Florida.

University Press of Florida
15 Northwest 15th Street
Gainesville, FL 32611-2079
http://www.upf.com

Contents

List of Figures   vii

List of Tables   ix

Acknowledgments   xi

Cuba Transnational: Introduction   xiii
Damián J. Fernández

1. Revisiting the Cuban Exception: A Comparative Perspective on
Transnational Migration from the Hispanic Caribbean to the United States   1
Jorge Duany

2. From Exiles to Transnationals? Changing State Policy and the Emergence
of Cuban Transnationalism   24
Sarah A. Blue

3. Myths and Mysticism: How Bringing a Transnational Religious Lens to the
Examination of Cuba and the Cuban Diaspora Exposes and Ruptures the
Fallacy of Isolation   42
Sarah J. Mahler and Katrin Hansing

4. Gay Sex Tourism, Ambiguity, and Transnational Love in Havana   61
Gisela Fosado

5. Locas al Rescate: The Transnational Hauntings of Queer *Cubanidad*   79
Lázaro Lima

6. Cosmopolitan, International, Transnational: Locating Cuban Music   104
Susan Thomas

7. Rap's Diasporic Dialogues: Cuba's Redefinition of Blackness   121
Alan West-Durán

8. Re-reading Revolution: *Gran Literatura* and Jesús Díaz's *Las palabras
perdidas*   151
James Buckwalter-Arias

9. ¿*Venceremos o Venderemos*?: The Transnationalization and Neiman
Marxistization of the Icon of Che Guevara   165
Denise Blum

10. *La Cubanía* in Exile   179
Alma DeRojas

Contributors   205

Index   207

Figures

2.1. Emigrant relationships with Cuban relatives by migration cohort   35
2.2. Remittance sending by immediate vs. extended relatives   36

Tables

1.1. Basic demographic characteristics of the Hispanic Caribbean population in the United States, 2000   4
1.2. Migration from the Hispanic Caribbean to the United States, 1900–2000   5
1.3. Top five states for Hispanic Caribbean residents in the United States, 2000   6
1.4. Top five metropolitan areas for Hispanic Caribbean residents in the United States, 2000   6
1.5. Occupational distribution of Hispanic Caribbean workers in the United States, 1997–2000   8
1.6. Industrial distribution of Hispanic Caribbean workers in the United States, 1997–2000   8
1.7. Occupational backgrounds of Cuban and Dominican immigrants admitted to the United States, 1996–2000   9
1.8. Migrant remittances to the Hispanic Caribbean, 1970–2000   10
2.1. Importance of remittances vs. dollars earned through work for Cuban families   31
2.2. Effect of remittances on Cuban household income   32
2.3. Remittances sent by Cuban emigrants by migration period   34
2.4. Amount of remittances sent by Cuban migrant cohorts   35

Acknowledgments

Cuba Transnational inaugurates the Cuban Research Institute's (CRI) series with the University Press of Florida (UPF). In this series we hope to offer the highest interdisciplinary scholarship on Cuban and Cuban American studies emanating from CRI associates and events. I would like to acknowledge the support of a number of individuals and institutions in making the series and the book possible. At UPF, Amy Gorelick has always been an enthusiastic editor. Without her vision, the series would not have been developed. Uva de Aragón organized the fifth CRI conference, "The Nation Transnational," on which *Cuba Transnational* is based. She had the able assistance of Susie Penley and the entire CRI staff. During the preparation of the manuscript Alisa Newman, editor for the Latin American and Caribbean Center, gave me a helping hand at a crucial moment. Alma DeRojas, CRI coordinator, put the final touches on the manuscript with her usual intelligence and diligence. Of course, without the collaboration of the eleven authors in the collection and the insightful and supportive comments of two reviewers, this book would not have become a reality. Although I have edited several collections in the past, this was by far the easiest to complete, thanks to the professionalism of the contributors. Finally, I would like to extend my sincere gratitude to Cristina Eguizábal and the Ford Foundation, who have generously supported the work of the CRI throughout the years.

Cuba Transnational

Introduction

Damián J. Fernández

One of the dominant images of Cuba, especially in the United States, is that of a geographically and politically isolated nation: an off-bounds place, caught in a retro time warp of the late 1950s and 1960s, quaint, romantic, shabby chic revolutionary, a sort of social Galapagos. The general public, the media, most policymakers, and even an influential segment of academics have accepted this view without question. The myth of isolation (to quote Mahler and Hansing in chapter 3) has served as a generator of symbolic capital, both domestically and internationally, and an excuse for political actions. The discourse on "Cuba as disconnected from the world" serves to promote interests in different, and usually contending, corners. It is profitable for new national and international entrepreneurs, who entice tourists with pictures of a seemingly exotic destination. The Cuban government has employed Cuba's apparent isolation to justify idiosyncratic national policies (usually based on national security and sovereignty criteria). In turn, policies such as curtailing, if not banning, Internet access have attempted with varying degrees of success to close off Cuban society as a defensive mechanism against the outside world—protecting the elite's position of power in the process. U.S. policy has often conspired to enhance isolation, apparent and real. Washington points to the nature of Cuba's political system—out of sync with the rest of its neighbors—as evidence of the need to isolate the island. Cyclical arguments abound on both sides of the diplomatic debate.

The portrait of isolation harks back to the notion of Cuban exceptionalism insofar as the island appears to be suspended outside real space and time, beyond the parameters of global social life. Such a portrayal highlights and magnifies Cuba's uniqueness. But has Cuba inexplicably fended off the force of globalization? Is the island's society beyond the reach of contemporary dynamics? Has globalization met its match? Have transnational norms, capital, identities, and mass culture stopped short of Cuban shores? These are the questions our book poses.

This book contains a selection of papers presented at the Cuban Research Institute's 2003 conference "The Nation Transnational." The overarching purpose of the conference, held at Florida International University, was to insert the analysis of Cuba into social theories of transnationalism, hyper-modernity, and the compression of time and space. Such a perspective frames the case of Cuba not as an exception but as the norm, a variation on a theme. It should not be surprising that most of the authors included in this volume are relatively young scholars influenced by cultural studies and postmodern approaches. They represent the cutting edge of scholarship on Cuba; their work signals a sea change in the study of culture and society in Cuba. It is fitting, therefore, that this book marks the beginning of the Cuban Research Institute's Cuba Series at the University Press of Florida.

We argue that, despite its political distinctiveness, Cuba is not outside the context of transnational culture; on the contrary, Cuban society is influenced by and influences transnational actors and forces. The island is insular merely in physical geography; it is not materially or normatively insulated from social relations typical of global culture in the twenty-first century, despite governmental attempts at isolation on both sides of the Florida Straits. By conducting grassroots fieldwork in Cuba (as well as in Little Havana and South Beach, Florida, among other locations) one can detect political and geographic connections across time, space, and borders. This is precisely what the authors of this anthology have done. By tightly focusing on diverse aspects of culture and society both in Cuba and abroad, they reveal patterns of cultural transnationalism that challenge both discourses of Cuban insularity and exceptionalism and standard disciplinary approaches to international relations.

The study of Cuba's international relations has been state-centric (Domínguez 1989; Erisman and Kirk 1991; Fernández 1992). *Cuba Transnational* expands this traditional perspective by including the global social field and dynamics that are not subsumed solely by state action. Without a doubt, states constrain or facilitate transnationalism through their policies. For example, the Cuban government's decision to limit Internet access restricts the space for transnational virtual linkages and the spread of a global mass culture, whereas its promotion of tourism does the opposite. The noteworthy aspect of Cuban transnationalism is that it reveals the limits of state power. In the Cuban case, even a central command economy cannot keep global capital (that is, remittances, joint ventures, and so on) and, perhaps even more important, global culture at bay.

The bulk of the literature on transnationalism in the Caribbean context has focused on migration and the sustained connection between migrants in the United States and their home countries and villages (Guarnizo and Smith 1998; Levitt 2001; Mahler 1998). The emphasis on migration at times has neglected wider dimensions of politics (this is especially true of international relations as a discipline, particularly in the Latin American setting) and culture (although transnational cultural studies has recently done much to remedy this neglect).

While addressing the migration dimension, this book also incorporates social and cultural manifestations beyond diasporas. We are especially interested in normative maps—the new cartographies of the mind that are generated in the transnational context (Appadurai 1990).

The perspective we offer depicts a society that is both an active agent in the generation of transnationalism (for instance, through music and as a space for cultural encounters, among other avenues) as well as a "receiver" of transnational currents that Cubans reinterpret and make their own (see the example of rap music discussed in chapter 7 by West-Durán). We conceptualize transnationalism as a condition of social life characterized by economic and ideational exchanges across borders by non-state actors, individuals, organizations, and networks.

Cuba, like most nations, was born transnational; colonialism, capitalism, and slavery marked the national experience structurally as well as culturally. In the Cuban case, transnationalism was facilitated by a number of factors, among them that Havana was a major port city, Florida was a boat ride away, ties of affection developed between Cuban residents and family members in Spain and the United States, and the Cuban economy grew and modernized rapidly during parts of the twentieth century. The economic development of the island when sugar was king supported the emergence of an elite that if not transnational was cosmopolitan. Moreover, Cuban nationalism was forged in no small measure in the transnational communities of Cubans in Tampa and Key West.

Indeed one could argue that transnationalism predated nationalism in many postcolonial societies. Modern-day transnationalism, however, is not quite the same as its precedent. In modern times the breadth and depth of social relations across borders is far reaching, due in part to what Harvey (1989) has called "time-space compression." Mass media, global capitalism, and mass travel have produced a sense that "it's a small world after all." Rather than domination by a strict, overly rationalized sort of capitalism and the cultural imperialism derived from it, what we see is a much more variegated, hybrid, and interactive cultural phenomenon.

In this book we bring together cultural studies and international relations under the paradigm of transnationalism to interpret how Cuba (and Cuban society specifically) is actor and subject in a transnational social space, with material and symbolic exchanges and human networks that link the people from here and there. At the level of theory, we push the disciplinary borderline of international relations by incorporating anthropology, sociology, literature, and cultural studies at different levels of analysis and by adopting a variety of approaches to relations between nations that include people and normative, day-to-day life. Cuba is a good case study because it reveals that despite physical insularity and political barriers (domestic and international), globalization and transnationalism are part and parcel of the contemporary physical and cultural landscape.

Only by including diverse disciplines can we sense the texture of social life in transnational modernity. Only through interdisciplinarity can we understand the social dimensions of what has traditionally been called "international relations." The international relations field has been concerned mainly with how power is expressed and distributed between states. State centrism has led to the neglect of other dimensions of social life in world affairs. Other approaches that focus on institutions and economic structures tend to disregard the social bases of everyday life as well. Most attempts to connect the domestic and the foreign have fallen short insofar as the domestic is defined as lobby groups and does not include the multiple dimensions that the transnationalist lens provides. Recent scholarship on constructivism and norm diffusion, although generally highlighting elite processes, is a step in the right direction but does not offer the view of the social landscape that transnationalism provides. Therefore, this book attempts to fill in what has been missing in the study of Cuban society and its international relations by bringing in a transnational cultural perspective. The approach offers possibilities in terms of theory building and the reconceptualization of politics.

Cuba Transnational also explores the multiple ways of being Cuban at the beginning of the twenty-first century. New identity categories have emerged as a result of the economic and social conditions of the island and the place of Cuba in an international political economy and a global imaginary influenced by transnational encounters (see Fosado's and Blum's chapters, chapters 4 and 9, respectively). Our approach introduces social dynamics to what used to be state-to-state—that is, international—relations. Again, despite political walls, from our vantage point the Cuban version of transnationalism is not unlike others. Take, for example, the issue of remittances. The fact that Cuban Americans send millions of dollars to family members and loved ones on the island (estimates range from $300 million to more than $1 billion annually) has recently received considerable attention and has been met with surprise. Yet remittances should not be seen as atypical or unusual; on the contrary, they are normal in the context of diasporas and poverty-stricken homelands. Perhaps most striking is that despite political distance, emotional intimacy still commands as great (or greater) a pull on heartstrings and purse strings as political passions.

What has received less attention is that social and cultural messages—ideas, behavior, social capital—are being transmitted concurrently with financial remittances. According to Levitt (2001: 11), social remittances "are the tools with which individuals create global culture at the local level." These tools allow for the emergence of new forms of being and foster experimentation and change, individually and collectively. As the chapters in this book reveal, the processes associated with social remittances are well underway on the island, although their effect is not always transparent or easy to analyze.

The chapters demonstrate patterns of accommodation and resistance to state authority on the island and provide a panorama of the dynamics of social change despite political continuity. The book starts with two core concerns of transnationalism, migration and remittances. Jorge Duany (chapter 1) offers an overview of the Cuban migration story in contemporary times. He places the Cuban case within a Caribbean framework to show that contrary to exceptionalist interpretations of the phenomenon, Cuban migration shares a profile with the experiences of other Caribbean nations. If that is the case, then the transnational paradigm can be equally applied to the Cuban context.

In chapter 2 Sarah Blue examines the influence of remittances on the Cuban population. Based on fieldwork on the island and a solid empirical foundation, Blue argues that remittances fuel social changes, not all of which are benign; inequality is on the rise as a result of the pattern of remittances.

The following chapters offer specific expressions of how transnationalism plays out on a quotidian basis, usually at a micro level of individuals and groups, and of its consequences. For example, in chapter 3 Sarah Mahler and Katrin Hansing debunk the myth of isolation by documenting the religious ties between communities of faithful in Miami and in Cuba. These religious networks have continued to bond groups of people and in so doing put into question whether the nation is the primary or sole form of community. Such religious transnationalism has been instrumental in other contexts, such as East and West Germany, and lays the groundwork for reconciliation at the national level.

Most of the contributions are based on recent ethnographic research on aspects of transnational encounters on or outside the island. The authors address the resulting new identities (Gisela Fosado in chapter 4 and Lázaro Lima in chapter 5, among others); the emerging zones of conflict between state and society and within different social sectors, national and international (Blue, Blum, DeRojas, West-Durán); the possibility of reconciliation (DeRojas, Blue, Mahler and Hansing); the economic impact of transnationalism (Blue, Fosado, Thomas); and the mental maps that are products of transnational cultural exchange (Blum, West-Durán). Transnationalism is addressed through multiple lenses: literary analysis and discourse (Buckwalter-Arias, West-Durán, DeRojas), social networks (Mahler and Hansing), as well as images and how they circulate in a global market (Blum).

In chapters 6 and 7 Susan Thomas and Alan West-Durán, respectively, listen to the story Cuban music tells about social change. Although music is perhaps the most transnational of all the island's cultural expressions, as Denise Blum points out in chapter 9, the image of Che Guevara is also a transnational icon of choice that has been circulated and redefined by the market. Redefinitions are typical results of transnational encounters. In chapter 8 James Buckwalter-Arias rereads a classic novel of the revolution from a transnational perspective, shedding light on ideological change among island intellectuals due to global cultural politics. The book ends with a poignant (self-)analysis by Alma DeRojas. In an attempt to define herself as a *cubanita*, she reviews how interpreters of the Cuban exile experience have created and re-created the notion of Cuba from a distance. She shows us that for diasporas, identity, imagination, and heart are always transnational.

Bibliography

Appadurai, Arjun. 1990. "Disjuncture and Difference in the Global Cultural Economy." In *Global Culture: Nationalism, Globalization and Modernity*, edited by Mike Featherstone, 295–310. London: Sage Publications.

Basch, Linda, Nina Glick Schiller, and Cristina Szanton Blanc, eds. 1994. *Nations Unbound: Transnational Projects, Postcolonial Predicaments, and Deterritorialized Nation-States*. Langhorne, Pa.: Gordon and Breach.

Domínguez, Jorge I. 1989. *To Make a World Safe for Revolution*. Cambridge, Mass.: Harvard University Press.

Erisman, H. Michael, and John M. Kirk, eds. 1991. *Cuban Foreign Policy Confronts a New International Order*. Boulder, Colo.: Lynne Rienner Publishers.

Fernández, Damián J. 1992. "Opening the Blackest of Black Boxes: Theory and Practice of Decision Making in Cuba's Foreign Policy." *Cuban Studies* 22: 53–78.

Guarnizo, Luis Eduardo, and Michael Peter Smith. 1998. "The Locations of Transnationalism." In *Transnationalism from Below*, edited by Michael Peter Smith and Luis Eduardo Guarnizo, 3–34. New Brunswick, N.J.: Transaction Publishers.

Harvey, David. 1989. *The Condition of Postmodernity: An Enquiry into the Origins of Cultural Change*. Cambridge: Basil Blackwell.

Keohane, Robert O., and Joseph S. Nye Jr. 1970. *Transnational Relations and World Politics*. Cambridge, Mass.: Harvard University Press.

Levitt, Peggy. 2001. *The Transnational Villagers*. Berkeley: University of California Press.

Mahler, Sarah J. 1998. "Theoretical and Empirical Contributions Toward a Research Agenda for Transnationalism." In *Transnationalism from Below*, edited by Michael Peter Smith and Luis Eduardo Guarnizo, 64–100. New Brunswick, N.J.: Transaction Publishers.

Ong, Aihwa, and Donald M. Nonini, eds. 1997. *Ungrounded Empires: The Cultural Politics of Chinese Transnationalism*. New York: Routledge.

1

Revisiting the Cuban Exception

A Comparative Perspective on Transnational Migration from
the Hispanic Caribbean to the United States

Jorge Duany

Most studies of the Cuban exodus have portrayed it as a unique experience
with few historical or contemporary parallels in other transnational migrant
flows, even from the Hispanic Caribbean.[1] A recent example of this academic
trend is Guillermo Grenier and Lisandro Pérez's book, *The Legacy of Exile:
Cubans in the United States* (2003), which reiterates several of the dominant
themes in current research on Cuban Americans. Like many other scholars,
Grenier and Pérez underline the special legal condition of refugees from the
Cuban Revolution, as well as the unusual programs for economic assistance
established by the U.S. government. Furthermore, they argue that "even
Cuba's emigration is marked by exceptionalism. . . . Emigration has maintained an exile ethos, created a powerful ethnic enclave, and exhibits relatively
high levels of economic and political influence at both the local and national
levels" (Grenier and Pérez 2003: 34). The authors also insist on certain
"unique" elements in Cuban history, such as the rapid elimination of the indig-
enous population, the long history of Spanish colonialism, and the island's
strategic position between the Old and New Worlds. (Actually, all of these
factors apply to Puerto Rico and the Dominican Republic as well.) Writing
about the period between 1902 and 1958, Grenier and Pérez grant that "Cubans had every reason to believe they occupied a unique and privileged position in the world order, reinforcing a sense of singularity and self-importance
in relation to their Latin American and Caribbean neighbors" (p. 33).[2]

For some time, I have been arguing that Cuban migration to the United
States is not as extraordinary as some scholars would have it (Duany 1997a,
1997b, 2001). The most recent migrant wave from Cuba (roughly since 1989,
during the so-called Special Period in Times of Peace) resembles other Caribbean population flows, including its legal status (much of it undocumented),

motivations (increasingly economic), and social composition (mostly working class), as well as the use of migration as a safety valve by the Cuban government (see Aja Díaz 1999; Castro 2002; Pedraza 2000; Rodríguez Chávez 1997). Also, in 1994, at the height of the *balsero* crisis, the U.S. Coast Guard began to return undocumented immigrants to Cuba, just as it has repatriated Haitian and Dominican "boat people" for decades. Moreover, during the 1990s, Cuban émigrés sent millions of dollars to their relatives back home and thousands of them visited the island, just as Puerto Ricans and Dominicans have done with their homelands (Barberia 2002; Eckstein 2003; Eckstein and Barberia 2001). Practitioners of Afro-Cuban religions such as *santería*—not to mention Catholic, Protestant, and Jewish faiths—have increased their participation in a transnational ritual economy through visits, telephone calls, letters, and other forms of communication (Burke 2002; Knauer 2002). As Lisa Maya Knauer points out, "Although Cubans do not experience the same ease and frequency of movement between 'here' and 'there' as many New York Puerto Ricans and Dominicans do, in most cases immigration to the United States has not meant a radical rupture with family and community ties" (Knauer 2001: 22; my translation),

I am not denying that Cuban immigration differs from other cases of contemporary transnational migration. For instance, most other migrants have not developed such an antagonistic relationship with their sending states as have Cubans living abroad. Even Cubans' self-definition as exiles is rare among recent transnational communities in the United States. The Cuban economic enclave in Miami and its exile politics are distinctive experiences in U.S. immigration history. Moreover, undocumented Cubans arriving in U.S. territory are not automatically deported like other groups, but are allowed to stay under the provisions of the Cuban Adjustment Act of 1966. Nonetheless, I would argue that Cubans in the United States are better understood from a transnational perspective that recognizes their basic similarities with other immigrants and does not exaggerate their singularity. Otherwise, one runs the risk of reproducing the myth of "the unique and privileged position" of Cuba in the world and of Cuban immigrants in the United States. A broader, comparative framework would help explain the historical roots of Cuban migration, its modes of incorporation into U.S. society, the transformation of cultural identities, and effects on both home and host countries. As María de los Angeles Torres (1999: 20) writes, "The burden of 'Cuban exceptionalism' [is] somehow lessened by understanding that there are comparable situations faced by all Latino groups—including their ambivalent relationship to homeland."

The purpose of this chapter, then, is to revisit the putative Cuban exception in transnational migration. I agree with the organizers of the Fifth Conference of the Cuban Research Institute (CRI 2003) that "many aspects of our past can be rethought with a new theoretical framework," such as transnationalism. In my mind, rethinking the Cuban diaspora transnationally would entail identifying common denominators between Cubans and other Hispanic immigrants, especially Dominicans and Puerto Ricans, in the United States. It would also imply sorting out the main themes of the conference from a comparative perspective, such as the multiple identities resulting from transnational migration; the increasing significance of transnational economic networks; the linkages (or lack thereof) among states, territories, citizens, and communities; the challenges of diasporic discourses to the image of the nation as a homogenous and well-bounded entity; the efforts of transnational communities to maintain their native culture and language; and the role of transnational communities in the future of their countries of origin. These dilemmas are not unique to Cubans but are widely shared by diasporic peoples everywhere.

In this essay, I underline the parallels between Cuban and other Hispanic Caribbean migrants and their multiple relationships with their homelands. First, I compare the basic demographic and socioeconomic characteristics of the three diasporas from the Hispanic Caribbean in the United States: Cubans, Dominicans, and Puerto Ricans. Second, I highlight how transnational migrants have become key actors in the economic and political systems of the Hispanic Caribbean over the past four decades. Third, I argue that many Cubans, as well as Dominicans and Puerto Ricans abroad, have retained strong ties to their homeland, particularly through remittances and family visits. Finally, I suggest that transnational migration has expanded the territorial and cultural boundaries of the nation for many Hispanic Caribbean immigrants and, to a lesser extent, for their sending countries as well. In short, I propose that Cuba is no exception to current trends in transnational migration; on the contrary, the island is experiencing many of the same forces as other "transnational nation-states" in the region as a result of a massive and continuing exodus.[3]

The Rise of Transnational Communities

The first set of data I would like to discuss relates to the volume of the Hispanic Caribbean population in the United States (table 1.1). In the year 2000, one out of ten Cubans, one out of twelve Dominicans, and nearly one out of two Puerto Ricans were living in the United States. Furthermore, almost 30 percent of the Cubans, compared to nearly 58 percent of the stateside Puerto Ricans and 10 percent of the Dominicans, were born in the United States. The free movement of Puerto Ricans as U.S. citizens between the island and the mainland helps explain the relocation of a high share of this population abroad. In contrast,

Table 1.1. Basic demographic characteristics of the Hispanic Caribbean population in the United States, 2000

Measure	Cubans	Dominicans	Puerto Ricans
Number of persons claiming ancestry	1,241,640	764,945	3,406,178
As percentage of the population with this ancestry[a]	10.0	8.3	47.2
Number of persons born in the country of origin	872,716	687,677	1,439,674
As percentage of the group in the United States	70.3	89.9	42.3
Number of persons born in the United States	368,969	77,268	1,966,504
As percentage of the group in the United States	29.7	10.1	57.8

Source: U.S. Census Bureau (2003).

[a] Includes the population of the sending country.

Cuba and the Dominican Republic, whose migrants are foreign citizens, have much lower proportions of their people living in the United States. Thus, the Cuban population is moderately transnational with regard to place of birth and residence.

The second feature I want to stress is the timing of each diaspora. The Cuban exodus dates back to the Ten Years' War in Cuba against Spain (1868–1878) and continued until the Spanish-Cuban American War (1895–1898). Statistics for Caribbean immigration to the United States suggest several waves and spurts throughout the twentieth century, drawing successively on different sending countries. During the first two decades, Cubans dominated regional outflows; their numbers dwindled thereafter, only to rise again during the 1940s and 1950s, especially after 1959 (table 1.2). The Puerto Rican exodus took off during the 1940s, intensified in the 1950s, and regained strength in the 1980s. In the 1940s, Puerto Ricans surpassed Cubans as the largest group of Caribbean migrants in the United States. The number of Dominican migrants was relatively small until the 1960s but has increased swiftly in every decade since then. By the 1980s, Dominicans had become one of the fastest growing segments of the foreign-born population in the United States. In the 1990s, the Dominican flow continued unabated, while the Cuban and Puerto Rican flows decreased temporarily. As Max Castro (2002: 5) notes, "Recent immigration from Cuba does not enjoy a privileged position relative to other large Caribbean nations, at least quantitatively."

The third demographic feature I will compare here is the settlement patterns of the three groups. In the year 2000, more than two-thirds of all U.S. Cubans lived in Florida, whereas almost three-fifths of the Dominicans and nearly one-third of the Puerto Ricans lived in New York (table 1.3).[4] The main contrast is that Puerto Ricans are scattered more widely than Cubans and Dominicans, who cluster in a single state. The extreme geographic concentration of Cubans

Table 1.2. Migration from the Hispanic Caribbean to the United States, 1900–2000

Decade	Cubans	Dominicans	Puerto Ricans
1900–1910	44,211	—	2,000
1911–1920	25,158	—	11,000
1921–1930	15,901	—	37,075
1931–1940	9,571	1,150	8,227
1941–1950	26,313	5,627	181,699
1951–1960	78,948	9,897	432,497
1961–1970	208,536	93,292	272,791
1971–1980	264,863	148,135	1,476
1981–1990	144,578	252,035	491,361
1991–2000	169,322	335,251	255,763
Total	987,401	845,387	1,693,889

Sources: Junta de Planificación de Puerto Rico (1972–2000, 2001b); Pérez (1994); U.S. Immigration and Naturalization Service (1997–2001).

in Florida and Dominicans in New York means that, for these groups, moving abroad (to *la Yuma* or *los países*, in Cuban and Dominican colloquial speech) is practically synonymous with moving to these two states. For Puerto Ricans, migrating to the mainland (*irse pa' fuera* or *brincar el charco*) means increasingly to relocate away from *los niuyores*, especially in Florida, New Jersey, Pennsylvania, and Massachusetts.

Within their primary places of destination, Hispanic Caribbean immigrants have carved out distinctive niches, especially in the metropolitan areas of New York, northeastern New Jersey, and south Florida (table 1.4). For Cubans, the top five settlements are in Miami, New York City, Union City–West New York, Tampa, and Los Angeles. For Dominicans, New York City, Miami, Bergen-Passaic, Union City–West New York, and Boston are the leading areas.[5] Puerto Ricans cluster in New York City, Philadelphia, Chicago, Newark, and Hartford. Many of these places have more people of Hispanic Caribbean origin than the largest cities in their countries of origin. For some time now, Miami has had more Cuban residents than Santiago de Cuba, Cuba's second largest city, while New York City has had more Puerto Rican residents than San Juan, the capital, and more Dominican residents than Santiago de los Caballeros, the second largest city of the Dominican Republic. Furthermore, Southwest Miami, the South Bronx, and Washington Heights in Manhattan have some of the highest densities of Cuban, Puerto Rican, and Dominican residents in the world.

What do these demographic trends mean? Above all, they suggest the sheer magnitude of physical and cultural displacement among Cubans as well as

Table 1.3. Top five states for Hispanic Caribbean residents in the United States, 2000

	Cubans				Dominicans				Puerto Ricans		
State	Population	Pct.		State	Population	Pct.		State	Population	Pct.
Florida	833,120	67.1		New York	455,061	59.5		New York	1,050,293	30.8
New Jersey	77,337	6.2		New Jersey	102,630	13.4		Florida	482,027	14.2
California	72,286	5.8		Florida	70,630	9.3		New Jersey	366,788	10.8
New York	62,590	5.0		Massachusetts	49,913	6.5		Pennsylvania	288,557	6.7
Illinois	18,438	1.5		Rhode Island	17,894	2.3		Massachusetts	199,207	5.8

Source: U.S. Census Bureau (2003).

Table 1.4. Top five metropolitan areas for Hispanic Caribbean residents in the United States, 2000

	Cubans				Dominicans				Puerto Ricans		
City	Population	Pct.		City	Population	Pct.		City	Population	Pct.
Miami	650,601	52.4		New York	424,847	65.1		New York	837,073	24.6
New York–Union City–	46,712	3.8		Miami	36,454	4.6		Philadelphia	160,076	4.7
W. New York[a]	44,502	3.6		Bergen-Passaic	36,360	3.7		Chicago	152,045	4.5
Tampa	41,602	3.4		Union City–W. New York	33,151	3.5		Newark	86,208	2.5
Los Angeles	38,664	3.1		Boston	25,057	3.1		Hartford	82,992	2.4

Source: U.S. Census Bureau (2003).

[a]Available data are for Union and Hudson counties.

Puerto Ricans and Dominicans. The vast number of Hispanic Caribbean people living abroad points to the need to rethink the islands' traditional geopolitical boundaries. For many Caribbean migrants, New York City and Miami are symbolic extensions of their homelands. Conversely, massive immigration from the Caribbean has inscribed Havana, San Juan, and Santo Domingo in the physical and cultural landscapes of those U.S. cities. The statistics show the historical depth of Cuban as well as Puerto Rican, and to a lesser extent Dominican, transnationalism, with more than three generations of immigrants in the United States. The concentration of Cubans in Miami is not exceptional, compared to Dominicans in New York City, though it differs from the growing dispersal of Puerto Ricans in the United States.

Transnational Workers and Their Modes of Economic Incorporation

Transnational migrants from the Hispanic Caribbean in the United States have been incorporated into a labor market that is highly segmented by class, race, and ethnicity. As is well known, Cubans have fared much better economically than Dominicans or Puerto Ricans abroad. On average, Cubans tend to hold better-paying and more prestigious jobs than other immigrants from the Hispanic Caribbean (table 1.5). Conversely, Puerto Ricans and Dominicans are relatively overrepresented in lower-skilled, blue-collar, and service occupations. Although the higher educational and occupational backgrounds of Cuban immigrants help explain this trend, other factors should also be taken into account, including age and sex composition, household structure, ethnic and racial discrimination, the dynamics of regional economies, local contexts of reception, and immigration policies (González-Pando 1998; Pedraza 1996; Portes and Rumbaut 1996). In any case, most Cubans in the United States are not employed in high-status occupations such as managers and professionals, but rather in middle- and low-status ones such as sales and service jobs. The myth of the prosperous self-made entrepreneur does not reflect the occupational situation of most Cuban workers.

Hispanic Caribbean immigrants in the United States specialize in the service sector, although Cubans are slightly better represented in professional services; construction; and finance, insurance, and real estate, than are the other two groups (table 1.6). Dominicans are relatively concentrated in manufacturing, trade, and transportation. None of the three groups is well represented in agriculture, communications, or public administration. Overall, Cubans do not differ markedly from Puerto Ricans and Dominicans in their industrial locations.

The Cuban enclave in Miami accounts for much of the exiles' legendary economic success (Pérez 2001; Portes and Bach 1985; Portes and Stepick 1993). This mode of incorporation is characterized by a spatial concentration

Table 1.5. Occupational distribution of Hispanic Caribbean workers in the United States, 1997–2000 (in percentages)

Occupation	Cubans	Dominicans	Puerto Ricans
Managerial and professional	24.8	10.9	17.3
Technical, sales, and administrative support	34.8	25.4	32.2
Service	24.4	33.3	29.6
Operators, fabricators, and handlers	16.0	30.4	20.9
Total	100.0	100.0	100.0

Source: Castro and Boswell (2002).

of immigrant-owned businesses in a wide range of economic activities, employing many of their compatriots and catering primarily to the ethnic market. Although most Cubans do not work within the enclave, those who do may avoid being absorbed by the secondary labor market, consisting of low-paying, unskilled occupations with poor working conditions and few opportunities for upward mobility. Some well-educated Cubans have entered the primary labor market, consisting of well-paying and highly skilled occupations, in the larger economy. Neither Dominicans nor Puerto Ricans have developed an ethnic enclave to the same extent as Cubans in Miami. Although Alejandro Portes and Luis Guarnizo (1991) have detected an incipient Dominican enclave in New York City, most Dominican immigrants have entered the secondary labor mar-

Table 1.6. Industrial distribution of Hispanic Caribbean workers in the United States, 1997–2000 (in percentages)

Industrial sector	Cubans	Dominicans	Puerto Ricans
Agriculture, mining, and forestry	0.8	2.0	1.2
Construction	5.7	4.3	4.0
Manufacturing	12.9	17.5	16.0
Transportation	7.1	8.0	5.4
Communications	2.4	0.5	1.0
Trade	21.8	27.8	21.4
Finance, insurance, and real estate	8.5	5.7	6.9
Business and repair services	7.1	7.0	8.1
Personal services	5.0	5.3	4.1
Professional services	24.1	20.0	26.6
Public administration	4.6	1.9	5.3
Total	100.0	100.0	100.0

Source: Castro and Boswell (2002).

Table 1.7. Occupational backgrounds of Cuban and Dominican immigrants admitted to the United States, 1996–2000 (in percentages)

Occupation	Cubans	Dominicans
Professionals and technicians	11.6	15.1
Executives, administrators, and managers	2.4	4.6
Sales	8.4	5.3
Administrative support	4.7	8.0
Precision production, craft, and repair	11.7	11.7
Operators, fabricators, and laborers	45.6	36.1
Service	14.6	13.1
Farming, forestry, and fishing	1.0	6.0
Total	100.0	100.0

Source: U.S. Immigration and Naturalization Service (1997–2001).

ket, especially in the service and manufacturing industries (Duany 1994; Torres-Saillant and Hernández 1998).

One of the main reasons for the emergence of the Cuban enclave in Miami was the exodus of a large portion of the middle and upper classes from prerevolutionary Cuba, especially between 1959 and 1962. Nevertheless, the occupational profile of recent Cuban immigrants is not more privileged than that of Dominican immigrants, at least for those who move legally.[6] Table 1.7 shows that more than 60 percent of Cubans admitted to the United States between 1996 and 2000 were either unskilled blue-collar or service workers. Dominicans had a higher proportion (nearly 20 percent) of professionals and managers than did Cubans (14 percent). The two groups had similar proportions of sales and administrative workers as well as skilled blue-collar workers. Dominicans were more likely than Cubans to be agricultural workers, however. These data suggest that the contemporary Cuban and Dominican exoduses draw primarily from the urban working class, and that recent Cuban immigrants are not exceptionally well qualified compared to earlier refugees or to other recent immigrants from Latin America and the Caribbean.[7]

Remittances as a Sign of Transnational Economic Linkages

Despite their relative disadvantage in earnings (even Cubans fall below U.S. standards), Hispanic Caribbean immigrants are playing increasing economic roles in their countries of origin. Their effect can be documented most clearly in the large amount of money they send back home. Remittances—along with other transactions related to migration, such as periodical visits to and direct investment in the homeland—have created a dense transnational economic

Table 1.8. Migrant remittances to the Hispanic Caribbean, 1970–2000 (in millions of US$)

Year	Cubans	Dominicans	Puerto Ricans
1970	—	25	95
1971	—	14	90
1972	—	24	87
1973	—	24	49
1974	—	27	78
1975	—	28	101
1976	—	112	102
1977	—	124	89
1978	—	132	95
1979	—	161	111
1980	—	183	137
1981	—	183	139
1982	—	190	174
1983	—	195	151
1984	—	205	160
1985	—	242	168
1986	—	225	175
1987	—	273	267
1988	—	289	281
1989	48	301	278
1990	13	315	293
1991	18	330	290
1992	43	347	306
1993	255	721	320
1994	310	757	317
1995	537	796	361
1996	630	914	239
1997	670	1,089	278
1998	690	1,326	312
1999	700	1,519	388
2000	720	1,689	449[a]

Sources: Barberia (2002); ECLAC (2003a, 2003b); Junta de Planificación de Puerto Rico (1972–2000; 2001a); *Migration News* (2003).

a. Preliminary figure.

field between the United States and several Caribbean and Latin American countries. Although Cuba entered this field relatively late, it has become one of the major recipients of migrant remittances in the region.

As Table 1.8 shows, private money transfers to Cuba increased fifteen-fold between 1989 and 2000, from US$48 million to US$720 million. In 2000, remittances generated half as much foreign currency as tourism, the leading sector of the Cuban economy today, and represented 15 percent of the value of all exports (ECLAC 2003a). Perhaps half of all Cubans now receive dollars from their relatives living abroad (*Migration News* 1998). Ironically, anti-Castro émigrés in the United States financed much of the modest recovery of the Cuban economy in the mid-1990s. Researchers have speculated that remittances may serve as startup capital for small businesses—such as *paladares* (private family restaurants)—self-employment, and the informal sector on the island (Duany 2001; Henken 2002; Núñez Moreno 1997; Smith 1999). The rapid expansion of a remittance economy in Cuba places it squarely within a Caribbean and Latin American mold.[8]

The value of monetary transfers sent home from workers living outside of the Dominican Republic multiplied more than sixty-fold over the last three decades (table 1.8). In the year 2000, Dominicans abroad remitted nearly US$1.7 billion, exceeding the value of all national exports and representing the second largest source of foreign currency after tourism in the Dominican Republic (ECLAC 2003b). A recent survey found that one out of five Dominican households receives remittances (Lizardo 2001). Although some of this money is invested in productive activities (Portes and Guarnizo 1991), most of it is devoted to meeting basic household needs, such as food, housing, health care, and education. The Dominican Republic is one of the prime examples of Latin American and Caribbean countries that depend on migrant remittances to maintain the living standards of their populations.

Money transfers from migrants on the U.S. mainland to Puerto Rico increased almost fivefold between 1970 and 2000, from $94.7 million to $448.6 million (table 1.8). Remittances now represent nearly four-fifths of the net income generated from tourism, the second economic sector after manufacturing (Junta de Planificación de Puerto Rico 1997). Puerto Rican remittances are much less voluminous than Dominican or Cuban remittances, because Puerto Ricans send less money on a per-capita basis than either of these groups. This trend is probably related to the economic situation in each of the countries of origin, as well as other variables such as the migrants' age, birthplace, education, occupation, and income (Díaz-Briquets 1994). One should also bear in mind that federal transfer payments to Puerto Rico (more than US$7 billion in 2000) far outweigh private remittances from the U.S. mainland.

Lately, migrant-sending states have capitalized on remittances as an untapped economic resource. Although remittances have mixed effects on economic development (Meyers 1998), many countries draw on them to square their balance of payments and generate new economic ventures. Like the Mexican, Dominican, and Salvadoran governments, the Cuban government now attempts to attract and capture remittances through official channels (Barberia 2002). In 2002, the cost of sending money to Cuba was the highest in the region, averaging $28 per $250 transferred (Orozco 2002a: 13). During the

1990s, Cuba deepened its reliance on transnational migration as a much-needed source of dollars to supplement, and sometimes even replace, local wages in *pesos*. As Susan Eckstein (2003: 14) writes, "Cubans, in the main, sought remittances for the same purposes as other Third World peoples. An estimated 96 percent of Cuban remittances are used to finance family consumption." Whether remittances will support or undermine the regime currently in power is still open to debate.

Transnational Citizenship and Political Incorporation

Hispanic Caribbean immigrants differ widely in their legal status, which in turn affects their political participation in the United States. Whereas Puerto Ricans are U.S. citizens by birth, 51.2 percent of all foreign-born Cubans and 33 percent of Dominicans were naturalized citizens in 1997 (U.S. Census Bureau 1998). Puerto Ricans are often considered internal rather than international migrants because they do not cross a state frontier when they move between the island and the mainland. As refugees fleeing a Communist country, Cubans were warmly received in the United States (until August 1994). The 1966 Cuban Adjustment Act reduced their residency requirement to only a year after arrival, facilitating their naturalization. As largely unwelcome economic migrants, Dominicans have faced strong obstacles to legal immigration to the United States, and thousands have done so illegally. They have one of the lowest naturalization rates among recent migrants to the United States.

Each of the three groups has developed a distinct mode of political incorporation in the United States. Puerto Ricans have achieved a relatively high degree of electoral representation at federal, state, and local levels, even though they continue to be underrepresented in proportion to their numbers (Cruz 1996). In 2005, the U.S. House of Representatives had three Puerto Rican members (Luis Gutiérrez, José Serrano, and Nydia Velázquez), in addition to the island's resident commissioner (Luis Fortuño). New York City has had a Puerto Rican borough president (in the Bronx) and several members on the city council and in the state senate. Cubans also have elected several public officials to Congress, state assemblies, and county governments, especially since 1980. Four Cubans (Lincoln Díaz-Balart, Mario Díaz-Balart, Bob Menéndez, and Ileana Ros-Lehtinen) serve in the U.S. House of Representatives. Although the House does not yet have a Dominican member, Adriano Espaillat and Guillermo Linares have served in the New York State Assembly and New York City Council, respectively. Based on the number of elected public officials, Cubans have gained more political influence than Dominicans but not much more than Puerto Ricans.

Because of low naturalization and voter registration rates, Dominicans are not as well represented in U.S. electoral politics as are Puerto Ricans or Cubans. In 1996, however, the Dominican legislature approved the granting of dual citizenship, allowing migrants to become U.S. citizens without relinquishing their Dominican nationality (Ríos 1996). Consequently, the number of naturalized Dominicans in the United States more than doubled in the second half of the 1990s. Still, nearly twice as many Cubans as Dominicans were naturalized during the entire decade (U.S. Immigration and Naturalization Service 2001).

Until very recently, Cubans had a stronger incentive to naturalize than did other groups because they lost their jobs, properties, and rights as citizens once they left their country. Hence, Cuban emigration has been primarily a one-way flow to the United States, unlike the Puerto Rican and Dominican diasporas, which have become substantial two-way flows. Although Fidel Castro's government has made some overtures toward the Cuban community abroad, it has not yet adopted a coherent approach to such issues as repatriation and investment by expatriates. Until now, émigrés have not been authorized to set up businesses in Cuba, unlike citizens of other countries. Entry visas for Cuban Americans continue to be more expensive than for non-Cuban tourists. Travel to and from Cuba is still restricted to a small proportion of Cubans on and off the island. For those living abroad, retaining a Cuban passport offers few practical advantages.

Transnational Policies and Politics

Thousands of Puerto Ricans constantly move between the Caribbean and North America. A recent airport survey in San Juan found that a third of those interviewed had traveled at least four times between Puerto Rico and the United States in the previous two years (Hernández and Scheff 1997). The 2000 census found that 112,788 persons who had lived in the United States in 1995 had moved to the island before the census was completed (U.S. Census Bureau 2003). Similarly, Dominicans are increasingly traveling back and forth to the Dominican Republic, as tourists, returnees, or circular migrants (Weyland 1998). Whereas few Cubans have returned recently to live in their homeland,[9] family visits to Cuba have become common for Cuban migrants as well. Between 1990 and 1999, the number of Cuban American visitors to Cuba rose from 7,000 to more than 140,000. By 1999, at least one out of ten émigrés had traveled back to Cuba (Eckstein and Barberia 2001). The main difference between Cubans and other migrants is that such visits are usually shorter and more infrequent for Cubans.

Another parallel in the transnational movement of people from the three islands is the sending state's approach toward emigration. Until the 1990s, Cuba curtailed emigration by age, gender, and occupation, but the prolonged economic crisis prompted a relaxation of the requirements for moving abroad

(Hernández 1995; Martín and Pérez 1998; Rodríguez Chávez 1997). For example, Cubans may now live temporarily in another country without losing the right to return home. By 1996, the Cuban government had issued about 10,000 permits for temporary residence abroad (Aja Díaz 1999: 11). As Lorena Barberia (2002: 25) notes, "Cubans who legally leave the island are no longer required to consider migration as permanent." Still, because of ideological tensions between Havana and Miami since 1959, the Castro government has tended to treat Cuban Americans with suspicion and animosity (and vice versa). Politically, the socialist regime consistently has used emigration as a way of exporting dissidence (Pedraza-Bailey 1985). In turn, the U.S. government encouraged Cuban immigration as a symbolic resource in the Cold War against Communism.

Since World War II, most Caribbean states have openly or covertly stimulated the relocation of surplus labor abroad. Puerto Rico's commonwealth government sponsored migration as part of its development strategy, Operation Bootstrap, during the 1950s (Stinson-Fernández 1996). In the Dominican Republic, Joaquín Balaguer's first administration (1966–1978) also used emigration to export political dissidents and excess workers (Torres-Saillant and Hernández 1998). For decades, Puerto Rican and Dominican planners and decision-makers viewed outmigration as a safety valve for demographic and economic pressures, such as overpopulation and unemployment. In the 1990s, Cuba followed suit. Migration and remittances have become two of the most common survival strategies of the Cuban people since the onset of the economic crisis in 1989.[10]

Postrevolutionary Cuba traditionally exemplified a "disinterested and denouncing state" that treated its migrants as if they no longer belonged to the homeland (Levitt and Glick Schiller 2003). During the 1990s, however, the Cuban government attempted to "normalize" its tortuous relations with the diaspora. As Eckstein (2003: 19) points out, "Cuba followed a growing trend among Third World governments, including those of the Dominican Republic and El Salvador, to reclaim their emigrant population." In 1994, Cuba established an office on the affairs of the Cuban community abroad under the Ministry of Foreign Relations. In 1995, the ministry launched a glossy magazine called *Correo de Cuba*, subtitled "the journal of the Cuban community," to publicize its activities. In June of the same year, the Cuban Union of Writers and Artists and the University of Havana cosponsored a symposium on national culture and identity, attended by twenty Cuban intellectuals living abroad (Unión de Escritores y Artistas Cubanos and Universidad de la Habana 1995). In November, the second "Nation and Emigration" conference in Havana gathered 357 representatives of the Cuban diaspora from thirty-seven countries (Aja Díaz 1999: 12). Nonetheless, efforts to extend the dialogue between Cubans on and off the island have proved feeble so far. For four decades, a policy of open confrontation has prevailed, except for two brief episodes in the late 1970s and mid-1990s (Torres 1999). It is probably necessary for the U.S. and Cuban governments to renew diplomatic relations before the émigrés can coexist peaceably with the current regime on the island.

The Dominican Republic has moved much farther than Cuba toward reclaiming its transnational community by allowing dual citizenship, reforming electoral laws, and recognizing the voting rights of Dominicans abroad. Like other countries in the Caribbean basin, such as Mexico, Colombia, and El Salvador, the Dominican Republic has enacted a constitutional amendment permitting dual citizenship (Ríos 1996). To the extent that the authority of the Dominican government "extends beyond the state's territorial boundaries and incorporates dispersed populations" (Glick Schiller and Fouron 2001: 20), it can be considered a "transnational nation-state" (Levitt and Glick Schiller 2003).

Despite its lack of sovereignty, the Puerto Rican government has acted as a transnational intermediary for its migrants for most of the twentieth century (Meléndez 1997). To serve its "migrant citizens," the Puerto Rican government set up several agencies on the U.S. mainland: the Identification and Employment Bureau (1930–1948); the Puerto Rico Office of Information (1945–1949); the Migration Division of the Department of Labor (1948–1989); and the Department of Puerto Rican Community Affairs in the United States (1989–1993). Among other initiatives, these agencies established an agricultural contract labor program, publicized job opportunities for Puerto Ricans in the United States, lobbied for the rights of migrant workers, negotiated low airfares between the island and the mainland, sponsored voter registration campaigns, and helped organize Puerto Rican communities abroad (Lapp 1990; Stinson-Fernández 1996). Of the three cases under consideration, Puerto Rico displays the longest-standing and widest variety of transnational migrant politics. As such, it could be considered a transnational colonial state.

Public Discourses of Transnational Migrants

Public opinion toward migration is surprisingly similar throughout the Hispanic Caribbean. In all three societies, transnational migrants are often viewed with a mixture of fear and admiration, envy and estrangement, familiarity and suspicion. For orthodox nationalists, leaving the country represents a betrayal of the homeland. For working-class families, migration is often a key survival strategy under harsh economic conditions. For the middle classes, it might be a way to maintain or improve social status. Each country has developed an ambivalent discourse on migration to the United States.

Until the 1990s, public rejection of migrants was strongest in Cuba, where the revolutionary government branded them as *gusanos* (worms). Using Cold

War rhetoric, Castro scorned the exiles as counterrevolutionary, reactionary, expatriate, elitist, corrupt, selfish, and pro-American. During the 1980 Mariel boatlift, official propaganda stigmatized the émigrés as *escoria* (scum), antisocial, and lumpen. After the 1978 dialogue with Cuban émigrés, Castro began to call them members of "the Cuban community abroad." Today, public discourse often uses the neutral term "emigration" rather than the emotionally charged "exile." Popular attitudes and practices toward émigrés in Cuba are more favorable than before, thus moving closer to Hispanic Caribbean standards (Hernández 1995; Martín and Pérez 1998; Martínez et al. 1996; Rodríguez Chávez 1997). It is no longer taboo to cultivate ties with relatives in the diaspora; such ties are now actively encouraged in Cuba. As a popular joke in Spanish goes, one must have *fe* (literally meaning faith, but also *familiares en el exterior*, or relatives abroad) to make ends meet. In 1996, as many as 436,277 Cubans—about 4 percent of the island's population—applied for the U.S. visa lottery in Havana. Informed sources estimate that at least half a million more Cubans would move to the United States if they could (Aja Díaz 1999). Daily life during the Special Period continues to be a struggle for survival that many would prefer to wage abroad.[11]

The migrants themselves have rejected negative stereotypes and sought alternative ways of asserting their identity. First-generation Cubans in the United States insisted that they were in exile, but the second generation prefers the hyphenated form Cuban-Americans (Pérez 2001). One of the crucial ideological transformations among Cubans abroad has been their shift in self-perception from exiles to immigrants to ethnics, a process still underway (García 1996; Pérez Firmat 1994; Torres 1999). For years, Dominican migrants were considered *dominicanos ausentes* (literally, absent Dominicans) or, more pejoratively, Dominican Yorks). During my fieldwork in New York's Dominican community of Washington Heights, I found that most immigrants disliked the categories Dominican York and Dominican American, and instead favored calling themselves simply Dominican (Duany 1994). While their descendants are slowly embracing the Dominican American label (Torres-Saillant and Hernández 1998), the official term in the Dominican Republic is now *dominicanos residentes en el exterior* (Dominicans living abroad). Of the three groups, Puerto Ricans are the most insistent on non-compound terminology. Perhaps because "Puerto Rican American" seems redundant or because they resist becoming another ethnic minority, stateside Puerto Ricans continue to define themselves primarily as *puertorriqueños* or *boricuas*. Except for some artists, writers, and intellectuals, Puerto Ricans in New York seldom use the derisive term Nuyorican. Despite their colonial status (or precisely because of it), Puerto Rican migrants seem more eager to assert their national identity than either Cubans or Dominicans, who come from independent countries (see de la Garza et al. 1992).

The migrants' reception in the United States has varied considerably from group to group and from time to time. Many Americans initially viewed Cubans more favorably than Puerto Ricans and Dominicans, who have been stigmatized for decades as lazy, violent, poor, and dark-skinned strangers. During the 1960s, the U.S. mass media tended to portray Cubans as hard-working, independent, law-abiding, and successful refugees from Communism (Pedraza-Bailey 1985). But after the 1980 Mariel exodus, Cuban émigrés were increasingly depicted as undesirable, economically deprived, and criminally prone aliens (García 1996; Masud-Piloto 1996; Pedraza 1996). In 1994, the Clinton administration reversed the "open-door" policy toward undocumented Cuban immigrants detained at sea but allowed them to apply for asylum if they made it to U.S. territory (the "wet foot–dry foot" policy). This change signaled the beginning of the end of the special treatment of Cubans and began their symbolic "Caribbeanization" or "Haitianization" (*Migration News* 1994). The new measure reflected a profound shift in U.S. public opinion toward Cuba in the post–Cold War period. Most Americans no longer consider Cuban exiles exceptional, if they ever did, compared to other Latin American and Caribbean immigrants.

Conclusion

The transnational framework helps to raise important issues about recent migration from Cuba to the United States. First, it serves to blur the artificial boundaries—including political ones—between sending and receiving communities that have been bridged through long-standing networks of social, economic, political, and cultural exchange. Second, it calls attention to the fact that Cuban lives may take place simultaneously in two or more separate but connected spaces, markets, polities, and often languages. Third, it locates contemporary Cuban migration within the regional and worldwide circulation of capital, labor, commodities, and technology, as well as images, identities, and practices. Finally, it encourages the interrogation of traditional discourses on statehood, nationality, citizenship, ethnicity, and language, grounded in nineteenth-century notions of sovereign, territorially bound, and culturally homogeneous entities. As I have argued elsewhere, "Recovering *lo cubano* within the diaspora forces one to transcend the insular territory, the juridical definitions of citizenship and nationality, the traditional postures of political ideology, and even the standard opposition between Spanish and English" (Duany 2000: 36).

At the same time, a comparative perspective on Hispanic Caribbean migration can help scholars rethink the distinctive features of Cuban transnationalism. Extensive transnational linkages between Cuba and the United States were forged during the nineteenth century (Pérez 1999). Furthermore, the massive movement of people from Cuba was initiated well before 1898, when the United States secured its hegemony over the Caribbean basin. More than many other countries of the region, Cuba developed an extreme form of economic and political dependence on its powerful neighbor to the north. (Only Puerto Rico, Mexico, and perhaps Panama have had such close links with the United States.) After 1959, the Cuban government adopted a "disinterested and denouncing" stance toward its émigrés, despising them as traitors to the homeland (Levitt and Glick Schiller 2003). As political refugees who until 1978 could not go back home, Cubans developed a more adversarial relationship to their sending state than either Dominicans or Puerto Ricans. Most Cubans now leave their country for economic reasons, however, much like other migrant workers. Many visit their families when they can and send money back home, as do Dominicans and Puerto Ricans. Transnational households and kinship networks, ambivalent attachments to home and host countries, hybrid cultural practices, and multiple identities characterize the Cuban diaspora as much as the Puerto Rican or Dominican diasporas.

Do Cubans, then, occupy a unique and privileged position in contemporary transnational migration? My basic argument throughout this essay has been that they do not. The most recent migrant wave from Cuba fits a well-established regional pattern that draws on relatively young, urban members of the working class seeking higher wages and standards of living through both legal and illegal means (Aja Díaz 1999; Rodríguez Chávez 1997). Cubans no longer enjoy a favored status under U.S. immigration laws, although the Cuban Adjustment Act is still in place and the "wet foot–dry foot" policy applies to undocumented Cubans. In turn, the Cuban government has become less "disinterested and denouncing" of its diaspora, partly because of the economic significance of remittances and family visits to Cuba, although it is not as openly accepting as the Puerto Rican and Dominican governments. More important for my purposes is that Cubans, like other Hispanic Caribbean migrants, have spun a dense web of social, economic, political, cultural, and even religious ties with their homeland (Burke 2002; Knauer 2002). Like Puerto Ricans and Dominicans, many Cubans abroad aspire to sustain a meaningful connection to their country of origin, even if they disagree with the Castro regime. This effort bodes well for any future attempts at reconciliation between Cubans on and off the island. For myself, I find intellectual comfort in the hope that sharing the immigrant experience with fellow travelers can lighten the burden of Cuban exceptionalism. Fortunately, we are not alone in our journeys back and forth.

Notes

1. The literature on Cuban migration to the United States is voluminous and growing. A sampling of recent works on the topic would include Aja Díaz (1999), García (1996), González-Pando (1998), Martínez et al. (1996), Masud-Piloto (1996), Pedraza

(1996, 2000), Pérez (1994, 2001), Pérez Firmat (1994), Portes and Stepick (1993), Rodríguez Chávez (1997), and Torres (1999). One of the key features of the bibliography is its narrow single-case approach that pays little attention to the comparative dimensions of the Cuban exodus (for important exceptions to this trend, see Pedraza-Bailey 1985; and Portes and Bach 1985).

2. For a recent overview of the historical roots of Cuban exceptionalism, see Whitehead (2003). For a critical position, see Buscaglia-Salgado (2002), who faults Cuban American historian Louis Pérez (1999) for promoting "the myth of Cuban primacy and uniqueness" in his account of U.S.-Cuban relations since the nineteenth century.

3. Nina Glick Schiller and Georges Fouron (2001: 19–20) define a transnational nation-state as "the reconstitution of the concept of the state so that both the nation and the authority of the government it represents extend beyond the state's territorial boundaries and incorporate dispersed populations" (see also Levitt and Glick Schiller 2003).

4. In addition, the 2000 Census enumerated 19,021 Cuban-born persons and 61,455 Dominican-born persons living in Puerto Rico (U.S. Census Bureau 2003).

5. Were Puerto Rico included in this calculus, the San Juan metropolitan area would have the second largest number of Dominican residents (54,711) in U.S. territory (U.S. Census Bureau 2003).

6. Comparable data on recent Puerto Rican immigrants are unavailable.

7. Other studies have confirmed that the average educational levels of Cuban immigrants have declined over time (Pedraza 1996; Rodríguez Chávez 1997).

8. For a recent comparative assessment of the impact of remittances on Central American and Caribbean countries, including Cuba, see Orozco (2002b).

9. A prominent example is that of Eloy Gutiérrez Menoyo, founder of the anti-Castro group Cambio Cubano. In August 2003, he decided to stay in Cuba after a brief family visit.

10. The other basic options have been self-employment or participation in the growing informal sector, including a huge black market that often provides services and goods stolen from state enterprises. Cubans commonly refer to such practices on the margins of the law as *resolver, inventar,* or *bisnear* (Holgado Fernández 2000).

11. Recent ethnographic fieldwork has documented the everyday difficulties of ordinary Cubans, such as the lack of sufficient food, the long lines to obtain rationed goods, the deteriorating housing stock, the collapse of public transportation, and the constant power outages (Holgado Fernández 2000; Rosenthal 1997). Social inequality has intensified due to economic reforms introduced by the Cuban government, especially the legalization of the U.S. dollar in 1993.

Bibliography

Aja Díaz, Antonio. 1999. "La emigración cubana en los años noventa." *Cuban Studies* 30: 1–25.

Barberia, Lorena. 2002. "Remittances to Cuba: An Evaluation of Cuban and US Government Policy Measures." <http://web.mit.edu/cis/www/migration/pubs/rrwp/15_remittances.doc>.

Burke, Nancy. 2002. *Pre-Paid Phone Cards, "Cosas," and Photos of the Saints: Trans-*

national Santería Practices in a Southwest City. Latin American Institute Research Paper 38. Albuquerque: University of New Mexico.

Buscaglia-Salgado, José F. 2002. "Leaving Us for Nowhere: The Cuban Pursuit of the 'American Dream.'" *The New Centennial Review* 2, no. 2: 285–98.

Castro, Max. 2002. *The New Cuban Immigration in Context.* North-South Center Paper, no. 58. Miami: University of Miami.

Castro, Max, and Thomas D. Boswell. 2002. *The Dominican Diaspora Revisited: Dominicans and Dominican-Americans in a New Century.* North-South Paper, no. 53. Miami: University of Miami.

CRI (Cuban Research Institute, Florida International University). 2003. Fifth CRI Conference on Cuban and Cuban American Studies: Call for Papers and Panels.

Cruz, José. 1996. "Los puertorriqueños y la política en los Estados Unidos: una evaluación preliminar." *Revista de Ciencias Sociales* (Nueva Época) 1: 86–111.

De la Garza, Rodolfo O., Louis DeSipio, F. Chris García, John García, and Angelo Falcón. 1992. *Latino Voices: Mexican, Puerto Rican, and Cuban Perspectives on American Politics.* Boulder, Colo.: Westview Press.

Díaz-Briquets, Sergio. 1994. "Emigrant Remittances in the Cuban Economy: Their Significance during and after the Castro Regime." In *Cuba in Transition,* vol. 4. Proceedings of the Fourth Annual Meeting of the Association for the Study of the Cuban Economy. <http://www1.lanic.utexas.edu/la/cb/cuba/asce/cuba4/diaz.html>.

Duany, Jorge. 1994. *Quisqueya on the Hudson: The Transnational Identity of Dominicans in Washington Heights.* Dominican Studies Research Monograph, no. 1. New York: CUNY Dominican Studies Institute.

———. 1997a. "Blurred Frontiers: Transnational Migration from the Hispanic Caribbean to the United States." Paper presented at the Caribbean and the United States since 1898: 100 Years of Transformation conference, October 13–15, Lehman College, City University of New York, Bronx, New York.

———. 1997b. "The Recent Cuban Exodus in Comparative Caribbean Perspective." In *Cuba and the Caribbean: Regional Issues and Trends in the Post–Cold War Era,* edited by Joseph Tulchin, Andrés Serbín, and Rafael Hernández, 141–61. Washington, D.C.: Woodrow Wilson International Center for Scholars.

———. 2000. "Reconstructing Cubanness: Changing Discourses of National Identity on the Island and in the Diaspora during the Twentieth Century." In *Cuba, the Elusive Nation: Interpretations of National Identity,* edited by Damián J. Fernández and Madeline Cámara Betancourt, 17–42. Gainesville: University Press of Florida.

———. 2001. "Redes, remesas y paladares: la diáspora cubana desde una perspectiva transnacional." *Nueva Sociedad* 174: 40–51.

Eckstein, Susan. 2003. *Diasporas and Dollars: Transnational Ties and the Transformation of Cuba.* <http://web.mit.edu/cis/www/migration/pubs/rrwp/16_eckstein.html>.

Eckstein, Susan, and Lorena Barberia. 2001. *Cuban American Cuba Visits: Public Policy, Private Practices.* <http://web.mit.edu/cis/www/migration/pubs/mellon/5_eckstein-barberia.html>.

ECLAC (Economic Commission on Latin America and the Caribbean). 2003a. *Cuba: evolución económica durante 2002 y perspectivas para 2003.* <http://www.eclac.cl/publicaciones/mexico/6/lcmexl566/lcmexl566e-completo.pdf>.

———. 2003b. *República Dominicana: evolución económica durante 2002 y perspectivas para 2003*. <http://www.eclac.cl/publicaciones/mexico/5/lcmexl565/lcmexl565e-completo.pdf>.

García, María Cristina. 1996. *Havana USA: Cuban Exiles and Cuban Americans in South Florida, 1959–1994*. Berkeley: University of California Press.

Glick Schiller, Nina, and Georges Eugene Fouron. 2001. *Georges Woke Up Laughing: Long-Distance Nationalism and the Search for Home*. Durham, N.C.: Duke University Press.

González-Pando, Miguel. 1998. *The Cuban Americans*. Westport, Conn.: Greenwood.

Grenier, Guillermo J., and Lisandro Pérez. 2003. *The Legacy of Exile: Cubans in the United States*. Boston: Allyn and Bacon.

Henken, Ted. 2002. "'Vale Todo' (Anything Goes): Cuba's Paladares." In *Cuba in Transition*, vol. 12. Proceedings of the Twelfth Annual Meeting of the Association for the Study of the Cuban Economy. <http://lanic.utexas.edu/project/asce/pdfs/volume12/henken.pdf>.

Hernández, David, and Janet Scheff. 1997. "Puerto Rican Ethnicity and U.S. Citizenship on the Puerto Rico–New York Commute." Paper presented at the Twentieth International Congress of the Latin American Studies Association, April 17–19, Guadalajara, Mexico.

Hernández, Rafael. 1995. "Cuba y los cubano-americanos: el impacto del conflicto E.E.U.U.-Cuba en sus relaciones presentes y futuras." *Cuadernos de Nuestra América* 12, no. 23: 4–47.

Holgado Fernández, Isabel. 2000. *¡No es fácil! Mujeres cubanas y la crisis revolucionaria*. Barcelona: Icaria.

Junta de Planificación de Puerto Rico. 1972–2000. *Estadísticas socioeconómicas*. San Juan: Junta de Planificación de Puerto Rico.

———. 2001a. *Balanza de pagos: años fiscales 1996–2000*. <http://www.jp.gobierno.pr/>.

———. 2001b. "Movimiento de pasajeros entre Puerto Rico y el exterior: años fiscales 1990–2000." Programa de Planificación Económica y Social, Negociado de Análisis Económico, Junta de Planificación de Puerto Rico, San Juan.

Knauer, Lisa Maya. 2001. "Afrocubanidad translocal: la rumba y la santería en Nueva York y la Habana." In *Culturas encontradas: Cuba y los Estados Unidos*, edited by Rafael Hernández and John H. Coatsworth, 11–31. Havana: Centro de Investigación y Desarrollo de la Cultura Cubana Juan Marinello; Cambridge, Mass.: David Rockefeller Center for Latin American Studies, Harvard University.

———. 2002. "Tourism, Santería, and the Cultural Economy of Race." Paper presented at the Fourth Conference of the Cuban Research Institute, March 6–9, Florida International University, Miami.

Lapp, Michael. 1990. "Managing Migration: The Migration Division of Puerto Rico and Puerto Ricans in New York City, 1948–1968." Ph.D. diss., Johns Hopkins University, Baltimore.

Levitt, Peggy, and Nina Glick Schiller. 2003. *Transnational Perspectives on Migration: Conceptualizing Simultaneity*. <http://www.peggylevitt.org/pdfs/cncptualzng_smltaneity.pdf> .

Lizardo, Freddy. 2001. *Altas las remesas en los últimos años.* . . <http://www.intec. edu.do/~indes>.

Martín, Consuelo, and Guadalupe Pérez. 1998. *Familia, emigración y vida cotidiana en Cuba.* Havana: Editora Política.

Martínez, Milagros, Blanca Morejón, Antonio Aja, Magaly Martín, Guillermo Millán, Marta Díaz, Inalvis Rodríguez, Lourdes Urrutia, and Consuelo Martín. 1996. *Los balseros cubanos: un estudio a partir de las salidas ilegales.* Havana: Editorial de Ciencias Sociales.

Masud-Piloto, Félix R. 1996. *From Welcomed Exiles to Illegal Immigrants: Cuban Migration to the United States, 1959–1995.* Lanham, Md.: Rowman and Littlefield.

Meléndez, Edgardo. 1997. "Transnational Puerto Rican Politics: Unresolved Issues and Research Problems." Paper presented at the Caribbean Diaspora: The Current Situation and Future Trends workshop, May 2, University of Puerto Rico, Río Piedras.

Meyers, Deborah Waller. 1998. *Migrant Remittances to Latin America: Reviewing the Literature.* Washington, D.C.: Inter-American Dialogue.

Migration News. 1994. "U.S. Sets Quota for Cuban Immigrants," vol. 1, no. 9 (October). <http://migration.ucdavis.edu/mn/more.php?id=436_0_2_0>.

———. 1998. "Cuba/Caribbean: Immigration, Remittances," vol. 5, no. 1 (January). <http://migration.ucdavis.edu/mn/more.php?id=1425_0_2_0>.

———. 2003. "Remittances: Dominican Republic." <http://migration.ucdavis.edu/mn/ data/remittances/remittances.htm>.

Núñez Moreno, Lilia. 1997. "Más allá del cuentapropismo en Cuba." *Temas* (Havana) 11: 41–50.

Orozco, Manuel. 2002a. "Challenges and Opportunities of Marketing Remittances to Cuba." <http://www.thedialogue.org/publications/country_studies/remittances/ Cuba_remittances.pdf>.

———. 2002b. "Globalization and Migration: The Impact of Family Remittances to Latin America." *Latin American Politics and Society* 44, no. 2: 41–66.

Pedraza, Silvia. 1996. "Cuba's Refugees: Manifold Migrations." In *Origins and Destinies: Immigration, Race, and Ethnicity in America*, edited by Silvia Pedraza and Rubén G. Rumbaut, 263–79. Belmont, Calif.: Wadsworth.

———. 2000. "The Last Wave: Cuba's Contemporary Exodus—Political or Economic Immigrants?" In *Cuba in Transition*, vol. 10. Proceedings of the Tenth Annual Meeting of the Association for the Study of the Cuban Economy. <http://lanic.utexas.edu/ la/cb/cuba/asce/cuba10/pedraza.pdf>.

Pedraza-Bailey, Silvia. 1985. *Political and Economic Migrants in America: Cubans and Mexicans.* Austin: University of Texas Press.

Pérez, Lisandro. 1994. "Cuban Catholics in the United States." In *Puerto Rican and Cuban Catholics in the U.S., 1900–1965*, edited by Jay P. Dolan and Jaime R. Vidal, 147–247. Notre Dame, Ind.: University of Notre Dame Press.

———. 2001. "Growing Up in Cuban Miami: Immigration, the Enclave, and New Generations." In *Ethnicities: Children of Immigrants in America*, edited by Rubén G. Rumbaut and Alejandro Portes, 91–125. Berkeley: University of California Press.

Pérez, Louis A., Jr. 1999. *On Becoming Cuban: Identity, Nationality, and Culture.* Chapel Hill: University of North Carolina Press.

Pérez Firmat, Gustavo. 1994. *Life on the Hyphen: The Cuban-American Way*. Austin: University of Texas Press.

Portes, Alejandro, and Robert L. Bach. 1985. *Latin Journey: Cuban and Mexican Immigrants in the United States*. Berkeley: University of California Press.

Portes, Alejandro, and Luis E. Guarnizo. 1991. *Capitalistas del trópico: la inmigración en los Estados Unidos y el desarrollo de la pequeña empresa en la República Dominicana*. Santo Domingo: FLACSO.

Portes, Alejandro, and Rubén G. Rumbaut. 1996. *Immigrant America: A Portrait*. 2nd ed. Berkeley: University of California Press.

Portes, Alejandro, and Alex Stepick. 1993. *City on the Edge: The Transformation of Miami*. Berkeley: University of California Press.

Ríos, Palmira. 1996. "International Migration, Citizenship, and the Emergence of Transnational Public Policies." Paper presented at the Annual Meeting of the American Ethnological Society, April 18, San Juan, Puerto Rico.

Rodríguez Chávez, Ernesto. 1997. *Emigración cubana actual*. Havana: Editorial de Ciencias Sociales.

Rosenthal, Mona. 1997. *Inside the Cuban Revolution: Everyday Life in Socialist Cuba*. Ithaca, N.Y.: Cornell University Press.

Smith, Benjamin. 1999. "The Self-Employed in Cuba: A Street Level View." In *Cuba in Transition*, vol. 9. Proceedings of the Ninth Annual Meeting of the Association for the Study of the Cuban Economy. <http://lanic.utexas.edu/la/cb/cuba/asce/cuba9/smith.pdf>.

Stinson-Fernández, John. 1996. "Hacia una antropología de la emigración planificada: el Negociado de Empleo y Migración y el caso de Filadelfia." *Revista de Ciencias Sociales* (Nueva Época) 1: 112–55.

Torres, María de los Angeles. 1999. *In the Land of Mirrors: Cuban Exile Politics in the United States*. Ann Arbor: University of Michigan Press.

Torres-Saillant, Silvio, and Ramona Hernández. 1998. *The Dominican Americans*. Westport, Conn.: Greenwood Press.

Unión de Escritores y Artistas Cubanos and Universidad de la Habana, eds. 1995. *Cuba: cultura e identidad nacional*. Havana: Unión de Escritores y Artistas Cubanos.

U.S. Census Bureau. 1998. *Current Population Survey, March 1997*. <http://www.census.gov/population/socdemo/hispanic/cps97>.

———. 2003. American FactFinder. <http://factfinder.census.gov/servlet/BasicFactsServlet>.

U.S. Immigration and Naturalization Service. 1997–2001. *Statistical Yearbook of the Immigration and Naturalization Service*. <http://uscis.gov/graphics/shared/aboutus/statistics/Immigs.htm>.

Weyland, Karin. 1998. "Dominican Women 'con un pie aquí y otro allá': International Migration, Class, Gender, and Cultural Change." Ph.D. diss., New School for Social Research, New York.

Whitehead, Laurence. 2003. "On Cuban Political Exceptionalism." <http://www.nuff.ox.ac.uk/Politics/papers/2003/On%20Cuban%20Political%20Exceptionalism.pdf>.

2

From Exiles to Transnationals?

Changing State Policy and the Emergence of Cuban Transnationalism

Sarah A. Blue

In the emerging field of transnational studies, the role of the nation-state has increasingly become a subject of discussion, if not of disagreement. Following the early coinage of the terminology "deterritorialized nation-states" (Basch, Glick Schiller, and Szanton-Blanc 1994), implying that the nation-state has extended its reach to include whichever territory its diaspora choose to settle in, several studies have emerged to clarify the important role that nation-states play in shaping transnational migration (Guarnizo and Smith 1998; Ong 1999; Smith 1999). Recent notions of transnationalism emphasize that nation-states continue to provide the context of opportunities and constraints against which transnational migrants act. The decline and subsequent rise of Cuban transnationalism is a clear example of how nation-states set the boundaries and often provide channels for transnational activity.

Recent empirical studies have emphasized the responsiveness of Cuban transnational activity to Cuban state policy (Barberia 2002). Little empirical evidence exists, however, to indicate which Cuban migrants have transnational links to their home country. Strong political incentives for Cuban migrants *not* to maintain transnational links through remittances (the money and goods that migrants send home) or home country visits often lead to assumptions that the majority of Cuban transnational activity is limited to recent migrants. After outlining how the home country context, including specific state policies, has influenced Cuban transnational ties, I use evidence from a recent household survey conducted in Havana to explore which groups of Cuban migrants have maintained or reestablished transnational links.

This chapter is structured as follows. First, I highlight the ways in which transnational links were encouraged or discouraged through Cuban state policy that roughly corresponds to three distinct periods of Cuban outmigration. Second, I evaluate evidence from a recent household survey to measure the importance and extent of transnational ties between migrants and their families in Havana. In December 2000 I led a team of Cuban researchers in conducting a household-level survey in Havana (hereafter called the 2000 Havana survey) from which I gathered detailed information on communication, visits, and remittances from each migrant relative for 334 households.[1] To complement the data gathered in the survey, I conducted twelve in-depth interviews in the summer of 2001. Case studies drawn from these interviews are presented later in the chapter to provide a context for quantitative analysis of the 2000 Havana survey. In the last section of the chapter I use this empirical evidence to focus on the transnational activity of early migrants, who are often assumed to abstain from transnational links because of overriding political disincentives to establish ties with remaining family and friends in Cuba.

Cuban Emigration, State Policy, and Transnational Links

One of the great contributions of the transnational approach has been to allow a consideration of the home country context, including not only the influence transnational migrants have on their home communities, but also the extent to which transformations in the home country affect the formation, maintenance, or decline of transnational communities (Al-Ali and Koser 2002). The same political and economic crises that receive attention as catalysts in stimulating outmigration in many cases have also led to an increase in transnational activity (Basch, Glick Schiller, and Szanton-Blanc 1994; Kemal Dorai 2002). The rise (or demise) of transnational communities often can be directly related to radical political change, acute economic crisis, or more subtle changes in the economy or migrant policy in the country of origin. Thus, while transnational migrants transcend the nation-state in their field of operation, their motivations and actions are shaped by state policy.

The increase in transnational ties to Cuba, here measured by increased visits and remittances, has been highly sensitive to the Cuban government's policies and initiatives from 1959 to the present (Barberia 2002). The effect of state policy on Cuban transnational ties is somewhat unusual in that both the home and dominant host countries have attempted to influence those ties through legislation and by influencing public opinion. As evidenced by the steady increase in visits and remittance flows to the island since the early 1990s, Cuban efforts to encourage transnational links have been much more successful than U.S. attempts to limit them (Barberia 2002; Eckstein and Barberia 2002). Ultimately, while some restriction of communication, visits, and remittances can be attributed to U.S. policy, the vast majority of changes in Cuban transnational activity can be attributed to Cuba's changing policy toward its emigrant population. Three distinct periods of Cuban emigration to the United States—1959 to 1979, 1980 to 1989, and 1990 to the present—roughly correspond to concurrent periods of Cuban state policy toward the emigrant population. In the next section, I trace the changing transnational links that correspond to each period (through visits and remittances) and discuss the importance of changing state policy in increasing or decreasing transnational activity.

Exile and Estrangement: 1959–1979

Tangible political barriers to family relationships across the Florida Straits strained transnational ties during the first decades of the Cuban Revolution. Entire family and friendship networks were disrupted as emigrants and those who chose to stay in Cuba were confronted by divisive political pressures in both countries. Cubans in the United States broke completely with revolutionary Cuba. The approximately 248,000 political exiles who left Cuba in the early years of the Revolution (1959–1962) were for the most part upper- or middle-class fiscal and political conservatives who set the fiercely anti-Communist tone that characterizes Cuban migrants to the present. In Miami in particular, a violent atmosphere endangered those who made any move toward reconciliation (Didion 1987; Pedraza-Bailey 1985). Cubans on the island, in turn, distanced themselves ideologically from those who had left, as participation in the Communist Party or even access to study at the university could be denied as a result of contact with them (Torres 1995). The complete estrangement of Cuban migrants from their relatives on the island often lasted for decades, threatening a permanent rupture.

The migration of another 300,000 relatives of the earliest migrants through the Camarioca boatlift of 1965 and U.S.-sponsored airlifts from 1965 through 1973 led to the eventual resettlement of entire families abroad (Masud-Piloto 1996). The massive outmigration and the decision to relocate entire families when possible were motivated by both loss of property and status in Cuba and favorable immigration policies in the United States. In Cuba, the revolutionary government confiscated the property of those who left and denounced the emigrants as enemies of the state. In the United States, the hundreds of thousands of Cubans fleeing Communist Cuba legitimized U.S. government ideology during the Cold War and were rewarded with unprecedented amounts of aid.[2] In 1960, President Eisenhower officially recognized Cuba as a Communist state, declared Cuban immigrants to be political refugees, and established the national Cuban Refugee Program. The Cuban Refugee Adjustment Act of 1966 eased the conversion of Cuban refugees into permanent residents (Pérez 1999). Still in effect today, it entitles Cubans to be processed for permanent status in the United States after residing in the country for one year.

The end of this period was marked by a short period of renewed transnational networks as a brief Cold War détente led to family reconciliation in the late 1970s. Beginning in late 1977, the Cuban government began to allow Cuban Americans to visit their homeland. Shifting from a previously consistent rhetorical treatment of emigrants in negative classist ("the bourgeois") and political-ideological ("counterrevolutionary") terms, President Castro encouraged reconciliation by referring to emigrants positively as "the community" (Martín Fernández 2000; Pedraza-Bailey 1985). Signaling a widespread suppressed desire to communicate with estranged family and friends, and in spite of strong political pressures not to return, more than 100,000 Cubans returned to visit in 1979 alone (Pedraza-Bailey 1985). The renewed consumerism introduced through these visits was partly responsible for a political backlash in Cuba that culminated in the Mariel boatlift of 1980 (Masud-Piloto 1988). Mariel became the second massive wave of outmigration, which in Cuba was accompanied by a campaign of renewed government-sponsored political hostility toward the emigrant population. Thus, the promising renewal of transnational ties came to a sudden halt with the rekindling of political hostilities.

Tentative Transnationalism: 1980–1989

Although political backlash in Cuba from Mariel in 1980 and the simultaneous conservative turn in the U.S. government temporarily interfered with the continued renewal of transnational links for early migrants, the arrival of 125,000 new Cuban immigrants in the United States set the stage for a Cuban immigrant population that was more likely to maintain transnational ties. More representative of their home country, the majority of the Marielitos were young, working-class men who, if married, had left their families behind (Pedraza-Bailey 1985). As opposed to the earlier groups, who had fled a society in transition from capitalism, these were largely people who had grown up in Communist Cuba and who had strong ties to the new society. Marielito immigrants and their families in Cuba, though facing the same divisive pressures as earlier immigrants, had an underlying understanding of the political and economic reality of revolutionary Cuban society and deep social and psychological roots in that society in spite of any ideological differences with it. Although both Cuban and U.S. government policy inhibited contact by complicating communication and remittance flows throughout most of the 1980s, the contacts established during visits in the late 1970s and strong family and friendship ties among recent immigrants resulted in a tentative transnationalism that was realized in tangible activity as soon as a shift in government policy allowed.

In the late 1980s the Cuban government once again adopted a conciliatory policy toward its emigrant population that included the encouragement of increased communication and visits between Cubans at home and abroad.

These political overtures to the emigrant population foreshadowed major fiscal policy changes that would usher in a new period of heightened transnational activity.

Growth and Reestablishment of Transnational Ties: 1990–Present

The 1990s in Cuba were characterized by growing transnational links in the context of a severe economic crisis, economic restructuring, and the depoliticization of emigration. This growth of transnational ties not only is true for recent migrants, but also represents the reconnection of earlier emigrants with their family and friends in Cuba.

With the collapse of the Soviet trading bloc (COMECON) in the early 1990s, Cuba's need for hard currency led to several radical policy changes that facilitated transnational ties, primarily by encouraging remittance-based consumption. Among the most important changes in this regard were the legalization of the U.S. dollar and the widespread expansion of dollar-only stores and currency exchange booths. Dollar remittances began to flow to Cuba on a large scale after the Cuban government authorized its citizens to use U.S. dollars for transactions within Cuba in July 1993. State-run retail stores, which sell goods at relatively high prices in U.S. dollars, were established throughout the country to recuperate dollar remittances that had been circulating on the black market.[3] Representing the only legal option for buying imported or higher-quality domestic goods, state-run dollar stores became the main destination of remittance spending. As of 1997, two-thirds of Cuba's total hard currency income came from sales at dollar retail stores, compared to 11 percent from exports and 22 percent from tourism (Monreal 1999, cited in Eckstein 2003). The government also established exchange booths (CADECAs) where dollars could be converted to pesos at rates approximately equal to the black-market rate, in another effort to stem the illegal exchange of dollars on the street and recuperate dollars into state coffers. These official exchange booths were often located next to farmers' markets, legalized in 1994, where fresh fruit, vegetables, and meat were available in Cuban pesos at free-market prices.

The legalization of the dollar and establishment of dollar retail stores and farmers' markets created an immediate demand for U.S. dollar remittances. While the majority of employment in Cuba remained in the peso sector, many staple household goods (for example, laundry detergent, soap, and cooking oil) became available only in dollars. A cutback in the food rations to each household resulted in a heightened need to buy food at the relatively expensive farmers' markets. The average salary in Cuba in 1999 was 217 pesos per month—slightly more than $10 at a 20:1 exchange rate.[4] While salaries for the most part remained constant (although there was an increase in the number of state workers receiving hard-currency incentives through their workplaces), the purchasing power of the peso declined dramatically as a result of severe inflation from 1989 through 1995. Purchasing power was further reduced by the shrinking number of products available as rationed goods. Moreover, an increasing number of basic goods, including domestically produced food, became available only in high-priced dollar stores (Ritter and Rowe 2002).

The economic crisis of the early 1990s resulted not only in a major restructuring of the Cuban economy, but in a depoliticization of migration, as individuals and the Cuban state began to see outmigration and remittances as a practical solution to household scarcity. As a result of growing material dissatisfaction and heightened attempts to leave the island illegally, the Cuban government announced in August 1994 that it would no longer intercept illegal departures, generating what became known as the rafter crisis. In the following month, the U.S. Coast Guard rescued approximately 36,800 Cuban rafters, most of whom were detained in military bases at Guantánamo Bay and in Panama for eight months, before they were eventually admitted to the United States (Pérez 1999). In the May 1995 bilateral negotiations that followed the crisis, Cubans lost some of their preferential status as the United States agreed to discourage illegal immigration and establish an orderly, legal procedure for all potential migrants. Illegal immigrants intercepted before they reached U.S. soil would be returned directly to Cuba, and the Cuban border patrol would actively detain all illegal migrants seeking to leave from Cuban shores.[5] Beginning in 1995, the United States established 20,000 visas annually for Cubans to enter the United States legally after winning a lottery in Cuba. Most of these migrants retain strong transnational ties to their homeland through immediate family members and friends who remained behind.

The severe economic crisis and subsequent restructuring of the economy have also facilitated a reconnection between earlier emigrants and their relatives in Cuba (Eckstein and Barberia 2002). Given the strong political antagonism of Cuban exiles toward the current Cuban government led by Fidel Castro, the assumption is often made that Cuban refugees—especially the earliest émigrés—would be unlikely to have transnational connections in Cuba (Díaz-Briquets and Pérez-López 1997). As the empirical evidence presented later in this chapter indicates, however, compassion for relatives in need of medicine, clothing, shoes, or food has quietly overruled political considerations and led Cuban expatriates to send material aid to family members in Cuba. In addition to material need, a general political disillusionment among Cubans on both sides of the Florida Straits may have contributed to a reconnection between previously estranged families. The persistence of the revolutionary government in spite of the Soviet Union's collapse and the end of the Cold War, as well as major economic reforms on the island that have compromised the government's revolutionary principles, are among the factors that have contributed to this disillusionment. A religious opening in Cuba, strengthened by Pope John Paul II's visit in January 1998 and his call for reconciliation, also helped bring alienated family members together (Eckstein and Barberia 2002). Finally, travel restrictions have also eased for migrants who want to return to visit, an option that increasing numbers of Cubans have exercised.[6] At least 100,000 Cuban émigrés are estimated to have visited annually between 1996 and 1999 (Eckstein and Barberia 2002).

Remittances as a Transnational Link in Contemporary Cuba

Common transnational activities, such as involvement in politics and financial investment in the migrant's home community, are limited in Cuba due to long-standing political hostilities between the United States and Cuba, favorable U.S. migration policies, a lack of economic opportunities that limits return migration, and restrictions on investment in private property in Cuba's socialist economy. Remittances are a concrete manifestation of transnational ties to the home country, and in Cuba they are one of the strongest indicators of transnational ties. Remittances have seen a dramatic increase worldwide since the early 1990s. The money and goods international migrants send to their home countries have outpaced official development aid, with an estimated $32 billion per year going to Latin American countries alone in 2002 (Hernández 2003; Martin and Widgren 1996; Taylor et al. 1996). Remittances are inherently difficult to measure (Lozano-Ascencio 1993), especially given the informal channels through which a significant proportion of the money travels (Orozco 2002). This is especially true for Cuba, where legal limits on the amount of remittances sent and a general distrust of government on the part of the migrant population have led to an extensive system of informal delivery on the island. Although estimates of remittances to Cuba vary widely, all agree that there has been a steady increase since the early 1990s (Díaz-Briquets 1995; Jatar-Hausmann 1999; Monreal 1999).

U.S. legal restrictions on remittances to Cuba, tied to the economic embargo, have changed several times in response to political pressures but have not stopped the dramatic increase in remittances. Cubans in the United States are allowed to send remittances under a general license controlled by the U.S. Treasury Department, which regulates the embargo. From March 1996 through March 1998, the U.S. government eliminated remittances in response to a political confrontation between the two countries, although some remittances were permitted for the purpose of emigration or extreme humanitarian aid. The general license was reinstated in March 1998 and was extended to any U.S. citizen in January 1999. The U.S. government restricts the amount of remittances that may be sent directly to relatives or acquaintances in Cuba to $300 every four months ($1,200 annually) (U.S.-Cuba Trade and Economic Council, 2001).[7] This amount is easily exceeded, however, by deliveries of in-

Table 2.1. Importance of remittances vs. dollars earned through work for Cuban families

	Total annual remittances	Annual household salary earned in dollars	Annual income from informal activities earned in dollars	Annual self-employment income earned in dollars
N (334)	114 (34%)	54 (16%)	40 (12%)	15 (4.5%)
Median	$425	$246	$330	$600
Minimum	$20	$60	$60	$60
Maximum	$3,900	$3,600	$3,600	$4,800

Source: 2000 Havana survey.

kind goods and cash sent through private couriers in the United States or third countries such as Canada and Mexico.

The 2000 Havana survey reflected the widespread influence and importance of remittances for both the Cuban economy and individual households. Of the 334 households surveyed, 51 percent (171) had at least one relative abroad,[8] and 34 percent (114) received cash remittances. Table 2.1 indicates that not only are cash remittances important for supplementing household income, but also the fact that they are in dollars greatly facilitates their recipients' access to the dollar economy. In the context of economic crisis and a gradual opening of the Cuban economy, dollar income has become particularly important. Fewer household necessities are rationed or subsidized, and many essential goods that were previously purchasable with pesos are now only purchasable with dollars. For the sample population, remittances were the easiest and most common way to access dollars. A third of all households surveyed received cash remittances (114 of 334), ranging anywhere from $20 to $3,900 annually (in the latter case from three different relatives). This compares favorably with other modes through which Cuban households acquire dollars. Sixteen percent (54 of 334) of the households earned dollars as productivity bonuses (*estímulos*)[9] at work, 12 percent (40 of 334) earned dollars through informal activities, and only 4.5 percent (15 of 334) earned dollars through self-employment.

Cash remittances also yielded more money in dollars than other sources (except for legal self-employment).[10] While the median amount received via remittances per household was $425, informal dollar earnings were $330 and salary bonuses were $246. The only source generating more dollar income was licensed self-employment, yielding an annual median of $600 per household. Licensed self-employment earning dollars is an option available to only a very small segment of well-situated *habaneros*, mostly through tapping into the tourist industry with private restaurants and bed-and-breakfasts.

The 2000 Havana survey found that remittances have a tremendous impact

Table 2.2. Effect of remittances on Cuban household income (in US$ equivalents)

	Non-remittance-receiving households	Remittance-receiving households	
	Annual household income	Annual household income	Income including remittances
N (334)	216	113	114
Median	$474	$468	$1,146
Minimum	$60	$89	$221
Maximum	$4,860	$5,520	$6,015

Source: 2000 Havana survey.

on household income. The households surveyed acquired a median of $425 annually via cash remittances.[11] Remittance income more than doubled the average household earnings for the 114 households that received it (table 2.2). Accounting for all sources of income (salary, including production bonuses; self-employment; and any informal sources of income) for each member of the household, the median annual income was $468. The pre-remittance income difference between those households that received remittances and those that did not was virtually nonexistent, but when remittance income was added, the difference was great.

The data from the 2000 Havana survey make clear the importance of remittances as a transnational link for Cuban households and the immense humanitarian stimulus to send money home. Clearly, with the market-based changes in the Cuban economy, even relatively small cash remittances have become extremely important for Cuban households.

From Exile to Transnational?

The degree of transnational activity among any migrant group inevitably shifts over time in response to changing conditions in both the host and home countries (Al-Ali and Koser 2002; Kemal Dorai 2002; Koser 2002; Smith 1999). Cuban migrants responded to the Cuban government's political shift in policy toward emigrants and to the restructuring of the Cuban economy, which facilitated the sending and spending of remittances. Given the diversity among migrants (in terms of class, race, gender, year of migration, and migrant generation), however, it would be erroneous to make claims about the transnational activity of all Cuban migrants. While certain changes in the home country context might motivate a specific segment of migrants to reestablish transnational ties (through increased remittances, investment, or visits), other groups never break their ties to home, and others break them altogether. The 2000

Havana survey allows an initial examination to determine which groups of Cubans have maintained or reestablished transnational links with their home country.

Operating under the premise that not all migrants are transnational migrants, and that transnational links are dynamic and influenced by the home country context, I use the 2000 Havana survey to provide a snapshot of those groups of Cuban migrants who are likely to have transnational links. Based on the survey results, I argue that the expansion of transnational links, encouraged by the changing political-economic context in Cuba, has occurred with all groups of Cuban migrants but has been especially strong with early migrants in terms of reestablishment of home country ties. In spite of decades of residence outside of the home country and in many cases of having few to no remaining immediate relatives on the island, early Cuban migrants appear to play an important role in the strengthening of transnational ties with Cuba.

Several scholars have argued that as political refugees Cuban migrants are less likely to send remittances to their home country. This argument has been applied especially to those who migrated in the early decades following the Cuban Revolution. Díaz-Briquets and Pérez-López (1997) argue that early Cuban migrants are less likely to send remittances due to political disincentives and the fact that many have few immediate relatives on the island. These authors further argue that opposition to the home country government, implied in the state of being a political refugee, may dissuade migrants from sending remittances home, given the role that cash remittances play in maintaining macro-level financial stability. Following this argument, those migrants who left Cuba between 1959 and 1979—those who fled the transition to a Communist system—are more strongly influenced by political disincentives than migrants who left after 1980—those who grew up in but later left the Communist system. The recent migrants are more familiar with current socioeconomic conditions in Cuba and are more likely to have immediate family living on the island.

The findings from the 2000 Havana survey indicate the importance of the changing home country context in motivating both long- and short-term migrants to "become" transnational—in this case, to send money to their relatives back home. In spite of what in many cases were decades of non-communication and probable strong feelings of political opposition to the current regime, Cubans who left the country more than twenty or thirty years ago were the group most likely to send remittances to their relatives back home. Among the Cuban households surveyed, relatives who migrated before 1980 were actually more likely to send money than were later migrant cohorts (table 2.3).[12] The earliest migrants also sent larger amounts of money than did later migrants, reflecting their stronger financial position in the host country.

Table 2.3. Remittances sent by Cuban emigrants by migration period

Migration period	Total remitters	Total migrants	% sending money	Amount of remittances sent (US$)			% sending >$600
				$20–$200	$201–$600	$601–$2,400	
1947–1979	41	57	72	16	11	14	34
1980–1989	47	86	55	18	15	14	30
1990–2000	63	106	59	18	32	13	21
Total	151	249	61	52	58	41	27

Source: 2000 Havana survey.

For the participants in the 2000 Havana survey, political ideology did not seem to deter remittance sending or limit the amount sent. Following Díaz-Briquets and Pérez-López's (1997) argument (that pre-1980 migrants are more likely to be influenced by political disincentives while post-1980 migrants are more likely to be influenced by their knowledge of current conditions in Cuba), the year of migration was used as a proxy for political ideology. Of 249 migrants reported, 83.5 percent (208) were in communication with their relatives, 53 percent (133) had returned to visit, 61 percent (151) had sent cash remittances, 56 percent (140) had sent medicine, and 46 percent (115) had sent goods (figure 2.1). There was little difference between the two groups in degree of communication with relatives: Approximately 84 percent of all relatives from each migrant cohort were in communication with their relatives in Cuba. Counter to commonly held beliefs, migrants from the earlier (pre-1980) cohort were *more* likely to have returned to Cuba at least once to visit (63 versus 52 percent) and *more* likely to have sent both money (72 versus 57 percent) and medicine (65 versus 54 percent) to their relatives. Both groups were equally likely to have sent non-medicinal in-kind remittances to their relatives (approximately 46 percent). Visits, letters, and telephone conversations facilitated a reestablishment of family connections, especially for pre-1980 migrants. Altruistic motivations to help relatives back home were ultimately stronger than political disincentives not to remit for this sample population.

In addition to being more likely to send money, the pre-1980 migrants were also more likely to send greater amounts of money per remitter (table 2.4).[13] The difference was not as great as anticipated, however, with 37 percent of the pre-1980 migrants and 25 percent of the post-1980 migrants sending more than $600 annually.

Individual family histories show how the political ideology and personal pride that once divided families have been surpassed in many cases by humanitarian concern for relatives. Among those still in Cuba, economic need and political disillusionment led them to overcome personal pride tied to ideologi-

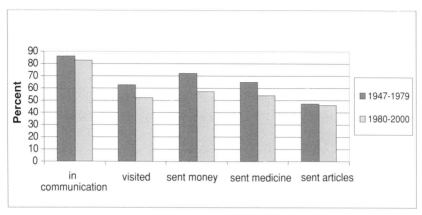

Figure 2.1. Emigrant relationships with Cuban relatives by migration cohort. (*Source:* 2000 Havana survey)

cal principles and to reach out to family members abroad. Alfredo (all names are pseudonyms), an active member of the Communist Party, for years had no contact with his younger brother, who left Cuba in 1980 as a political refugee. Even acknowledging that he had a brother in Miami could have caused him trouble at work and with the party. Before the economic crisis of the 1990s, his political principles would not have allowed him to accept any money or gifts from his brother, had he received any. Likewise, his brother's political ideals stopped him from making contact with his family in Cuba. Through a mutual friend who visited in the mid-1990s, however, the brothers reestablished contact. Motivated by correspondence with his family, and without ever mentioning politics, the younger brother began sending $100 every three months to be split between his elderly mother and two brothers on the island. Another example is the case of Gabriel. Gabriel's sister, who emigrated in 1970, had always maintained communication but had not sent money until 1990, at the onset of the Special Period, when Gabriel first became ill due to stress and a poor diet. When he again fell ill in 1992–1993, his sister began to send $50 a

Table 2.4. Amount of remittances sent by Cuban migrant cohorts

Migrant cohort	Remittance dollars sent						Total
	$20–$200		$201–$600		$601–$2,400		
1947–1979	15	37%	11	27%	15	37%	41
1980–2000	36	33%	47	43%	27	25%	110
Total	51	34%	58	38%	42	28%	151

Source: 2000 Havana survey.

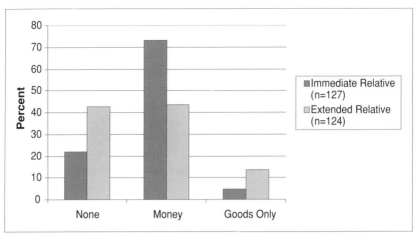

Figure 2.2. Remittance sending by immediate vs. extended relatives. (*Source:* 2000 Havana survey)

month so that his family of five could eat well again. He quickly recovered, but his sister maintained the monthly payments through 2001.

Increased visits to the island by Cuban Americans and foreign tourists alike have also led to an increase in transnational activity. For several of the families interviewed in 2001, initial contact after many years of separation came when a tourist or friend who had visited the island delivered a letter or made a phone call on behalf of family members. Adriana asked a tourist to deliver a letter to her half-sister in Houston, whom she had never met. The sister replied and, after months of letters and telephone calls, began to send an annual remittance of $300. Lucía recounted how her husband's reconciliation with his relatives in Miami was initiated by a video that a Cuban American friend took of her family in the mid-1990s and shared with her in-laws abroad. After her brother-in-law heard that Lucía's daughter needed a respirator for her asthma, he began to send medicine and cash remittances on a regular basis.

As the 2000 Havana survey shows, transnational ties do not have to be among immediate family members. In the Cuban case, an economic crisis and a sudden policy change resulted in remittance sending on the part of both immediate and extended family. Although immediate relatives were more likely to send remittances than were extended family members, more than half of all extended relatives sent remittances: 78 percent (99 of 127) of all immediate relatives and 57 percent (71 of 124) of all extended relatives sent money, goods, or both. The presence of immediate family in Cuba, however, did result in stronger transnational ties for this surveyed population. Immediate family members sent more money more reliably, whereas extended family members sent less money less frequently (figure 2.2). Emigrants with immediate relatives in Cuba were likely to send money, regardless of the year in which they migrated. Seventy-three percent (93 of 127) of all immediate relatives but only 44 percent of extended relatives (54 of 124) sent money.[14] Distant relatives were more likely to send necessary medicine or articles of clothing to their extended relatives in Cuba and to send cash remittances to their immediate relatives.

The increased transnational activity of early Cuban migrants who do not necessarily have immediate family remaining in their home country is illustrated by the 2000 Havana survey results and by individual case histories. Manuel related how his elderly uncle in Miami began to send between $100 and $200 a year after hearing of Manuel's inability to work due to semi-blindness caused by optic neuritis, which he contracted in 1993. The uncle now sends money regularly to both Manuel and a surviving brother in Cuba.

The data from this empirical study indicate that short- and long-term migrants, as well as immediate and extended relatives, have all maintained or established transnational links to Cuba. Even early migrants, who are most strongly identified as political exiles, have established transnational links to family members in Cuba through visits and remittances. The severe economic crisis of 1990–1993, combined with a shift in Cuban state policy toward emigrants and economic restructuring that facilitated remittances, led to an increase in transnational activity, highlighting the critical role of the home country context in influencing a migrant group's level of transnational activity. Contrary to common perceptions that political exiles who migrated decades earlier and have few to no immediate relatives will not engage in transnational activity, early Cuban migrants are important actors in the move toward strengthened transnational ties with Cuba.

Conclusion

Implementing a transnational perspective allows for a more comprehensive picture of the impact of international migration, including the importance of the home country context and changing state policy for migrants' connections to family and community in the country of origin. While advances in travel and communication technology have facilitated a new level of transnational activity among international migrants, the nation-state continues to play a major role in shaping that activity. As illustrated by the responsiveness of transnational activity among Cuban migrants to shifts in state policy, nation-states provide the context of opportunities and constraints within which transnational migrants act. Legal restrictions on visits and remittances and shifts in government discourse toward the emigrant population have alternately restricted and expanded the boundaries of possible transnational activity over the past forty-five years. The restructuring of the Cuban economy in the early

1990s, including the legalization of the dollar and the establishment of dollar-only stores, created a heightened demand for remittances and provided channels for consumer spending.

Through analysis of remittances and visits reported in a household survey conducted in Havana in December 2000, I have explored which groups of Cuban migrants were likely to maintain or reestablish transnational links to Cuba. In the absence of the transnational ties found among other migrant groups, such as political participation and investment in home communities, visits and remittances are Cuba's most concrete manifestation of transnationalism. A focus on year of migration revealed that Cuban migrants, regardless of when they migrated, were strengthening their transnational ties through visits and remittances. Unexpectedly, however, Cubans who migrated before 1980 were actually more likely to visit and send remittances than were more recent migrants. The 2000 Havana survey also revealed that many Cuban migrants were reestablishing connections with extended as well as immediate relatives, indicating that the presence of immediate relatives on the island was not a necessary condition for reestablishing transnational ties. Connecting with extended relatives, such as aunts, nephews, or cousins, has been both a humanitarian response to economic crisis and a means of seeking or reestablishing cultural roots in Cuba.

While politics undoubtedly still acts as a barrier to a full manifestation of transnationalism for certain groups of Cuban migrants and other political refugees, the transnational angle allows an examination of equally interesting questions regarding which migrants have established transnational ties and the nature and effect of their transnational activity. Shifts in Cuban transnational activity, culminating in the most recent period of heightened ties, make clear the dynamic nature of transnationalism as migrants and their families respond to political and economic changes in the countries where they live.

Notes

The research presented in this article was generously supported by NSF Grant #0117931.

1. See Blue (2004) for a more detailed discussion of my research methodology.

2. From 1961 to 1974, the U.S. government spent more than $957 million in relief and services to Cuban immigrants (García 1996: 45). This amount included millions of dollars the CIA funneled to exile groups to support various attempts to undermine the Cuban Revolution.

3. One of the first chains of state-run dollar stores was explicitly named TRD (*tiendas recuperadoras de divisa*, or stores for the recuperation of dollars).

4. In the new dual economy, Cubans tend to calculate their peso earnings according to their dollar equivalent, without considering the social wage paid by the government:

a subsidized monthly food ration in pesos (which generally needs to be supplemented with food purchased at free-market prices); free health care and education; subsidized rent (Cubans pay no more than 10 percent of their wages for housing); and social security coverage (Eckstein 2003; U.S.-Cuba Trade and Economic Council 1999).

5. The Cuban Refugee Adjustment Act is still in effect, however. This act grants protections, including eventual permanent residency, to Cubans who overstay temporary visas, as well as rafters and other illegal entrants "who manage to elude Cuban and U.S. authorities and successfully arrive in the U.S." (Pérez 1999: 207).

6. Reversing a decade-long trend, the U.S. government initiated new policies that restrict travel to Cuba as of June 1, 2004. These new policies limit legal visits by Cuban Americans to once every three years, with a two-week maximum stay, and exclude visits to extended family. It is yet to be seen what effect these restrictions will have.

7. In 2004 the Bush administration further restricted remittances, which now may be sent only to immediate relatives, excluding aunts, uncles, and cousins, who were formerly on the list of eligible recipients.

8. Six friends who were sending remittances were included here.

9. This number may not include the *java*, or bag of toiletries valued at $10–$20, given to workers in certain industries each month.

10. Cubans have few opportunities to own their own businesses. Self-employment accounts for only 3 percent of national economic activity.

11. It was not possible to approximate the value of goods and medicine sent.

12. These tables are meant to be descriptive and should not be considered representative of the larger population.

13. Relatives identified a total of 249 migrants in the 2000 Havana survey. Twenty-three percent (57) migrated before 1980; 77 percent (192) migrated in 1980 or later. When compared to approximations of the number of Cubans who have migrated in distinct cohorts since 1959, the sample reflects a bias toward more recent migrants. According to a recent estimate of Cuban outmigration from 1959 to 1997, 64 percent (678,757) emigrated between 1959 and 1979 and 36 percent (379,938) between 1980 and 1997 (Díaz Fernández and Aja Díaz 1998). The higher number of recent migrants in this sample most likely reflects a tendency for earlier migrants to have emigrated with the majority of their immediate families, whereas later migrants are more likely to have left immediate relatives behind in Cuba.

14. These figures do not include seven senders of remittances: six "friends" and one relative whose relationship was not reported. All sent both cash and in-kind remittances. Immediate relatives were defined as parents, children, and siblings, as well as in-laws and ex-spouses—who were likely to be immediate relatives to household members other than the interviewee. Extended relatives included aunts, uncles, nieces, nephews, cousins, and godparents.

Bibliography

Al-Ali, Nadje, and Khalid Koser. 2002. "Transnationalism, International Migration and Home." In *New Approaches to Migration?: Transnational Communities and the*

Transformation of Home, edited by Nadje Al-Ali and Khalid Koser, 1–14. New York: Routledge.

Barberia, Lorena. 2002. *Remittances to Cuba: An Evaluation of Cuban and U.S. Government Policy Measures*. Rosemary Rogers Working Paper Series 15. Cambridge, Mass.: Inter-University Committee on International Migration.

Basch, Linda, Nina Glick Schiller, and Cristina Szanton-Blanc. 1994. *Nations Unbound: Transnational Projects, Postcolonial Predicaments, and Deterritorialized Nation-States*. New York: Gordon and Breach.

Blue, Sarah. 2004. "Socio-Economic Costs of Global Integration: Remittances, the Informal Economy, and Rising Inequality in Contemporary Cuba." Ph.D. diss. University of California, Los Angeles.

Díaz-Briquets, Sergio. 1995. "Emigrant Remittances in the Cuban Economy: Their Significance during and after the Castro Regime." *Cuba in Transition* vol. 4. Proceedings of the Fourth Annual Meeting of the Association for the Study of the Cuban Economy. <http://www1.lanic.utexas.edu/la/cb/cuba/asce/cuba4/diaz.html>

Díaz-Briquets, Sergio, and Jorge Pérez-López. 1997. "Refugee Remittances: Conceptual Issues and the Cuban Nicaraguan Experiences." *International Migration Review* 31, no. 2: 411–37.

Díaz Fernández, María, and Antonio Aja Díaz. 1998. "Análisis comparativo de la emigración cubana hacia los Estados Unidos según año de entrada." *Anuario CEAP 1997–1998: emigración cubana*, 54–79. Havana: Centro de Estudios de Alternativas Políticas, Universidad de la Habana.

Didion, Joan. 1987. *Miami*. New York: Simon and Schuster.

Eckstein, Susan. 2003. *Diasporas and Dollars: Transnational Ties and the Transformation of Cuba*. Rosemary Rogers Working Paper Series 16. Cambridge, Mass.: Inter-University Committee on International Migration.

Eckstein, Susan, and Lorena Barberia. 2002. "Grounding Immigrant Generations in History: Cuban Americans and Their Transnational Ties." *International Migration Review* 36, no. 3: 799–838.

García, María Cristina. 1996. *Havana USA: Cuban Exiles and Cuban Americans in South Florida, 1959–1994*. Berkeley: University of California Press.

Guarnizo, Luis Eduardo, and Michael Peter Smith. 1998. "The Locations of Transnationalism." In *Transnationalism from Below*, edited by Michael Peter Smith and Luis Eduardo Guarnizo, 1–33. New Brunswick, N.J.: Transaction.

Hernández, Daisy. 2003. "With Fewer Dollars to Go Around, More Are Going around the World." *New York Times*, July 14, sec. B, p. 1.

Jatar-Hausmann, Ana Julia 1999. *The Cuban Way: Capitalism, Communism and Confrontation*. West Hartford, Conn.: Kumarian Press.

Kemal Dorai, M. 2002. "The Meaning of Homeland for the Palestinian Diaspora: Revival and Transformation." In *New Approaches to Migration? Transnational Communities and the Transformation of Home*, edited by Nadje Al-Ali and Khalid Koser, 87–95. New York: Routledge.

Koser, Khalid. 2002. "From Refugees to Transnational Communities?" In *New Approaches to Migration? Transnational Communities and the Transformation of Home*, edited by Nadje Al-Ali and Khalid Koser, 138–52. New York: Routledge.

Lozano-Ascencio, Fernando. 1993. *Bringing It Back Home: Remittances to Mexico from Migrant Workers in the United States*. Center for U.S.-Mexico Studies Monograph, no. 37. San Diego: University of California at San Diego.

Martin, Philip, and Jonas Widgren. 1996. "International Migration: A Global Challenge." *Population Bulletin* 51, no. 1: 1–47.

Martín Fernández, Consuelo. 2000. *Cuba: vida cotidiana, familia y emigración*. Centro para el Estudio de Migración Internacional (CEMI), Universidad de la Habana. Photocopy.

Masud-Piloto, Félix R. 1988. *With Open Arms: Cuban Migration to the United States*. Totowa, N.J.: Rowman and Littlefield.

———. 1996. *From Welcomed Exiles to Illegal Immigrants: Cuban Migration to the U.S., 1959–1995*. Lanham, Md.: Rowman and Littlefield.

Monreal, Pedro. 1999. *Migraciones y remasas familiares: veinte hipótesis sobre el caso de Cuba*. Centro de Investigaciones de Economía Internacional (CIEI), Universidad de la Habana. Photocopy.

Ong, Aihwa. 1999. *Flexible Citizenship: The Cultural Logics of Transnationality*. Durham: Duke University Press.

Orozco, Manuel. 2002. "Globalization and Migration: The Impact of Family Remittances to Latin America." *Latin American Politics and Society* 44, no. 2: 41–67.

Pedraza-Bailey, Silvia. 1985. *Political and Economic Migrants in America*. Austin: University of Texas Press.

Pérez, Lisandro. 1999. "The End of Exile? A New Era in U.S. Immigration Policy toward Cuba." In *Free Markets, Open Societies, Closed Borders? Trends in International Migration and Immigration*, edited by Max Castro, 197–211. Miami: North-South Center Press.

Ritter, Archibald R. M., and Nicholas Rowe. 2002. "Cuba: From 'Dollarization' to 'Euroization' or 'Peso Reconsolidation'?" *Latin American Politics and Society* 44, no. 2: 99–123.

Smith, Robert. 1999. "Reflections on Migration, the State and the Construction, Durability and Newness of Transnational Life." In *Migration and Transnational Social Spaces*, edited by Ludger Pries, 187–219. Brookfield, Vt.: Ashgate.

Taylor, J. Edward, Joaquín Arango, Graeme Hugo, Ali Kouaouci, Douglas S. Massey, and Adela Pellegrino. 1996. "International Migration and National Development." *Population Index* 62, no. 2: 181–212.

Torres, María de los Angeles. 1995. "Encuentros y encontronazos: Homeland in the Politics and Identity of the Cuban Diaspora." *Diaspora* 4, no. 2: 211–38.

U.S.-Cuba Trade and Economic Council. 1999. "Economic Eye on Cuba: 31 May–6 June 1999." <http://www.cubatrade.org>.

———. 2001. "2000 Commercial Highlights." <http://www.cubatrade.org>.

3

Myths and Mysticism

How Bringing a Transnational Religious Lens to the Examination of Cuba and the Cuban Diaspora Exposes and Ruptures the Fallacy of Isolation

Sarah J. Mahler and Katrin Hansing

In the winter of 2003, Fidel Castro imprisoned dozens of dissidents whose criticism of the regime in Cuba was attracting high levels of international attention. His action was quickly condemned by governments around the world, including his previous supporters in the European Union, who proceeded to curtail trade and aid to the island. In May 2002, President George W. Bush included Cuba in his list of countries forming an "axis of evil" which, he argued, threatened not only the United States but every free nation. And just two years before that address, the Elián González custody battle erupted on a world screen, with camera shots cutting from scenes of outraged Cubans in the streets of Havana to scenes of outraged Cubans storming the streets of Miami. These events, with their hostile rhetoric and confrontational images, serve as recent reincarnations of the Cold War politics that have characterized Cuba and its relationship to the United States, in particular, for nearly fifty years. On the U.S. side, these events help justify that country's embargo and policy of isolation against the Castro government. Cuba has continuously responded via a carefully crafted and dramatized tale of David versus Goliath, showcasing how resilient and righteous Cuba remains despite the unfair and unjust actions of the superpower to its north.

For decades, then, U.S.-Cuba relations have been heated by constant accusations of just versus unjust policies of isolation. How true is this portrayal of these relations? We hold that isolation is more myth than reality. Furthermore, we argue in this chapter that examining these relations with a religious lens brings a little-recognized dimension to the fore; that is, there have always been and continue to be religious ties between Cuba and other nations, ties that disrupt the convenient fiction of modern-day Cuba as an isolated outpost of

Communist zeal. Moreover, we have found and documented that the activities of religious organizations and the practice of a variety of faiths on the island constitute one of the few, and certainly the most autonomous, civic spaces on the island. In recent years and largely due to transnational ties to Cuba from abroad, as we document later, this space has grown considerably. The purposes behind this transnational investment by Cubans on the island, Cubans in the diaspora, and non-Cubans alike are complex, and their importance is consistently overlooked in scholarly and popular discussions of Cuba and its future in the world system. We are in the process of redressing this critical oversight, and we present some of our findings in this chapter.

Our overall research, of which this chapter is an excerpt, investigates the roles that religion plays and has played in both U.S.-Cuba relations and exile-island ("the two Cubas") relations. To date, we have interviewed more than 150 religious leaders and congregants in both Miami and Cuba, documented scores of religious services and organizational meetings in both locations, and conducted archival research. We have (1) traced the histories of various faiths (Catholic, Protestant/Evangelical, and Afro-Cuban) both within Cuba and in relationship to the United States; (2) documented the emigration of the vast majority of Cuban religious professionals and congregation members in the years following the 1959 revolution and the subsequent development of Cuban religious communities in Miami; (3) recorded the persistence of religious praxis in post-1959 Cuba, emphasizing efforts by the religious to keep open an alternative, religio-civic space for dialogue within Cuba and between the island and the United States; and (4) traced the multitudinous transnational religious ties that link Cuban clergy and laity on the island with diasporic communities in the United States, particularly in Miami.

Bias from a Framework Featuring International Relations

Cuban-U.S. relations have overwhelmingly been couched in historical, diplomatic, and international relations genres (Arboleya 1996; Benjamin 1990; Brenner 1988; Domínguez and Hernández 1989; Fernández 2000; Gunn 1993; Ortega 1998; Paterson 1994; Pérez 1990; Pérez-Stable 1993). While understandable, this political science/international relations approach has so dominated the literature that other ways of viewing the issue have been clouded if not completely obscured. What roles, for example, do *non*-state actors play in shaping Cuban-U.S. relations? We will discuss in detail religious actors as one key constituency of this nongovernmental sphere of influence. More generally, non-state actors—civil society in particular—have customarily been excluded or downplayed as participants in the construction and perpetuation of international and domestic relations and security, though recent scholarship has challenged this narrow viewpoint (Brysk 1993, 2000; Keck and Sikkink 1998; Mato 1997; Rudolph and Piscatori 1997; Smith 1994). In Cuba, the state so dominates civil institutions that they can barely function, underscoring the need to consider the role of the church—arguably the only semiautonomous social institution in the country—in Cuba's domestic and international security issues. A small literature addresses this gap but only through the early 1990s (Domínguez 1989; Fernández 1991; Pedraza 1998; Pérez 1994). Our research begins where these texts end. Moreover, we use a very different analytical framework to examine our data: a transnational, not an international relations framework.

The Transnational Analytical Framework

"Transnationalism" has become a buzz word in recent years and its overuse has led many to lament that the term and its frequent counterpart, "globalization," have become "empty conceptual vessels" (Guarnizo and Smith 1998). We do not have the space to go into a thorough etymology and discussion of these terms here; rather, we provide a much abbreviated discussion of these concepts and their relationship to migration and religion as a foundation for understanding how we apply this framework to analyzing the myriad transnational religious ties we have found that link Cuba to Miami, the United States more generally, and other countries and localities.

A critical initial step for distinguishing "transnational" from "global" can be found in the work of Michael Kearney. He argues that "whereas global processes are largely decentered from specific national territories and take place in a global space, transnational processes are *anchored in* and transcend one or more nation-states" (Kearney 1995: 548, emphasis added). His use of the expression "anchored in" communicates that transnational ties are grounded in "specific social relations established between specific people, situated in unequivocal localities, at historically determined times" (Guarnizo and Smith 1998: 11). Transnational relations are often "trans-local," linking localities within states that are separated by international borders.

The work of Glick Schiller continues this process of distinguishing "transnational" from "global" by adding issues of scope and agency:

> "Global" is best reserved for processes that are not located in a single state but happen throughout the entire globe. Processes such as the development of capitalism are best understood as global because capitalism is a system of production that was developed not in a single state or between states but by various emerging European bourgeois classes utilizing resources, accumulated wealth, and labor throughout the world. On the other hand, I employ the word transnational to discuss political, economic, social, and cultural processes that extend beyond the borders

of a particular state, *include actors that are not states*, but are shaped by the policies and institutional practices of states. (Glick Schiller 1999: 96, emphasis added)

We follow Glick Schiller's lead in making this distinction, which at once emphasizes the continued importance of borders—certainly true in the Cuban-U.S. case—and the fact that some participants in transnational processes must *not* represent states' interests. In this way, transnational relations differ from international relations, a distinction first advanced by Daniel Mato (1997). Advocates of the transnational framework use the word "international" in a more limited sense, using it to signify "between nations," as in international relations between states.

The particular usage of "transnational" we develop here is not universally adopted by either scholars or non-scholars, so there continues to be great confusion regarding its application. We trace our lineage directly to those scholars who innovated the transnational perspective on migration (Basch, Glick Schiller, and Szanton Blanc 1994; Glick Schiller, Basch, and Blanc-Szanton 1992). This is appropriate since many, but certainly not all, of the transnational religious ties we have found are between Cubans who emigrated from the island and their brothers and sisters, both biological and religious, who stayed in Cuba. The transnational perspective on migration examines the reasons why many people who migrate to new countries do not cut themselves off completely from their societies of origin, but rather retain transnational ties and build new linkages. This approach diverges sharply from traditional research on migration, which construed it as a unidirectional process of travel across international borders, leading to settlement and assimilation in the new society. In contrast, transnational migration has come to be defined as

a pattern of migration in which persons, although they move across international borders and settle and establish social relations in a new state, maintain social connections within the polity from which they originated. In transnational migration, persons literally live their lives across international borders. That is to say, they establish transnational social fields. . . . Transmigrants are people who claim and are claimed by two or more nation-states, into which they are incorporated as social actors, one of which is widely acknowledged to be their state of origin. (Glick Schiller 1999: 96)

"Transnational" is not only a term of choice adopted by scholars of migration, but also a popular word among intellectuals who focus on religious faith and practice. In the first paragraph of *Transnational Religion: Fading States*, for example, Susanne Rudolph and James Piscatori state, "Religious communities are among the oldest of the transnationals. Sufi orders, Catholic missionaries, and Buddhist monks carried word and praxis across vast spaces before those places became nation-states or even states" (Rudolph and Piscatori 1997: 1). The authors imply an expansive definition of transnational religion, one that makes us uncomfortable. Why? Because our use of "transnational" is founded on the existence of nation-states, whereas they refer to a period of history that predates this political formation. We *are* however interested in comprehending what another scholar characterizes as the "fluidity of religion across political borders" (Levitt 2001: 8).

Unfortunately, little published research to date focuses on transnational religious activities undertaken by either migrants or nonmigrants, though the literature is growing (Ebaugh and Saltzman Chafetz 2000; Levitt 2001, 2003; Menjivar 1999; Vásquez 1999; Vásquez and Marquardt 2003). We see our work as contributing directly to these lacunae both substantively and analytically. To anticipate, in the next sections of our chapter we will discuss a little known and highly diverse set of historical and contemporary transnational religious ties linking Cuba to Miami and the United States. Indeed, before Cuba's gaze turned northward in the years of the wars of Cuban independence and the U.S. military occupation, the island was joined at the hip to Spain. Among the thickest of the many strands of Spanish colonialism in Cuba were religious ties that served not only cultural but also ideological purposes. Although these colonial bonds were severed more than a hundred years ago, they retain vestiges of their earlier importance. Similarly, we will show that despite more than four decades of "isolation," transnational religious ties between Cuba and the United States have endured, strengthening significantly in recent years.

Transnational Religious Ties between Cuba and the United States: The Historical View

Cuba today is teeming with a religious fervor that reflects both domestic and international factors. To many religious peering at Cuba from outside, the island appears to be one of the last great, nearly virgin grounds for evangelization, at least in the Western Hemisphere. According to dozens of Cuban religious leaders and scholars we interviewed, the island is attracting thousands of religious "tourists" from many countries, most notably the United States, anxious to establish beachheads for what they feel will be fertile ground for their faith after Cuba opens in the post-Castro era. Internally, the prolonged economic crisis has helped shift Cubans' faith away from socialism and toward spirituality and institutionalized religion, aided by the gradual political warming toward religious expression and the zeal of evangelists from home and abroad.

The contemporary effervescence contrasts sharply with Cuba's history as perhaps the least churched country in Latin America (Kirk 1989; Pérez 1994; Tweed 1997). For hundreds of years the Catholic Church reigned alone, yet its parishes were concentrated in urban areas and underserved the great masses of peasants in the countryside. As recently as 1954, a nationwide survey revealed that the overwhelming majority of Cuba's population had minimal or no contact with the institutional church and 19 percent did not profess any religion at all (Echevarría Salvat 1971). Protestants appeared in the late nineteenth century; the first pastors were political refugees from the wars of independence with Spain who converted to Protestantism in Florida and returned to Cuba just before the U.S. occupation. Given that the early mainline Protestant church institutional structure was formed during the occupation, most denominations—such as Presbyterians, Methodists, and Southern Baptists—were incorporated into home missions instead of foreign ones. This initiated deep-seated institutional, economic, and emotional ties between Cuban Protestants and their counterparts in the United States, ties that endure to this day. Protestant pastors evangelized by building schools alongside churches. Some schools became premier institutions in Cuba and trained its leadership, but they did not convert much of the general population. In sum, by 1959 institutional churches could claim a mere fraction of Cuba's faithful, predominantly among the country's urbanites and elite (Kirk 1989; Yaremko 2000); instead, the spiritual needs of the overwhelming majority of Cubans were addressed by a host of African-based faiths, including Santería, Palo Monte, and Espiritismo (Pedraza 1998).

In the years leading up to Castro's victory in 1959, numerous Catholic and Protestant clergy supported the revolution and a few fought alongside the revolutionaries (Crahan 1989; Kirk 1989). But when Castro declared Cuba an atheist state in 1961, the resulting discrimination against, and sometimes incarceration of, those who professed their faith inspired a near complete about-face in the clergy's view of the new regime and a mass emigration of both clergy and laity (Pedraza 1998). The enmity escalated rapidly and endures to this day, particularly among Catholics. Three Spanish priests exiled from Cuba participated in the Bay of Pigs invasion, and all who fought wore shoulder patches bearing crosses as a sign of their belief that their mission represented God against the atheists (Kirk 1989: 95). Castro countered by curtailing religious liberties, forbidding religious to join the Communist Party, and precluding the entry into Cuba of denominations that were not already present as of 1959. The ensuing climate of fear and intimidation against the faithful decimated congregations, and the few pastors and priests who remained behind were scorned by their exiled and embittered colleagues who resettled abroad, especially in Miami. The conditions of the exodus meant that as religious leaders built new communities in exile, resentment and anger were principal ingredients. Thus, Cuban churches in the United States, particularly in Miami, became powerful and outspoken anti-Communist institutions seeking confrontation over reconciliation. Underlying the thick air of politics were deep-seated feelings and accusations: Pastors who fled Cuba were often burdened with guilt—and sometimes blame—for abandoning their flocks, while those who remained behind were labeled puppets of Castro. While the Miami religious exiles strove to reconstitute their institutions in their new setting, often giving their churches and schools names identical to those they had left in Cuba (Pérez 1994), the diminished ranks of the religious leadership in Cuba struggled to keep some vestige of a religious life on the island despite overwhelmingly adverse conditions. And when the United States declared its embargo, pastors who had received salaries, pensions, or benefits from denominational headquarters in the United States were cut off (Corse 1989; Greer 1989). For most clergy, whose churches had never reached self-sufficiency even in the best of times, this sudden severing of their religious—and economic—umbilical cords to their mother churches in the north was cataclysmic at first. This abrupt orphaning gave rise over time, however, to these churches' Cubanization.

For the first ten years following the revolution, religious and political animosities in Cuba grew in tandem and transnationally. Not until the late 1960s did the first cracks in the ice appear through, among other factors, the Latin American Bishops Conference in Medellín, Colombia, where the "preferential option for the poor" was adopted. This new social agenda represented a liberalization of the Catholic Church in the Americas, casting Cuba in a better light than before. In the 1970s Castro toured Chile during the administration of leftist president Salvador Allende and was exposed to liberation theology (Crahan 1989; Kirk 1989: 134). As it dawned on Castro that Christianity could coexist with a socialist revolution, he began to entertain dialogues with religious leaders from the United States as well as Cuba, culminating in 1985 with the publication of *Fidel y la religión* (Fidel and religion; Betto 1985). As these dialogues proceeded, they slowly expanded the space for religious devotion in Cuba. They also constituted one of the slim strands of transnational communication linking the island to the outside prior to the present era.

In sum, during the early revolutionary era religious communities on both sides of the Florida Straits suffered rapid, wrenching transformations and in the process frequently developed an omnipresent hostility that would endure for decades; some would say it still characterizes relations. Regardless, a thin space for transnational dialogue and reconciliation stayed open, primarily due to efforts among liberal Protestants on both sides. Given the fact that Catholics had been tied transnationally primarily to Spain and the Vatican, this is not surprising; Protestants, with their thick and deep, multifaceted ties to their mother denominations in the north, had the most to lose—and gain—in this period. Remarkably, despite all the adversity, relations between religious on the island and in the United States remained open, albeit only slightly. This condition of restriction would change abruptly with the end of the Cold War.

Contemporary Transnational Religious Ties

Religious leaders on both sides of the Florida Straits date the present religious renaissance to 1990, when the Special Period began after the former USSR unraveled and with it the economic subsidies on which Cuba depended. In the years immediately afterward, hunger and dashed hopes fostered disillusionment among the populace. During this time, people were attracted to the church to fill material as well as spiritual needs. Reports of suffering in the early 1990s stimulated churches in Miami to invent ways to supply medicine and other scarce goods to the island without drawing the wrath of either the Cuban or U.S. governments. Indeed, many clergy in Miami and elsewhere are pushing hard to take advantage of the last decade of increased religious tolerance—including the Cuban government's abrogation of the long-standing policy of official atheism in 1991. During a meeting of Protestant clergy and laity in the fall of 2003, for example, one pastor urged the audience to get involved immediately and not to wait. Referring to how inexpensive evangelism on the island is now, given the strength of the dollar and the impoverishment of the masses, he argued, "In a few years we won't be able to do with thousands of dollars what we can do with ten dollars today!"

Before proceeding with the analytical framework we have developed to organize and comprehend the myriad transnational linkages that now span the Cubas, we present a short series of ethnographic examples of the transnational religious ties we have observed and describe the people who enact them to give a sense of their diversity and multidimensionality.

Among the most ingenious projects we found and one that survives to this day is a Catholic radio program broadcast from Miami that reaches the north coast of Cuba. Beginning in 1994, an exile priest who recently succumbed to cancer would transmit religious homilies to Cubans on the island and solicit them to write to him with their medical needs. Thousands of letters have been sent and, in an effort underwritten by wealthy Cuban exiles and staffed by a team of volunteers, each request is fulfilled. The desired medicine is packaged along with a rosary and a small religious pamphlet. These *paqueticos* are delivered by Miami Cuban American "mules" who can travel back to the island legally every three years (until 2004 they could travel once a year). The priest's organization pays for their travel if they agree to carry a suitcase filled with medicine packets. Obviously, the Castro regime is privy to this operation and the myriad others that discreetly provide material aid to Cuba, but it does not intervene unless participants draw public attention to their work that would make the regime lose face as a state unable to meet the basic needs of its population.

This example is but one of many we have discovered that illustrate the ways in which transnational religious ties built on the foundation of Cuban migration to the United States cultivate more than faith. In this particular case, humanitarian aid delivers a dual message: The external aid helps to bolster the regime, but it also exposes the regime's inability to meet much of its population's basic needs, a vulnerability that undermines its credibility.

Another example of religious ties with political undertones is the itinerant missionaries who enter Cuba as "tourists" with the express purpose of starting new, usually conservative Pentecostal congregations. We have both heard stories about and witnessed these missionaries, many of whom are Cubans from Miami who entice converts with promises of gifts in dollars or goods. Frequently, they also offer to pay religious leaders regular salaries to lead new congregations initiated and supported by the missionaries. Given that the average salary in Cuba is a mere $10 per month, Cuban religious leaders are enticed by offers of $20 to $100 a month—a ransom in Cuba but a pittance for religious evangelical organizations abroad. Over and again, established pastors in Cuba have lamented to us that their carefully cultivated leadership is being drawn away by these offers, which they admit are hard to refuse given the deteriorated economy. This is not merely shrewd evangelization; in many of our interviews we have heard a distinct subtext of "saving souls" in Cuba. The objective is also distinctly anti-Communist, for Communism is deemed the handiwork of the Antichrist. Cuban lay leaders are tempted by these offers because stature as a religious leader enhances their chances of acquiring a coveted prize—a visa to travel abroad. Interviews with clergy on the island point to a little known truism, namely, that clergy have greater access to international travel than virtually any other sector of society except top Communist Party members.

The availability of religious visas from both the United States and Cuba has facilitated not only travel, and hence emigration, but also dialogue. The escalating enforcement of Bush administration restrictions on travel between the countries since 2003 is affecting these religious visas. Still, Catholic transnational ties are among the most dense and active. Cuban Catholic priests from the island come to Miami every month. They celebrate Mass in one of the many Cuban Catholic churches in Miami, meet with former congregants from their parishes in Cuba, and even perform sacraments—weddings, baptisms, and so on. These priests serve as balm to long-divided communities by sharing local and personal news, and many preach a theology of reconciliation during their homilies. During their stays in Miami they also collect large sums of money for their churches back in Cuba.

In fact, Protestant as well as Catholic churches in Miami take advantage of this "religious tourism" by inviting traveling clergy to speak, and often preach, to their congregations. They frequently solicit financial aid to support projects led by their churches in Cuba, such as the restoration of church buildings and the creation of soup kitchens and homes for the elderly. Such donations build transnational rapport. In addition, since 1997 high-level meetings between clergy on both sides of the Florida Straits, known as Reuniones para Conocerse Mejor, have encouraged a culture of dialogue over discord. These exchanges, coupled with the thousands of family visits to the island by émigrés, promote a face-to-face diplomacy that buttresses and expands the existing religious space. This space is expanding rapidly and constitutes, in our opinion, one of the few legitimate arenas for rapprochement and reconciliation between Cubans on the island and in the United States.

Leaving the confines of institutional church transnational religious ties, we have found that Afro-Cuban religions also thrive transnationally, for several reasons. Santería, Palo Monte, and other faiths have drawn attention to Cuba from overseas in recent years owing in no small part to the perception that they are purer in Cuba given the island's marginal engagement with the global economy and its trappings, especially commercialization. A popular notion is that the *aché*, or energy/power, of the *orishas* (Afro-Cuban gods) is more powerful and potent in Cuba than elsewhere. Another determining factor is no doubt the fact that it is cheaper to be initiated in Cuba than in most other locations. As a result, many Miami-based Cubans and others travel to the island for induction, guidance, and initiation from resident *babalaos, santeros,* and *paleros*. Arriving with suitcases full of ritual garments and other paraphernalia—often purchased in Miami along their transnational routes—many of these individuals have established or reestablished links to the island through their newly formed religious families. The Cuban government has sought to capitalize on this global interest by sponsoring the construction of the Yoruba Cultural Center in Havana as well as other attractions that appeal to tourists and their dollars but alienate many established practitioners. These dynamics represent one of the newest waves of transnational religious ties that link Cuba to Miami and other sites, virtually all of which have yet to be documented and published.

Finally, we will end this overview of the transnational ties we have witnessed, which illustrate that Cuba is far from the isolated outcast nation portrayed in the media and in much rhetoric in Miami, by focusing on the transnationalization of performances of key Cuban religious festivals that occur simultaneously in Cuba and south Florida. These not only serve to reproduce "traditions" but also promote the imagined community of the Cuban diaspora. In that spirit, please imagine the following scenes:

American Airlines Arena, downtown Miami, 7 p.m., September 8, 2001. One after another they come, eleven couples, each carrying carafes of water from their home diocese in Cuba, bowing to Caridad (Our Lady of Charity) before emptying the vials into a crystal bowl on the altar of the makeshift sanctuary. Eleven exile couples, eleven waters blessed by diocesan priests on the island before being commingled and sprinkled by Miami priests upon the exiles in attendance, tens of thousands strong. Cheers of "Cuba libre!" and strains of "Virgen Mambisa"[1] punctuate the hours-long performance of the patron saint festival, now in its fortieth year. A thousand miles away in El Cobre, Cuba, hundreds of pilgrims file past rum-sweetened revelers into the teeming, sultry sanctuary where another gold-draped Virgin awaits them in the dark before dawn. Some come to petition her and others to thank her for providing help. Times are hard and could she spirit them a visa or watch over a loved one about to embark for Miami on a raft? They come despite the difficulty of finding transportation and food and under the watchful eyes of the authorities.

Imagine now El Rincón de San Lázaro, Cuba, a few minutes before midnight on December 17, 2001. It seems as if the 100,000 who make the annual pilgrimage to the shrine are trying to cram into the sanctuary simultaneously. The tension builds as those in penance drag their exhausted, gunnysack-clad bodies across the floor to the altars. The final inches of a miles-long journey are the most arduous—squeezing in between the Santería practitioners smoking cigars to summon Babalú Ayé (San Lázaro to Santería devotees), the sick and infirm with their makeshift wheelchairs and crutches, the innumerable pilgrims bearing offerings of purple flowers, the groups of jovial transvestites and "rockers." Above the cacophony, "Our Father" is broadcast every five minutes as if to bring orthodoxy to the syncretic, chaotic scene below. Just before the stroke of midnight, a priest asks everyone to make final preparations, to cleanse their hearts and minds to receive the saint. Then the bells chime the dawn of the saint's day and people clap wildly while the priest cries, "Long live San Lázaro! Blessings this day to all Cubans, the Cuban family!"

Meanwhile, across the Florida Straits in Miami's Cuban enclave of Hialeah, pilgrims arrive by the hundreds to El Rincón, a shrine to San Lázaro presided over by a priest not recognized by the archdiocese. Much of the scene there is a simulacra, but on a much smaller scale, of El Rincón, Cuba. As the sun sets and night falls, the stream of pilgrims to the altar grows. Work has ended and it is time to give thanks. An occasional devotee prostrates himself upon entry into the shrine, wiggling the twenty-five feet to the altar where the life-sized statue of San Lázaro is encased in Plexiglas and surrounded by large barrels of purple and yellow flowers. The pilgrims kneel at the altar, light candles, pray, and leave by the side door to the outdoor sanctuary where Mass is held at 6:30 followed by a procession at 8:00.

These examples of transnational religious ties are just a few of dozens we have documented during our research. Given the fact that there is little precedent for analyzing such religious ties and few publications of any kind that map transnational linkages between Cuba and other nations, we found it useful and necessary to begin our analysis by developing an analytical framework as we describe next.

Typology and Analysis of Ties

Over the course of documenting transnational religious ties we have identified three broad categories useful for analyzing them: (1) a typology of the main types of ties; (2) a typology of agency; and (3) an examination of the intentions behind the ties. In the following section we outline these categories and then provide some concrete examples from our fieldwork. As illustrated in the extract that follows, the first typology distinguishes the very palpable kinds of material items that travel across the Florida Straits from the more esoteric links. This typology focuses on the ties themselves. We expect that the distinctions are sufficiently basic and the brief examples so immediately intelligible that they need no further explanation.

General types of transnational religious ties

Broadly speaking, we have identified three main types of ties:
- *Material ties*, which mainly manifest themselves in face-to-face visits and transfers of monetary, food, and medical donations
- *Media/mass-communication ties*, which include religious radio programs, periodicals, and the Internet, as well as videos containing some sort of religious content
- *Ties of a "particularly" a symbolic nature*, which connect two communities through such rituals as prayer, patron saint's day festivals that are celebrated in both communities, sister church relationships, and *promesas* (religious vows) that have a transnational component.

> - We recognize that material and mass-communication ties are also symbolic, but we highlight in this category certain ties in which the symbolism and ritual are especially rich and often identifiable by practitioners.

The second typology in our data centers attention on the locations from which people forging transnational ties act. In our larger project we locate these agents themselves within the multiple constellations of social relationships that shape their agency—hierarchies of class, race, gender, citizenship, and so on. We do not have sufficient space here to provide a deep and extensive analysis of each actor's embeddedness in these hierarchies. Nor can we show how, despite these hierarchies' effects, facilitations, and constraints on individuals, people's actions also include a measure of their own motivation. What we can offer given this limited space is a structural analysis of agency as illustrated in the extract below. We have observed that people who enact transnational ties fall along a continuum, from those who act in an official or institutional capacity to those who act primarily as individuals and informally. Of course, the same individuals can engage in ties officially one day and informally another. We also know that over time informal ties can develop into institutional linkages, a point we develop more thoroughly later. For the time being, we merely assert that in the course of our analysis of transnational religious ties we have found it useful to distinguish agency by level of formality and also by the degree of institutionalization of the actors involved in these ties. The extract depicts institutionalization as a tripartite typology for heuristic reasons but we conceptualize it more as a continuum between the poles of macro and micro levels. At the highest, or macro, level we find transnational ties that link religious denominations or major institutions, such as those between the Archdioceses of Miami and Cuba. At the micro level we have witnessed many individuals who participate in transnational ties for solely personal reasons or on behalf of their churches or church committees. In between, in what we call the meso, or intermediate, level of agency, we find group-to-group relations such as sister church ties and small- to medium-sized organizations such as ECHO-Cuba, a group of Evangelical clergy and laity in Florida who collect donations and sponsor social service projects in limited areas of Cuba.

Degrees of formality and levels of agency

Degree of formality
- ties that are official or formal
- people-to-people ties of a mainly informal and unofficial nature

Continuum of agency
- macro (denominational or large institution level)
- meso (church or small organization level)
- micro (individual or small-group level)

A good example of how these two dimensions of agency interweave is the Bridge of Hope Cuba-Florida Covenant sister church relationship between Florida and Cuban Methodist congregations. The sister church program was the brainchild of a now deceased Methodist bishop in Florida. It initiated formal transnational linkages where each church in Cuba was affiliated with one or more churches in Florida. (Some Miami churches do not participate for political reasons.) We characterize this arrangement as an example of agency orchestrated officially and formally at the macro level. As Methodists in both countries have explained to us, however, each sister church relationship reflects the interests and energies of congregants. Some have evolved into regular visitations between groups from each church while others have focused primarily on the transfer of material aid from the Florida church to its Cuban sister or sisters. These continued ties occupy a middle ground in the continuum of for-mality, as the churches involved often must seek assistance from their denomi-national hierarchies to obtain the visas necessary for the visits or to transfer aid that cannot be carried in visitors' personal luggage. Similarly, as efforts at the congregational level, these ties occupy what we refer to as the meso level of agency. We have however heard of cases where sister church relations have declined over time but person-to-person ties begun through these sisterhoods have endured. Thus, we observe in the Methodist case an evolution from for-mal to informal and from macro to micro.

This example is not unusual, and it is one of the ways that we develop in our larger project what we characterize as "transnationalism of the middle" (Mahler and Hansing 2005). We argue that too much current research and theorizing on contemporary social processes focus on the global-local divide; that is, too rigid a distinction is made between processes that are understood to operate globally versus their manifestations on the ground, or locally. We are critical of this division because we have seen in our own research how fluid these processes and their effects are, particularly when observed over time. Small-scale actions evolve into large-scale processes while huge institutions implode or devolve. More important, many activities and agents operate nei-ther at the top nor at the bottom but in the middle—or they meet in the middle. Unfortunately, we cannot develop this analytical and theoretical point here, but we will have in another publication (Mahler and Hansing 2005).

The final typology we have devised for organizing our data for analysis is to focus on why people participate in transnational religious linkages. This is the arena of purposes. Theorists studying transnational ties have slowly identified a range of intentions behind their construction and perpetuation, ranging from the altruistic to the self-serving and reflecting everything from secular to sacred interests. In our research we have observed a range of reasons or motivations behind why people get involved in or even initiate transnational religious ties. These include

- *Humanitarian*: to send or receive economic or other material aid
- *Religious*: to evangelize and save souls; to save people from Commu-nism and other forms of government that limit religious freedoms
- *Communication*: to get in touch with friends and family separated by borders
- *Personal*: to improve one's status or prestige; to find ways to leave a country in order to improve one's future; to improve one's material wel-fare

In our Cuban-U.S. study, the reasons people offer for their transnational reli-gious activism differ based on where they are located vis-à-vis the Florida

Straits. On the one hand, the main intentions people in Cuba give for their involvement reflect at least to some degree the country's current economic and political crisis. People of faith living on the island are motivated to pursue transnational linkages to expand their horizons and opportunities in a multitude of ways. They can gain information that otherwise is restricted or difficult to obtain on the island; they often find new ways to express their faith and to commune with their religious brothers and sisters abroad; and they may be able, for example, to study to become a pastor more easily. Additionally, leaders often seek transnational ties to obtain resources from the outside that aid in their delivery of social services. Of course, there are always some people who pursue religious ties primarily because they facilitate the achievement of essentially personal goals, such as securing a visa to leave Cuba or obtaining a higher salary.

In Miami, on the other hand, participants express much stronger motivations to evangelize, to save souls long lost to Communism. Other actors cite humanitarian reasons; they point to deteriorated economic conditions on the island, such as the lack of basic foodstuffs, and focus their attention on sending material aid. Numerous transnational actors take advantage of the greater religious spaces opened up between the island and Miami to pursue more personal objectives, such as reconnecting with relatives and reconciling with old church friends who used to attend the same congregation in prerevolutionary times. It is important to note as well that the motivations of the Miami-based actors vary greatly depending on when they emigrated. The first wave often still feel the pangs of forced exile and the twinge of guilt over having abandoned church and family. Subsequent waves of emigration, such as the 1980 Mariel boatlift and the more recent legal immigration of relatives of exiles and those arriving through the *bombo*, or visa lottery system,[2] are people who have greater experience with life in Cuba under Castro. Their desire to sustain contacts is often very personal and immediate when compared to that of the first exiles, who generally cut almost every tie for decades.

Given these generational factors, as well as the current tense political climate between the two Cubas, it is not surprising that most of the reasons mentioned for transnational engagement are influenced by political factors and motivations. This is also true in the official discourses of the dominant denominations, the Catholics in particular. As such, we have organized intentions along a continuum of political purposes that range from rancor to reconciliation, from pressing for change to seeking common ground. In other words, most ties, whether humanitarian, religious, personal, or communicative, are tinged by an antipathy toward the Castro or U.S. government combined with advocacy for change or an orientation toward acceptance, rapprochement, and reconciliation. There is, of course, much middle ground between these two.

Conclusion

Much is at stake as the day draws closer when the aging Castro will die and a future chapter will be written in Cuban-U.S. relations and those of the two Cubas divided by the Florida Straits. The anxiety is palpable and contributes to further rounds of myth making, of portraying Cuba and the United States as inextricably fixed in Cold War animosities. Decades of anger, distrust, and bitterness have left deep wounds in this nation divided territorially, socially, politically, economically, and emotionally. But the story does not end on this note. As much as there have been division and isolation, there have also been dialogue and bonding, much of the latter fostered through the healing balm of faith and faith-based activities.

Although not nearly as appreciated as we feel it ought to be, a sliver of space for transnational communication was preserved by the faithful even during the worst years of repression against religion in Cuba. This small space has grown into a considerable conduit, yet it remains underappreciated. Among the faithful whose activities are responsible for this growth, the inattention is more likely a blessing than a curse. They know they must keep a low profile in order to accomplish their goals without incurring the wrath of the Cuban or U.S. government. Quietly yet steadily, and only occasionally with any fanfare, transnational religious activities take place. We cannot predict their long-term impact or whether they will be targeted for termination. We can assert from our study, however, a number of key findings. First, God truly knows no borders between Cuba and the United States. Over the course of its history, Cuba has been bridged to other lands and peoples via the activities of people of faith. This is no less true today than it was centuries ago. And even in the years of greatest constraints on religious expression on the island, the bridges did not collapse. Second, we can affirm that the existence and persistence of these religious bridges and buttresses are testaments to the fact that Cuba is not the isolated state so often depicted in both island and U.S. mainland portrayals. Certainly, Cuba has in no way achieved the status Castro has desired as patriarch of the family of nations. Neither has the island fallen into complete international disrepute as an excommunicated infidel land, the persona non grata designation sought by hard-liners in the United States, Cuban and non-Cuban alike. These portrayals and the people behind them form the Cold War endpoints to a spectrum of opinions and representations on Cuba. Somewhere in the middle of these extremes lies a truer description of reality. Does this mean that the two opposing camps will come to meet in the middle and face the truth? We do not know for sure, but if religious history is any guide and if faith plays any role, that day of meeting peacefully in the center may be closer than anyone imagines.

Notes

1. The *mambises* were those Cubans who fought for Cuba's independence from Spain. The name Virgen Mambisa claims Caridad as a nationalist as well as a religious figure.

2. *Bombo* is a Cuban nickname for a legal visa program instituted by both the Cuban and U.S. governments as a consequence of the 1994 *balsero,* or rafter, crisis. The United States agreed to offer 20,000 legal permanent resident visas annually to Cubans on a lottery basis in addition to visas already available for relatives of residents in the United States The intention was to alleviate some of the pressures building in Cuba for people to flee the island and attempt to enter the United States illegally, often crossing in unsafe boats.

Bibliography

Arboleya, Jesús. 1996. *Havana-Miami: The U.S.-Cuba Migration Conflict.* Melbourne: Ocean Press.

Basch, Linda, Nina Glick Schiller, and Cristina Szanton Blanc. 1994. *Nations Unbound: Transnational Projects, Postcolonial Predicaments and Deterritorialized Nation-States.* Amsterdam: Gordon and Breach.

Benjamin, Jules R. 1990. *The United States and the Origins of the Cuban Revolution: An Empire of Liberty in an Age of National Liberation.* Princeton: Princeton University Press.

Betto, Frei. 1985. *Fidel y la religión: conversaciones con Frei Betto.* Havana: Oficina de Publicaciones del Consejo de Estado.

Brenner, Philip. 1988. *From Confrontation to Negotiation: U.S. Relations with Cuba.* Boulder: Westview Press.

Brysk, Alison. 1993. "From Above and Below: Social Movements, the International System, and Human Rights in Argentina." *Comparative Political Studies* 26, no. 3: 259–85.

———. 2000. *From Tribal Village to Global Village: Indian Rights and International Relations in Latin America.* Stanford, Calif.: Stanford University Press.

Corse, Theron. 1989. "Presbyterians in the Revolution: An American Missionary Church and the Challenge of Castro's Cuba, 1959–1970." *Cuban Studies* 31: 1–33.

Crahan, Margaret E. 1989. "Catholicism in Cuba." *Cuban Studies* 19: 3–24.

Domínguez, Jorge I. 1989. "International and National Aspects of the Catholic Church in Cuba." *Cuban Studies* 19: 43–60.

Domínguez, Jorge I., and Rafael Hernández, eds. 1989. *U.S.-Cuban Relations in the 1990s.* Boulder: Westview Press.

Ebaugh, Helen R., and Janet Saltzman Chafetz. 2000. *Religion and the New Immigrants: Continuities and Adaptations in Immigrant Congregations.* New York: AltaMira Press.

Echevarría Salvat, Oscar A. 1971. *La agricultura cubana, 1934–1966: régimen social, productividad y nivel de vida del sector agrícola.* Miami: Ediciones Universal.

Fernández, Damián J. 1991. "Revolution and Political Religion in Cuba." In *The Reli-*

gious Challenge to the State, edited by Matthew C. Moen and Lowell S. Gustafson, 57–58. Philadelphia: Temple University Press.

———. 2000. *Cuba and the Politics of Passion*. Austin: University of Texas Press.

Glick Schiller, Nina. 1999. "Transmigrants and Nation-States: Something Old and Something New in the U.S. Immigrant Experience." In *The Handbook of International Migration*, edited by Charles Hirschman, Philip Kasinitz, and Josh DeWind, 94–119. New York: Russell Sage Foundation.

Glick Schiller, Nina, Linda Basch, and Cristina Blanc-Szanton, eds. 1992. *Towards a Transnational Perspective on Migration: Race, Class, Ethnicity, and Nationalism Reconsidered*. Annals of the New York Academy of Sciences 645. New York: New York Academy of Sciences.

Greer, Harold. 1989. "Baptists in Western Cuba: From the Wars of Independence to Revolution." *Cuban Studies* 19: 61–77.

Guarnizo, Luis E., and Michael P. Smith. 1998. "The Locations of Transnationalism." In *Transnationalism from Below*, edited by Michael P. Smith and Luis E. Guarnizo, 3–34. New Brunswick, N.J.: Transaction Publishers.

Gunn, Gillian. 1993. *Cuba in Transition: Options for U.S. Policy*. New York: Twentieth Century Fund Press.

Kearney, Michael. 1995. "The Local and the Global: The Anthropology of Globalization and Transnationalism." *Annual Review of Anthropology* 24: 547–65.

Keck, Margaret E., and Kathryn Sikkink. 1998. *Activists beyond Borders: Advocacy Networks in International Politics*. Ithaca, N.Y.: Cornell University Press.

Kirk, John M. 1989. *Between God and the Party: Religion and Politics in Revolutionary Cuba*. Tampa: University of South Florida Press.

Levitt, Peggy. 2001. "Between God, Ethnicity, and Country: An Approach to the Study of Transnational Religion." Paper presented at the SSRC International Migration Program, ERSC Transnational Communities Programme, Princeton University Center for Migration and Development Workshop on Transnational Migration: Comparative Perspectives, Princeton N.J.

———. 2003. "You Know, Abraham Was Really the First Immigrant: Religion and Transnational Migration." *International Migration Review* 37, no. 3: 847–73.

Mahler, Sarah J., and Katrin Hansing. 2005. "Toward a Transnationalism of the Middle: How Transnational Religious Practices Help Bridge the Divides between Cuba and Miami." *Latin American Perspectives* 32, no. 1: 121–46.

Mato, Daniel. 1997. "On Global Agents, Transnational Relations, and the Social Making of Transnational Identities and Associated Agendas." *Identities: Global Studies in Culture and Power* 4, no. 2: 167–212.

Menjivar, Cecilia. 1999. "Religious Institutions and Transnationalism: A Case Study of Catholic and Evangelical Salvadoran Immigrants." *International Journal of Politics, Culture and Society* 12, no. 4: 589–612.

Ortega, Luis. 1998. *Cubanos en Miami*. Havana: Editorial de Ciencias Sociales.

Paterson, Thomas G. 1994. *Contesting Castro: The United States and the Triumph of the Cuban Revolution*. New York: Oxford University Press.

Pedraza, Teresita. 1998. "'This Too Shall Pass': The Resistance and Endurance of Religion in Cuba." *Cuban Studies* 28: 16–39.

Pérez, Lisandro. 1994. "Cuban Catholics in the United States." In *Puerto Rican and Cuban Catholics in the U.S., 1900–1965*, edited by Jay P. Dolan and Jaime R. Vidal, 147–207. Notre Dame, Ind.: University of Notre Dame Press.

Pérez, Louis. 1990. *Cuba and the United States: Ties of Singular Intimacy*. Athens: University of Georgia Press.

Pérez-Stable, Marifeli. 1993. *The Cuban Revolution: Origins, Course and Legacy*. New York: Oxford University Press.

Rudolph, Susanne H., and James Piscatori, eds. 1997. *Transnational Religion: Fading States*. Boulder: Westview Press.

Smith, Michael P. 1994. "Can You Imagine? Transnational Migration and the Globalization of Grassroots Politics." *Social Text* 39 (Summer): 15–33.

Tweed, Thomas A. 1997. *Our Lady of the Exile: Diasporic Religion at a Cuban Catholic Shrine in Miami*. New York: Oxford University Press.

Vásquez, Manuel A. 1999. "Pentecostalism, Collective Identity, and Transnationalism among Salvadorans and Peruvians in the U.S." *Journal of the American Academy of Religion* 67, no. 3: 617–36.

Vásquez, Manuel A., and Marie F. Marquardt. 2003. *Globalizing the Sacred: Religion across the Americas*. New Brunswick, N.J.: Rutgers University Press.

Yaremko, Jason M. 2000. *U.S. Protestant Missions in Cuba*. Gainesville: University Press of Florida.

4

Gay Sex Tourism, Ambiguity, and Transnational Love in Havana

Gisela Fosado

From 1998 to 2002 I interviewed countless young men who had migrated to Havana from across Cuba to sell gay sex to tourists (and sometimes to locals). I met with them day after day in the spaces where they awaited wealthy gay men, and I quickly became part of their community. These young men, who range from sixteen to thirty years of age, are called *pingueros* because of the way they use their *pinga* (prick) to make money. They form part of a large group of young adults who, since the beginning of the current economic crisis, have participated in the underground economy by hustling tourists in a wide variety of ways as a means to upward mobility. Their mode of hustling, or *luchar*,[1] ranges from selling cigars to earning commissions from hotels and restaurants and explicitly or implicitly selling sexual pleasure and romance.

In 2001 and 2002 I also interviewed many of the gay tourists who slept with these young men and who sometimes became their long-term partners. Often from Europe and Canada and often middle-aged, these gay men spent much of their time in confusion about the exact nature of their relationship with *pingueros*. This essay explores the nature and power dynamics of these complex relationships.

Although some tourists travel to Cuba specifically for cheap sex, countless others become sex tourists of an entirely different sort. Ambiguity and love are so prominent in the experiences of the latter, and sometimes the former as well, that I chose to focus my dissertation project on these important characteristics of sex tourism[2] relationships—characteristics that are often ignored since they exist outside the simplistic hierarchical relationships that scholars often depict in their writings. This chapter, then, focuses on long-term relationships between Cubans and foreigners, but also includes analysis of the role of ambiguity and love among short-term relationships as well.

Most of the recent media attention given to sex tourism, and even the vast majority of scholarly work, has focused on the commercial aspects of sex tourism relationships because they fit more neatly into the victimized, exploited image of the sex worker that we hold in our Western imagination. My work forms part of an emerging backlash that creates a fuller, more accurate, and less sensationalized view of the experiences of Cuban men and women with their tourist-lovers.

The transnational marriage bonds that create migration possibilities for young Cuban women are well represented in the media and in recent academic work (Cabezas 1998; Fusco 1998). The focus of this essay, however, is the transnational relationships that are formed between gay tourists and Cuban men.[3] I argue that within the long-term relationships I studied, both Cubans and tourists work to maintain love and ambiguity at the center of their relationships during key moments, each for different reasons. Although Cubans form strong bonds with the tourists they sleep with, they also feign emotions in order to manipulate the tourists into giving more money. And although tourists are clearly aware of the importance of money in their relationships at some points, they overlook many of the commercial aspects of their relationships in order to focus on love—a more socially legitimate justification for sexual relations. These are but a few of the reasons why tourists and Cubans alternately focus on the money and love aspects of their transnational relationships in different contexts and at different moments.

Ambiguity in Other Sites

Scholars studying other parts of the world have noted that sex tourists are confused due to the ambiguous nature of their sexual relationships with locals. Erik Cohen, a pioneer in sex tourism ethnography, noted in much of his work that sex tourism relationships in Thailand were "ridden with ambiguities" (Cohen 1982: 411). Most of the scholars who have written about ambiguity, however, have described it as a veil tourists use to delude themselves into legitimizing their relationship with Third World Others. Sánchez Taylor, for example, points to the "difference" of sexual transactions in the Caribbean and other resorts that allows "tourists and some sex workers to convince themselves that what is happening is not like straightforward prostitution" (Sánchez Taylor 2000: 42). This type of political emphasis on exploitation and victimization has been criticized by many recent scholars who argue that such a focus is inaccurate and creates public policies that are not helpful to sex workers and, in fact, further marginalize them (see, for example, Bernstein's [2001] groundbreaking work).

I argue that the "difference" Sánchez Taylor diminishes in her research is substantial, largely because both parties experience the relationships differently. These relationships therefore represent something between a noncommercial, "socially legitimate" relationship and one that foreigners and locals label as "fully commercial." Scholars such as O'Connell Davidson and Sánchez Taylor seem to prefer black-and-white terms. They claim that tourists "deceive themselves about the true nature of their sexual interaction with local people first because prostitution takes a number of different forms in the countries they visit and second because they too buy into highly sexualized forms of racism" (O'Connell Davidson and Sánchez Taylor 1999: 65). These authors are clearly invested in maintaining the victim-centered discourse within sex tourism studies that is dangerous in the Caribbean context, as it is in other contexts.

While I agree that some tourists might deceive themselves, and while they clearly engage in highly racially informed modes of sexualizing locals, I also believe that most of the long-term relationships I looked at are truly confusing and ambiguous to both participants because they push the limits of "legitimate" and "illegitimate" sexual encounters by being commercial in some ways and not in others. I argue that both the ambiguous and the hierarchical aspects of these relationships must be represented in ethnographic work. *Pingueros*, like their counterparts in other cultures, have clear motives for perpetuating ambiguity in these relationships and themselves feel confused by many aspects of their relationships with tourists.

"Love No Longer Exists in Cuba" and *Relaciones de Interés*

> Here in Cuba there are no friends. Once a foreigner was with me and he started flirting with a friend of mine and he fucked him too. . . . My friend fucked him for money, because there is no love in Cuba. So what did he do? He took the money instead of my friendship. . . . He traded me in for money. . . . There is no love in Cuba. Everyone is after money and nothing else.

When Yusnaldy, an eighteen-year-old *pinguero* from Havana Province spoke these words to me in 2001, they resonated with phrases that I had heard from countless other Cubans within and outside of sex tourism areas, within and outside of Havana. The repeated use of this expression, as well as other related expressions, signaled to me that the relationship between money and sex had experienced a radical shift during my fieldwork time and during the 1990s generally. These expressions were not used casually and thoughtlessly, but often were surrounded by a discourse that emphasized the confusing, disturbing, and depressing state of relationships that lacked love. The main idea of this particular expression is that love does not exist in Cuba because people are driven by economic mobility first and foremost. Love in Cuba, therefore, can only exist between two people who place the other person's financial well-being before their own.

In this case, Yusnaldy's friend had violated the common friendship etiquette of not interfering with a friend's *lucha*. Yusnaldy's friend took away his tourist and thereby gave up the friendship for his own *lucha*. On other occasions when I witnessed Cubans using this expression, they were referring to giving up love relationships for more lucrative relations, whether with other Cubans or with tourists.

Although I heard this expression used in various parts of the country, there was agreement among the Cubans I spoke to that people from the countryside were more *sano* (innocent, healthy) than people from Havana, who were more prone to do things *por interés* (with ulterior motives). Even outside of Havana, however, people I spoke to agreed that Cubans in general were becoming more and more *dolarizados* (dollarized, commercialized) every day.

The men I interviewed expressed deep concern over whether relationships were economically motivated (in other words, whether or not they were *relaciones de interés*). I asked a twenty-nine-year-old hustler named Salvador whether he ever bought drinks or gifts for his girlfriends. He replied,

Almost never because I would be buying her. I want them to do it for love. I think what really happens in Havana is that women are with you *por interés*, not because they like you or anything like that, but because you're going to satisfy her necessities. . . . I have youth. I'm not a model, but I'm not ugly either and so I can have a relationship without *interés*. Everything in life is an *interés* because you can be with a girl, even if you don't buy anything for her, but they're with you because you take them out to eat or drink, or to parties, or because you joke around with her. It's another kind of *interés*. Everything in life is either an economic *interés* or a social *interés*.

The fear of economically motivated relationships goes against a general idea that is even more widespread in Cuba—that people who have more than average resources should share them, since equality is the official, state inculcated ideal and since sharing is integral to loving someone, sexually or otherwise. Indeed, one of the main modes used to establish friendships among the street people I studied was gift giving and sharing. It became a difficult issue for me to negotiate as I was expected to participate in gift giving according to my means, which were always assumed to be the same as those of other tourists.

Marcel Mauss argued in his seminal work, *Essai sur le don* (1923), that there are expectations of return behind every gift and that these expectations constitute shared culture. This is certainly true in Cuba, a place where gift giving is surprisingly prolific during most holidays and even at other times and where there is a shared expectation of reciprocity (according to one's means). I received more gifts for Valentine's Day, Christmas, and my birthday than I had ever received on those days before. On these special days most people I knew went out of their way to give me food or knickknacks or anything they could. On ordinary days people regularly invited me for meals and always said, "Where there's enough food for four, there is enough for five." The hustlers I interviewed, who did not eat regular meals, would invite me to share the peanuts or candy that they bought on the street to show that they appreciated me. They would also offer to take me to movies (which cost ten cents during my fieldwork time), to the beach, or out dancing at peso clubs at night. The Cubans I knew received the same treatment from their friends and were expected to return the favor when they could. Gifts and social relations are indeed intricately connected to each other (Komter 1996) in culturally specific ways in Cuba. The ambiguity between requesting reciprocal gifts as an appreciation of love and swindling money from wealthy people is of course what makes hustling in Cuba so effective, because if you do not return gifts according to your means then you deviate from expectations and are labeled *camaján*, *codo*, or another label for stinginess.

The essence of my point regarding *relaciones de interés* is that although certain ideologies contribute to inequality in social relations in Cuba, the assumed ideal has been economic equality since the revolution began. Although men might control the money in a household as part of the ideology of *machismo*, a prenuptial financial agreement, for example, would be contradictory to the meanings associated with love relationships.

During the Special Period in Time of Peace—the name given to the current economic crisis—uncertainty has grown about whether or not relationships are *por interés*. This is especially the case as the tourism industry and remittances from family abroad create deep divides in incomes (especially in Havana and within tourist areas). This uncertainty has brought a shift in the way that Cubans conceptualize love because money has taken an increasingly large role in culturally specific narratives regarding love. Although men have long paid for women's meals and other expenses during courtship without verbally highlighting these exchanges, the increasing disparity between those with means and those without has made the subject of money exchanges prominent in love narratives.

As Salvador noted, if one is young and attractive, then relationships without ulterior motives are more easily attainable, but once these qualities are lost, people might date you for money or other resources. As he astutely explained, many other qualities or resources are exchanged, such as humor, food and drink, access to social events, and so on. The term *relaciones de interés*, however, marks the uneven and critical exchange of resources that are necessary to live on a day-to-day basis or that change one's economic status by orders of magnitude. This uneven exchange in a *relación de interés*, furthermore, creates a situation where sincerity is questioned since money, not love, might be the main glue binding two people together. This economic and resource inequality within relationships is what Cubans describe as a *relación de interés*. In cases where relationships are deemed to have clear ulterior motives, and the types of exchanges become suspect, the existence of love is suddenly questioned and a confusing, ambiguous state emerges where the sincerity of feelings is never quite certain. This is not only true in relationships among Cubans; as one might imagine, it is even more pronounced in relationships between Cubans and foreigners, where wealth, marriage, or migration become suspected ulterior motives.

Benicio, an eighteen-year-old *pinguero*, commented,

> Tourists tell me that they love me and I think they're lying so I tell them that I love them too. It's a way to get more money out of them. I tell them, "I love you, I adore you, I want you" . . . and so they grow even more fond of me and they love me more. I don't know if it's real or not that they love me, but shit, right away they say, "Wow, this boy loves me, and I'm going to please him so that his love for me doesn't end and he enjoys being with me. I'll treat him well." That's when I get all the money out of him.

Both the tourists and the young men I interviewed were not sure what was "real" in their sexual relationships. Young men in Cuba who hustle tourists see the tables turn after they walk away from these relationships with dollars in their pockets because they subsequently date women and are never sure how much of those heterosexual relationships are "real" or *por interés*.

Being able to manipulate tourists into ambiguous relationships and making them lucrative is a skill called *la mecánica*[4] (the swindle). A young man named Yamil explained,

> Yamil: If young people would use their head in the first moment when they speak to the foreigner, they'd realize that the most correct thing to do is not to ask for money. What happens if you ask for money is that you get to know the foreigner and he invites you to go out, you might do something physical and he'll pay you and "bye, bye." But then we have the other scenario: You can meet a foreigner, he can invite you to go dance, you can have sex without you telling him a price, he still might pay you well, and then the next day he might invite you to go out again. Those who are intelligent and who are professionals at this do this. That's how I think anyway.
>
> Gisela: But there must be some *camaján*[5] (stingy) tourists who don't want to spend any money.
>
> Yamil: Those with enough education and enough *psicología* (psychology) can soften any cheapo.

Pingueros who are good at swindling are said to have *psicología* and *inteligencia* (psychology and intelligence). These terms point to the fact that successful hustling entails careful social maneuvering, planning, and acting. This was the *pingueros'* view of their relationships with tourists and wealthy gay men when they spoke generally about their hustling activities. When I spoke to them about individual gay tourists or individual wealthy gay Cubans with whom they spent days or weeks, however, they noted feeling a tenderness for them that they associated with fatherly love. Because of this appreciation, *pingueros* would often become confused when attempting to understand and talk about the long-term relationships they formed with individual men. And mixed in with these contradictory feelings of love and hustling were sometimes deep homophobic feelings that I often associated with the way they treated the women in their lives, but that is a topic for another essay. These are some of the many elements that make these relationships precarious and confusing.

Sincerity, Ambiguity, and *La Mecánica*

Inexperienced tourists who confront experienced *pingueros* are easily swindled, especially when approached in non-sexualized zones. One winter afternoon I met such a tourist while I sat on a bench with a few friends in Havana's Central Park. I noticed Juan, an eighteen-year-old *pinguero* whom I knew quite well, sitting at the opposite end of the park with an attractive tourist in his late thirties or early forties. Juan came over to me and asked me to help translate because he did not understand if the tourist wanted to have sex with him. He also asked me to ask the tourist if he had any old shoes or clothes that he wanted to give him. Wolfgang, the tourist, was German. I explained that I was an anthropologist studying the park community and that I would be willing to translate and listen to what Wolfgang had to say. He recounted his initial encounter with Juan and his subsequent feelings of confusion as to whether or not he was being hustled. As he spoke, Juan wandered away to talk to his girlfriend and their two-month-old baby, who quietly observed from the same bench at the other end of the park where I had been seated minutes earlier. There was an unspoken understanding between Juan and me that I would only say things that would help Juan earn some money. He left me alone with Wolfgang for about fifteen minutes, which gave me a chance to interview the German. Wolfgang told me that they first met on a main tourist drag in Old Havana a few blocks from the park:

> First, I saw him putting his hands through his hair. And then I sort of looked at him and I noticed quite soon through the look in his eyes and the duration of the eye contact that he might be interested. Like other times when I've cruised, I passed him and since I thought he was inter-

ested, I looked over my shoulder. Then I saw that he was also looking back, so then I passed a bit further, and again, I looked over my shoulder and I saw him look again. And then we turned around and passed each other again, and we kept looking at each other. . . . I first came back to this bar where he was standing, on a street corner. He gave a glance every fifty seconds or so, not too obvious and then I recognized that he was looking at me, so I went back to this street and I noticed that he was following me and then I sort of sat down on the corner of a very small bar near Obispo [Street] and, well, he sort of passed me and I shook his hand and introduced myself.

Because this initial interaction so closely resembled average "cruising" exchanges that Wolfgang was familiar with, he remained hopeful that money was not a motivator. Wolfgang requested that I tell him whether or not I thought Juan might be hustling him. I made it clear that I could not help him on that or any other matter regarding the people I interviewed because I could not disclose any information that I learned while conducting my fieldwork. He nevertheless agreed to continue with the interview. I was afraid that my refusal to give him information would implicitly suggest that Juan was indeed a sexual hustler, but in fact, Wolfgang remained thoroughly confused. Perhaps he was too excited about the potential romantic encounter with Juan to carefully analyze our conversation.

> Gisela: And you are hoping that it's just sexual interest, that there is nothing monetary or anything?
>
> Wolfgang: I hope, yes, I definitely hope so. I know there are, at least I think there are, lots of tourists who are prepared to pay for this. But because he was not directly seeking contact with me and also because he said he was a bit afraid of the whole situation, I'm hopeful it's not hustling. But I'm a very careful type; I'm a very suspicious type also because I've had some bad experiences. Here in Cuba it's pretty safe. I think in the rest of South America it's much less safe than it is here. Especially in the beginning, I'm very much keen on how he reacts, how he behaves, and I sort of gathered that he's not hustling, but you never know.

Wolfgang explained to me that during his two weeks of traveling in Cuba, he often felt that he did not know who was sincere because he sensed that everyone expected something material from him. Wolfgang longed for "real," or sincere, interaction with Cubans, and he used various methods to determine whether people were more interested in him or his money. Later in the interview he also mentioned people's gazes as primary clues to figure out if they were hustling him. Some things made him suspicious that Juan was a hustler, he added. Juan had told him that he paid one dollar per day for housing and that he was a student. Wolfgang wondered how any Cuban could afford to pay this unless he hustled for a living. By this time Juan had returned, and he nudged me and reminded me to ask if Wolfgang had old clothes or shoes to give away. I translated and Wolfgang offered to give him the tennis shoes he was wearing if Juan walked him back to his hotel room to change shoes. Juan was content with this and decided not to have sex with Wolfgang since the shoes were all he really wanted anyway. I suspect that Wolfgang was left confused by the entire interaction.

Other hustlers like Juan who want to capitalize from these types of ambiguous *relaciones de interés* might lie about their occupation, feign attraction during courtship, or avoid mention of payment for sex (although it is quite common for the hustler to remind tourists after sex that he has no money and that anything they can give would be a tremendous help). It is also common to give a small gift to the tourist, as to a friend or lover, so that he feels the need to reciprocate with a larger gift. The *pinguero* might then feel even more obliged to engage in enthusiastic sexual relations.

Sex Tourism Mirroring My Anthropology

> Travel and travellers are two things I loathe—and yet here I am, all set
> to tell the story of my expeditions.
> —Lévi-Strauss, *Tristes tropiques*, 17

The similarity between my activities and Wolfgang's is striking and merits discussion in an essay about transnational relations. Wolfgang and I both traveled from First World countries to Cuba in search of Otherness—the traditional substance of anthropology. We form part of a Cuba boom in which hundreds of thousands of tourists, including many scholars, have taken an interest in and traveled to Cuba. Ruth Behar calls this the Buena Vista Socialization of the world, referring to the way the Buena Vista Social Club music and film sparked the popularization of salsa, *mojitos*, and all things Cuban.[6]

Wolfgang and I, like many of these tourists, both spent our time trying to understand the power dynamics and meanings of sexual and love relationships in Cuba. Both of us acted as voyeurs and created a forced distance between ourselves and the hustlers we observed as we methodically analyzed their behavior. (This is not to say that the hustlers we observed were not also actively observing and analyzing us, because they were indeed.) The parallels between my actions and the actions of tourists like Wolfgang, as we search for "authentic" adventures and objects in exotic lands so that we can tell stories about and make sense of them back home, is a process that has a long history in anthropology, colonialism, and tourism. Dean MacCannell noted some of these parallels between tourists and researchers in his groundbreaking book on tourism: "Modern tourists," he wrote, "share with social scientists their curiosity about primitive peoples, poor peoples and ethnic and other minorities" (MacCannell 1999: 5). Although much contemporary work by anthropologists breaks this tradition, mine does so in only limited ways. While I studied poor, marginalized people in Cuba, I myself emerged from a similar marginalized community in Mexico and thereby identified with the people I studied in ways that many tourists did not.

Tourists Comfortable with Ambiguity

Unlike Wolfgang, Carter, a Canadian in his sixties, was not bothered by the monetary aspect of his relationship with *pingueros* and was therefore not interested in pursuing the question of whether or not the experience was "real" and "sincere." Like many tourists, he assumed that the young men were attracted to them and liked having sex with them on *some* level. He explained why he was so happy in Cuba:

> Carter: It's easier here to meet the kind of men I like, because in Canada there's absolutely nothing to do, because there are black people and Arabic people and Latinos and everything but they're out of bounds and out of reach and I couldn't meet them. I don't go out to bars that much, and even if I do, there's not that many of them there, and if there are, they just look through me as if I were invisible.
>
> Gisela: And here more people seem to be interested?
>
> Carter: More people, and you're not invisible here at all. Of course you stand out and everything. It's definitely easier.
>
> Gisela: And it doesn't bother you that they might be attracted to you because you have dollars?
>
> Carter: No, it doesn't bother me at all, no. 'Cause I'm sure there's more than that, 'cause I've asked myself that question very, very, very often and I know that there's more than that. Yes they do need money and dollars and things but they need more, 'cause they do give a lot. When it's only for money, it's bang, bang, bang and cold and distant and mechanical, which it isn't here at all.
>
> Gisela: You think they might be good actors, or you think there's something very sincere too?
>
> Carter: I think it's something very sincere 'cause if they're actors, at times they would drop the act or would forget about the act and their natural side would come out but, no, I think they're quite sincere as far as I know.

Carter felt that the sexual and other interactions he had with young men in Cuba were enough to convince him that they were sincere, even if he was paying them regularly. As a first-time visitor to Cuba, Carter had met few *pingueros*. The sole *pinguero* lover he had had was also new to the scene and did not make explicit demands for money or gifts as more experienced *pingueros* often do. Or perhaps his lover's goal was to migrate abroad or maintain a continual source of money, and he therefore wanted to act as sincere as possible in his efforts to establish a long-term relationship.

Yusmani, a twenty-year-old *pinguero* from the outskirts of Santa Clara, was one of the very few young men I knew who managed to migrate to Spain during my fieldwork time. He had lived in an orphanage most of his life and had set his mind on leaving Cuba in order to prosper financially. He explained to me why he never asked for money from any tourist he slept with. Although he never said that it was because he wanted to leave the country, I believe that this can be inferred from the following interview:

> Yusmani: I never asked for money. And that's why many times they didn't even pay, but I never have regretted acting like that.
> Gisela: Why?
> Yusmani: Because the people who don't give you money, the ones that don't help you in that way, maybe if you would have obligated them to give you money, they would give you the money without good intentions, you know? They give it to you but then they talk behind your back. They say, "Look, that boy charged me" and who knows what else, and "that boy isn't worth it." I'm glad I did what I did. I'm just too ashamed to ask. I wasn't born for that. I wasn't born to prostitute myself for money. That hurts me, because maybe someone wants to get to know you with good intentions—with intentions, perhaps, to have a relationship with you. . . . I put myself in the place of that person. I don't want to do to people what I don't want them to do to me. Because in the past I've liked a girl a lot and I've tried to get close to her and that girl has asked me, "Do you have a car?" and I've told her no. And then she asks me, "Do you have a motorcycle" and I've said no. And then she asks, "Where are you going to invite me to go out?" And I've said, "to the movies," or "to the park," and you know what she said? "You're not going to invite me to an expensive disco?" And I've had to say, "I'm not the man you're looking for then." But suppose that you like a boy, if you had to sit in a park to talk, well, you'd do it because you fall in love. So, I'm looking for one of those people. I'm not interested in meeting anyone else. Not prostitutes, or businessmen, or prostitute men. I like to be around people

who are like me, open-minded, that understand me so that there are no secrets. If I ever marry a woman, I would like her to know everything about my life: that I once had gay relations, that I once lived in Cuba, that I was poor, that I lost my parents, that she knew everything.

Yusmani pointed to many reasons why he would never ask for money. He noted that it could create gossip, create barriers and limits in the relationship, bring him shame, and that he is uninterested in relationships where money is important (*relaciones de interés*) and he assumes that tourists would feel the same way.

Explicit Sex and Money Exchange

The other general strategy the *pingueros* I interviewed used to make money from tourists was explicitly to exchange money for sex, often in response to tourists who directly offered money for sexual services. Tourists looking for explicit sex-for-money exchanges were often repeat tourists who had visited Cuba and other poor countries for sex many times. Morocco and Eastern European countries seemed to be particular favorites. Many of these tourists were bargain hunters who found Cuba to be cheaper, safer (in terms of violence and sexually transmitted diseases), and more sexually *caliente* (hot, insatiable, horny, talented) than other countries. Such exoticizing tourists travel to places where they can act and treat others differently from the way they do at home.

Several sex tourism researchers describe tourists' experiences as existing in a state of liminality (following Arnold Van Gennep's 1909 rites of passage framework). One claim made by scholars is that tourism offers a liminal environment away from the constraints of home, which reduces inhibitions and provides increased opportunities for sex (Clift and Forrest 1999; McKercher and Bauer 2003: 10). Pruitt and LaFont (1995), for example, found that tourist women feel regarded as more voluptuous and sexy abroad. Eiser and Ford (1995) call the feeling of being a "different person" abroad "situational disinhibition." Sánchez Taylor claims that this liminal state that tourists find themselves in is related to the "obscene disparity of wealth between rich and poor nations" (Sánchez Taylor 2000: 41). Given this disparity, she notes, "even relatively low-paid workers from affluent countries can 'live like kings/playboys' in the Third World countries they visit, and enjoy the kind of economic power they cannot hope to enjoy at home" (Sánchez Taylor 2000: 41). She adds that many tourists use this power to obtain sexual services.

Sex tourism scholars argue not only that tourists feel "different" abroad but that they treat locals as inherently "different" from them as well. Laurie Shrage

(1994) and Kamala Kempadoo (1999) have both noted that historically and cross-culturally, sex customers overwhelmingly seek sex workers whose ethnic and class identities are different from their own. Citing Henriquez (1965) and Bush (1990), Kempadoo notes that in the Caribbean specifically, historians have noted that ideologies and practices have "situated a woman of mixed African/European descent (the mulatta) as the object of white male sexual desire and fantasy, constituting her as the sexual servant, concubine or mistress, and whore" (Kempadoo 1999: 74). This stereotype has present-day manifestations in the tourist industry since "sensual mulattoes" are often illustrated in advertisements (Bolles 1992; Dagenais 1993; Kempadoo 1999). Sánchez Taylor claims that locals must then play along with the myth and "be the bearers of very specific racialized and gendered identities. . . . The myth thus becomes a self-fulfilling prophecy as the interplay of race and gender limit the opportunities for Blacks in the formal economy and shape their entry into the informal economy" (Sánchez Taylor 2000: 48–49). Kempadoo notes that tourists see locals dancing, drinking, and smooching with other tourists and this validates racist fantasies of the hypersexual Other as "living in idyllic pleasure, splendid innocence or Paradise-like conditions—as purely sensual, natural, simple and uncorrupted beings" (Kempadoo 1995: 76). And Cuban mulattas have been exoticized not only by foreign men; male Cuban writers, artists, and poets "enshrined the erotic image of Cuba's *mulatas* long before the advent of tourism" (Schwartz 1997: 86).

Lee (1991: 90) found that tourists in Asia often engage in sex tourism as a backlash to the women's movement in the West because female passivity is a scarce resource back home; even travel advertisements explicitly advertise "docility and submission." As I show elsewhere (Fosado 2004), sexual exploitation and sexual ideologies are still highly linked to ideas that emerged during colonial rule, when Western men projected racist fantasies about the "primitive" Other (Collins 1991; Gilman 1985; Hooks 1992; Kempadoo 1999; Sánchez Taylor 2000).

Sex tourism scholars rarely address the differing experiences of male and female tourists and male and female locals. Sánchez Taylor found that white female tourists, like white male tourists, do not challenge the racial hierarchy when they develop relationships with black men abroad but instead happily accept their superior position since "they are allowed to be in control of masculinities which are 'Black,' hypersexual and 'dangerous.'" She also noted that this type of female tourist does not plan on establishing "a loving relationship with a Jamaican man . . . nor does she challenge racism back home but rather accepts the racial hierarchy and her position in it" (Sánchez Taylor 2000: 47).

The experienced sex tourists I interviewed were usually not fully taken in by *pingueros* who lied. Most tourists, experienced or not, preferred to think that on some level, the young man loved them and enjoyed the sexual encounters.

Roy, a sixty-six-year-old Canadian, explained to me why he confronted many sex workers about their overt lies:

> Roy: Well, you know what's going on here is that when people ask you, "Oh, I want to go with you, I want to go with you," at my age I'm always surprised. And what I do is I ask them "Why? Why me?" But I know down there in their mind that it's the money that they want, but when I'm not interested in them, I ask them that joke. I say, "Why do you want to go with me? You don't want me. You want money" and so on, and "I don't have any money. Do you want to come with me if I don't give you any money?" At that point they're not going to come. They don't say no, but they don't say yes.
>
> Gisela: It's an uncomfortable question, I've noticed. They don't like to be confronted.
>
> Roy: I know that it's a very uncomfortable question, but I only ask this question when I'm not interested. First of all, I don't take a boy every hour, so I choose them. I'm a man—I chase them (laughs). I always chase people who don't talk to me and don't look at me. Hard to get is my type.

Despite his skepticism, Roy believed many lies in other encounters with men he wanted to have sex with. He wanted desperately to believe that the young men he liked felt the same way about him. Although Roy is a bargain-hunting sex tourist in most of his encounters, his dream was to find a boy who sincerely liked him and with whom he could develop a stable relationship. In the meantime, he offered ten to fifteen dollars for sex.

Many *pingueros* who dealt with explicit sex-for-money exchanges were resentful that tourists offered so little. As one young man put it, "Tourists treat us like merchandise. They say, 'Let's look for cheap sex, because it's the cheapest in the world,' because of how needy we are in Cuba. The whole world knows it."

Practitioners of the straightforward method often charge on a sliding scale depending on the age, attractiveness, and nationality of the client, and also depending on how desperate they are for money. As the day wears on, prices get lower. Many older Cuban gays stay out until four or five in the morning if they want to find a desperate *pepillo* (trendy, attractive young man) to go home with them for food and shelter, or perhaps five dollars. A marketable young man might charge tourists as much as fifty dollars but the average going rate is twenty dollars.

When *pingueros* hustle, either explicitly or through some form of *mecánica*, they often tap into the vast black market commission system. Cubans are not allowed inside hotels, so they must have sexual relations with locals in private rental rooms and sometimes do the same with foreigners. When a Cuban takes a foreigner to a private room or restaurant or bar, he earns a commission from the owners of the establishment or the bartender. The average commission for a rental room is five dollars per night. For restaurants, it is five dollars per meal, and for bars it is three dollars per mixed drink. Some experienced hustlers can increase their commissions threefold quite easily. They make arrangements with the establishment personnel to charge naïve tourists excessive amounts of money, threatening to take the tourist to another establishment if the personnel do not comply. In either case, the tourist is overcharged and the *pinguero* returns the next day to collect his commission. These are merely a few of the most common ways of getting money from tourists.

In this essay I have made a case for not making cut-and-dried distinctions among sex tourism, prostitution, and love in relationships between Cubans and foreigners. By looking closely at the way the men I interviewed experienced and spoke about their relationships, I have concluded that these categories are inadequate for understanding sexual relationships in contemporary Cuba be-cause they obfuscate the role of money in sexual relationships. These catego-ries, furthermore, are ethnocentric and deserve careful deconstruction when used in cross-cultural analysis.

I have argued that there is much confusion about the role of money in transnational love relationships in contemporary Cuba, particularly since the economic crisis of the 1990s. As in any other society where love relationships are based on exchange and are continually in flux, it is important to examine the ways those exchanges take place and how they are conceptualized in a specific time and place. Through my exploration of the ubiquitous expression "there is no love in Cuba" and use of the category *relaciones de interés* (rela-tionships with ulterior motives), I have shown the need for a new theoretical framework that allows for uncertainty and ambiguity as defining factors in relationships. While I draw attention to important aspects of these relation-ships, I am certainly not implying that sex tourism relationships lack deep-seated levels of exploitation and injustice. I am arguing, however, that focusing solely on hierarchical power relationships ignores some of the important as-pects of the way both tourists and Cuban men experience these long-term relationships. My framework, I argue, is necessary for understanding the power dynamics in sex tourism relationships and other love relationships in contemporary Cuba.

Notes

1. Since the early 1990s, *luchar* has been used to refer to the daily struggle to make ends meet. Among *pingueros* it means to swindle or hustle sexually. Militarized terms that previously referred to the revolutionary struggle toward socialism and the common good now refer to the daily struggle to hustle dollars or goods in the black market for

individual gain, thus marking a clear shift in the political economy. Although Cubans used *luchar* occasionally to describe what we consider "sex work" in the early twentieth century, the term was not as developed and popular as it has been postrevolution. *Luta*, the Portuguese equivalent of *lucha*, is likewise used in Brazil to denote the everyday life struggles of poverty, portraying "life as a veritable battleground" (Scheper-Hughes 1992: 188).

2. For reasons that I have detailed elsewhere (see Fosado 2004) I have chosen to use an extremely broad definition of sex tourism. Like Chris Ryan, I take sex tourism to mean "sexual intercourse while away from home" (Ryan 2000: 36). While this definition may seem absurdly broad, it is particularly useful in places like Cuba where sex tourism practices are incredibly diverse, as should become clear in the examples that follow.

3. Hodge's (2001) provocative article on gay sex tourism, "Colonization of the Cuban Body," follows the past trend in sex tourism studies to focus on the exploited sex worker, as the title suggests. His work, however, is the first published scholarly work that focuses on the relatively less visible gay sex tourism scene in Cuba.

4. This expression (*mecaniquear*) is also used to refer to swindling people, not just tourists, out of anything.

5. I use *camaján* here because it is a term commonly used by *jineteros* (male prostitutes) and *pingueros* to describe tourists who refuse to give money away, either because they want to make sure the interaction is sincere or because they keep a tight hold on their money.

6. From a Cuban Research Institute Conference presentation, 2000, Florida International University. See Behar (2002: 658) for her views on this phenomenon.

Bibliography

Behar, Ruth. 2002. "While Waiting for the Ferry to Cuba: Afterthoughts about *Adio Kerida*." *Michigan Quarterly Review* 41, no. 4: 651–67.

Bernstein, Elizabeth. 2001. "The Meaning of the Purchase: Desire, Demand and the Commerce of Sex." *Ethnography* 2, no. 3: 389–420.

Bolles, A. Lynn. 1992. "Sand, Sea and the Forbidden." *Transforming Anthropology* 3: 30–34.

Bush, Barbara. 1990. *Slave Women in Caribbean Society: 1650–1838*. Bloomington: Indiana University Press.

Cabezas, Amalia. 1998. "Discourses of Prostitution: The Case of Cuba." In *Global Sex Workers: Rights, Resistance, and Redefinition*, edited by Kamala Kempadoo and Jo Doezema. New York: Routledge.

Clift, Stephen, and S. Forrest. 1999. "Gay Men and Tourism: Destinations and Holiday Motivations." *Tourism Management* 20: 315–25.

Cohen, Erik. 1982. "Thai Girls and Farang Men: The Edge of Ambiguity." *Annals of Tourism Research* 9: 403–28.

Collins, Patricia Hill. 1991. *Black Feminist Thought: Knowledge, Consciousness, and the Politics of Empowerment*. London: Routledge.

Dagenais, Huguette. 1993. "Women in Guadeloupe: The Paradoxes of Reality." In *Women and Change in the Caribbean: A Pan-Caribbean Perspective*, edited by Janet H. Momsen. Bloomington: Indiana University Press.

Eiser, J. Richard, and N. Ford. 1995. "Sexual Relationships on Holiday—A Case of Situational Disinhibition." *Journal of Social and Personal Relationships* 12, no. 3: 323–29.

Fosado, Gisela. 2004. "The Exchange of Sex for Money in Cuba: Masculinity, Ambiguity and Love." Ph.D. diss., University of Michigan.

Fusco, Coco. 1998. "Hustling for Dollars: *Jineterismo* in Cuba" In *Global Sex Workers: Rights, Resistance, and Redefinition*, edited by Kamala Kempadoo and Jo Doezema. New York: Routledge.

Gilman, Sander L. 1985. "Black Bodies, White Bodies: Toward an Iconography of Female Sexuality in Late Nineteenth Century Art, Medicine and Literature." *Critical Inquiry* 12, no. 1: 204–42.

Henriquez, Fernando. 1965. *Prostitution in Europe and America*. New York: Citadel Press.

Hodge, Derrick. 2001. "Colonization of the Cuban Body: The Growth of Male Sex Work in Havana." *NACLA Report on the Americas* 34, no. 5: 20–29.

Hooks, Bell. 1992. *Black Looks: Race and Representation*. London: Turnaround.

Kempadoo, Kamala. 1995. "Prostitution, Marginality and Empowerment: Caribbean Women in the Sex Trade." *Beyond Law* 5, no. 14: 69–84.

———, ed. 1999. *Sun, Sex, and Gold: Tourism and Sex Work in the Caribbean*. New York: Rowman and Littlefield.

Komter, Aafke E. 1996. Introduction to *The Gift: An Interdisciplinary Perspective*, edited by Aafke E. Komter. Amsterdam: Amsterdam University Press.

Lee, Wendy. 1991. "Prostitution and Tourism in South-East Asia." In *Working Women: International Perspectives on Labour and Gender Ideology*, edited by Nanneke Redcliff and M. Thea Sinclair. London: Routledge.

Lévi-Strauss, Claude. 1968. *Tristes tropiques*, translated by John Russell. New York: Atheneum.

MacCannell, Dean. 1999. *The Tourist: A New Theory of the Leisure Class*. Berkeley: University of California Press.

Mauss, Marcel. 1923. *Essai sur le don*. Reprint, *The Gift: The Form and Reason for Exchange in Archaic Societies*. New York: Routledge, 1990.

McKercher, Bob, and Thomas G. Bauer. 2003. "Conceptual Framework of the Nexus between Tourism, Romance, and Sex." In *Sex and Tourism: Journeys of Romance, Love, and Lust*, edited by Tomas G. Bauer and Bob McKercher. New York: Haworth Hospitality Press.

O'Connell Davidson, Julia, and Jacqueline Sánchez Taylor. 1999. "Fantasy Islands: Exploring the Demand for Sex Tourism." In *Sun, Sex, and Gold: Tourism and Sex Work in the Caribbean*, edited by Kamala Kempadoo. New York: Rowman and Littlefield.

Pruitt, Dean G., and Suzanne LaFont. 1995. "For Love and Money: Romance Tourism in Jamaica." *Annals of Tourism Research* 22: 422–40.

Ryan, Chris. 2000. "Sex Tourism: Paradigms of Confusion?" In *Tourism and Sex: Culture, Commerce and Coercion*, edited by Stephen Clift and Simon Carter. New York: Pinter.

Sánchez Taylor, Jacqueline. 2000. "Tourism and 'Embodied' Commodities: Sex Tourism in the Caribbean." In *Tourism and Sex: Culture, Commerce and Coercion*, edited by Stephen Clift and Simon Carter. New York: Pinter.

Scheper-Hughes, Nancy. 1992. *Death without Weeping: The Violence of Everyday Life in Brazil*. Berkeley: University of California Press.

Schwartz, Rosalie. 1997. *Pleasure Island: Tourism and Temptation in Cuba*. Lincoln: University of Nebraska Press.

Shrage, Laurie. 1994. *Moral Dilemmas of Feminism*. London: Routledge.

Van Gennep, Arnold. 1909. *The Rites of Passage*. Reprint, Chicago: University of Chicago Press, 1960.

5

Locas al Rescate

The Transnational Hauntings of Queer *Cubanidad*

Lázaro Lima

Can we speak of a distinctly queer Cuban transnationalism?[1] If so, what practices of freedom—the classic Foucaultian ethic of the care of the self[2]—might
this migratory variant adopt to cope with political exile and emotive sexile?
This chapter explores these two heuristic propositions by analyzing the practices of freedom initiated by a group of self-identified queer Cuban *balseros*
(rafters) and Marielitos who were known as the Locas al Rescate (Queens [or
queers] to the Rescue) on the South Beach (SoBe) club circuit of the early
1990s.[3] The group explicitly parodied the rightist-identified organization
Hermanos al Rescate (Brothers to the Rescue) and its humanitarian work of
rescuing rafters at sea by "rescuing" unsuspecting club goers from the club
fashion faux pas and, more important, from the historical amnesia surrounding the most present of the group's concerns: the plight of Cuban rafters in
SoBe's hypervisual culture of surface but politically vapid cultural geography
and the evocation of those who disappeared at sea during the height of the raft
exodus following Cuba's Special Period (Período Especial) of economic collapse and energy shortages after the fall of the Soviet bloc.

I take the Cuban rafter experience as emblematic of Cuban transnational
identity and community making outside the traditional, empirically driven
economy of transnational studies.[4] I do this to question how forms of
unquantifiable queer loving through the performances of Cuban American
cultural memory can produce practices of freedom that fall outside the grasp of
traditional social science accounts of the transnational, accounts that too often
lack the critical vocabulary of feeling.[5] These practices of freedom are more
subtle but no less engaging than those imagined on a national scale, because
they participate in public life by making private history, needs, and desires
publicly visible and rendered on the terms established by Cuban American
queers. The performances of freedom staged by Locas al Rescate can therefore

be understood as self-constituting identity practices that name the terms of engagement with the memory of the Cuban national culture, the sexiled queer forms of being, and the Cuban exiled community's marginalization of queer forms of *being* Cuban through abjectification (see note 14). In its strictly Foucaultian sense, these practices of freedom constitute an "ethics of self-making" that produce spectacles of Cuban and Cuban American history by minoritarian subjects who position themselves within a history that has been dismissive of their participation. As José Esteban Muñoz reminds us, these types of identity practices "cannot be undervalued in relation to the formation of counterpublics that contest the hegemonic supremacy of the majoritarian public sphere" because these spectacles, he notes, "offer the minoritarian subject a space to situate itself in history and thus seize social agency" (Muñoz 1999: 1). In this sense, these queer Cuban practices of freedom create an alternative and visible cultural memory that foregrounds those modes of being Cuban that fall outside hegemonic understandings of what it means to be Cuban or Cuban American.

The story of the cultural networks forged by Cubans, as well as by other immigrants, has usually been narrowly focused on the empiricist grounds of knowing, on the quantifiable world of numbers, demographics, political affiliations, and the attendant methodologies of the quantifiable world. I come to this engagement as both witness and scholar in an auto-ethnography of self interpolated in community networks too often ignored by the limits of quantifiable experience. Yet the autobiographical act in scholarship, the interpolation of self within the confines of an academic discipline, is a risky proposition. Not surprisingly, the fusion of subject and object of study in disciplines that require evidentiary protocols supported by statistics is usually seen as suspect. How can the subject, after all, know the dancer from the dance when she is subject, object, and choreographer at once? In almost any act of self-disclosure one's motives are never disinterested, and I do not pretend to be an exception. But to rely almost exclusively on the measurable world is to rely too singularly on an Enlightenment legacy that cannot always account for the contradictions and possibilities of complex personhood. Transnational studies, coming from a social science as beleaguered as anthropology,[6] has relied too singularly on empirical explanations for processes embedded in *affective* motivations—the heavy density of feeling surrounding what García Canclini (1995) has termed *las estrategias para entrar y salir de la modernidad*, the strategies for stepping in and out of the binds and incomplete promises of modernity. There is intellectual and human impoverishment, too many missed opportunities, when we neglect the private worlds we inhabit and all the personal and cultural hauntings that tie us to those geographies of memory that clamor for attention when we least expect it. I feel and hear it all too often, more than I care to: "Mi hijo, lo sacrificamos todo por ti. . . . Lo sacrificamos todo por ti" (My son, we've sacrificed it all for you. . . . We've sacrificed it all for you).[7] But more about that later.

Balseros

Balseros cross national boundaries, both literal (the nation) and imaginary (the seascape of ambivalent citizenship), in rafts made of flimsy found objects ranging from particle board to the inner tubes of tires, all in the hope of being swept into the mostly placid northerly movement of the Gulf Stream that swirls objects, people, and desires ashore. The rafter experience itself has galvanized a series of literary, cultural, and political interventions on the status and presumed privilege of Cuban exiles seeking refuge in south Florida. As a subject of fiction, Cuban rafters have been interpolated in the American literary imagination in novels such as John Sayles' *Los Gusanos: A Novel* (1991) and J. Joaquín Fraxedas' *The Lonely Crossing of Juan Cabrera* (1993). In diatribes in the local and national press about Elián González's plight (1999), in films such as Luis Felipe Bernaza's *Estado del Tiempo/Changing Tides* (1994) and Bosch and Domènech's *Balseros* (2002), and in Hermanos al Rescate's search for rafters—both literal and political—the *balsero* experience reactivated a generational rift in the way the Cuban diaspora has been represented and understood in the public sphere (Habermas 1989).

The queer manifestations of this rift were interpolated in club circuit spaces by a group of self-described *locas* (literally, "crazy women"; pejoratively, "queer men" or "queens") who hounded the 1990s SoBe club scene with fashion pointers that derided both Lycra-clad *musculosos* and self-styled Cuban *sofisticados* whose near-dead political pulse was suddenly and ardently charged through the public-space takeovers staged by this group. Locas al Rescate takeovers often parodied and at times satirized many of the public humanitarian pronouncements of Hermanos al Rescate by drawing attention to the plight of recent Cuban arrivals, rafters, and other "dry footers"[8] who were the symbolic beneficiaries of Hermanos al Rescate's largesse but seemed to be forgotten once they made it ashore. Before addressing the Locas al Rescate's practices of freedom, their move from parody to activism, and queer ethnic remembrance as a practice of freedom, I situate their parodic referent within the Cuban American imaginary.

From its inception, Hermanos al Rescate attempted to consolidate a public identity inflected with its stated humanitarian goals—saving rafters fleeing Castro's Cuba—rather than with its overtly political associations with the so-called Cuban mafia, the exiled political right. What interests me here, however, are not the well-known and complex political invectives for or against caricatures of either the right or the left. I am interested, rather, in the potential of performances of *cubanidad* to tell us about Cuban American negotiations of a queer identity vis-à-vis the appropriation of community-specific modalities of political expression through the evocation of love and loss. Ultimately, the question is, How does one engage with a political discourse so preoccupied with authenticating Cuban identity by righting past political slights that it becomes difficult to imagine a Cuban or Cuban American identity outside the context of national borders or that nostalgic longing for the restoration of a wholeness that may never have been? As I noted, I am particularly interested in moving away from Cuban and Cuban American studies' dependence on an empiricism and a "proof"-driven academic imperative that ultimately depoliticize the realm of the imaginary worlds we inhabit and the feelings that drive much of what we can quantify as the locus of exilic consciousness, the observable world manifested through feeling.

Mi hijo, lo sacrificamos todo por ti. . . . Lo sacrificamos todo por ti.

Cuban Transnational Hauntings

It is haunting to hear your parents' explanation of that prolonged state of melancholia they've lived in as exiles. You see and hear it in your sleep when you dream them in syllables and smell, the textures of their past imagined from frayed black-and-white photographs that come to life when you least expect it. In your sleep you see someone's parent, a woman pregnant with thought, on her wedding day, distracted in white and knowing that her beloved would soon leave the island. Se tuvo que ir . . . por puente aéreo a España (He had to leave . . . via Spain), or so the story goes. It is a narrative about your father, you realize. There are constants in the narrative, with subtle changes over the years: his exact age at the time, his last words to her before leaving on Cubana de Avia- ción, the poems he wrote to her about longing and loss, a lost wedding ring, and ultimately a memory of betrayal that through the years accu- mulated details so subtle they beg questions impossible for a son to ask. It could be someone else's story but it is your own.

The personal history of feeling is the emotional fuel that feeds actions quan- tifiable by social science methodologies. Indeed, that is Avery F. Gordon's con- tention in her brilliant book, *Ghostly Matters: Haunting and the Sociological Imagination* (1997). Gordon (1997) engages Horkheimer and Adorno's cri- tique of modernity *in The Dialectic of Enlightenment* (1944),[9] in order to designate a space of meaning that recognizes the weight of memory, the con- tours of feeling, and the shape of longing. She does so by pointing out significant limitations and oversights in the way social science is conducted and social life is observed and described. For Gordon this requires a fundamental change in the way we know and make knowledge, and entails a "thoroughgoing epistemological critique of modernity as what is contemporaneously ours with an insurgent sociological critique of its forms of domination" (Gordon 1997: 10–11). Further, it requires scrutinizing one's hauntings:

> To be haunted and to write from that location, to take on the condition of what you study, is not a methodology or a consciousness you can simply adopt or adapt as a set of rules or an identity; it produces its own insights and blindnesses. To be haunted and to write from that location . . . is about making a contact that changes you and refashions the social relations in which you are located. It is about putting life back in where only a vague memory or a bare trace was visible to those who bothered to look. It is sometimes about writing ghost stories, stories that not only repair representational mistakes, but also strive to understand the conditions under which a memory was produced in the first place, toward a countermemory, for the future. (Gordon 1997: 22)

I have focused on the intersections of personal and cultural history in order to contextualize the *intrahistorias* (inner stories, inner histories) that drive our intellectual will to power, our own objects of study, and how and why we produce knowledge about *cubanía* in the present for the future. The narrative textures of personal experience that manifest themselves in our own work, as well as the affective ties we discard or refuse to recognize, bind us to an unexplored realm of knowledge that will remain depoliticized until Cuban and Cuban American studies recognizes—perforce—the space of feeling in the production of knowledge about *cubanía* (in or outside of the Miami bubble) and the performances of nationalism that presumably define a *cubanidad* at large which must be interrogated.

One of the fundamental problems that results when individual *intrahistorias* begin to saturate public consciousness is that they begin to stand in for the whole community. This creates a hegemony of feeling, if you will, that makes dissenters prisoners in *cubanía*'s house of meaning, genealogical isolates who are not Cuban American, much less Cuban, because they cannot remember or they remember differently the narratives of nationalism that bestow permanent residency in Cuba's house of mirrors—a symbolic citizenship in the public sphere of *cubanidad* in exile. To say that you stand outside of *cubanía*'s hegemony of feeling is to say that you stand outside of history.

In New York City you meet dancers from a Cuban troupe whose name you will not mention. You let them know that you are Cuban and convivial warmth turns to stolid rhetoric: "¿Tú, cubano? No señorito, tú no eres cubano. Tú vives aquí" [*You, Cuban? No sir, you are not Cuban. You live here*].

The hegemony of feeling is a Janus-like coin, monolithic and impenetrable on either side of the political façade.

You learn that one of the dancers from the troupe attempts to defect but after "falling ill from fatigue," he is returned to Cuba for a rest.

There are tremendous emotional investments involved in saving face, regardless of which side of the *cubanidad* coin you are on.

Queer Transnationalism and the Politics of Place

Performances of presumed Cuban affective authenticity are re-created every day in the media markets of Miami. For those of us born shortly before or after 1970 and raised in the United States, SoBe became the locus of a legitimated *cubanidad*. Whether we lived in Miami or not, the SoBe scene had an identity that marked *cubanidad* as hip, culturally identifiable, and legitimate. And for those of us who were coming of age intellectually in the late 1980s and early 1990s, it became evident that the two most public versions of *cubanidad*—the 1959 and Mariel generations—were giving way to a transnational *cubanidad* whose two most defining features at the time were the Cuban-inflected SoBe scene and the rafters who were arriving in droves as a result of Cuba's Special Period.[10] I say transnational *cubanidad* because it was not just the rafter experience that highlighted the obvious crossing of national borders but also the SoBe scene's highly visual economy of signs that were disseminated throughout and cemented in the North American and European imaginary through tourism. Miami and SoBe became the destination of choice for European travelers, according to European tour operators catering to the upwardly mobile, hip, and pretty wannabes from the other side of the pond (Germans, Spaniards, and Italians, in particular). This commodified and marketed *cubanidad* had a curious outcome: It fabricated a ready-made identity for young urban Cuban Americans (Yucas) both in and outside of Miami, an identity that made Cuban affiliation in the United States analogous to a previous generational tension among Cuban Americans. Like the exiled post-1959 Cuban Americans who disidentified from the often-derided Marielitos who came after them, the Yucas identified with the presumed progenitors of Miami's transformations; that is, the post-1959 Cubans who presumably had created the social architecture that could allow SoBe to thrive. It was an identification that disidentified Yucas from rafters, in much the same way as pre-1980 Cubans disidentified themselves from Marielitos. This mythic nationalistic recourse to the presumed origins of an exile identity rooted in the 1959 diaspora, of course, obscured a very different reality that had more to do with the influx of foreign capital into SoBe's economy. (I am thinking of tourism again, in particular, the German rediscovery of SoBe's Art Deco district as well as the bustling drug trade.) Another reality was the influx of gays, many of whom were Marielitos themselves, who found—at least until the late 1980s—affordable housing and creative space to thrive: Cuban queers with nothing to lose who left Cuba not only because they were hungry but because they wanted to believe that across the Florida Straits one could be a *maricón con plumas* (a fag with feathers), *muchas plumas*. It was and is the desire for political *and* sexual personhood that makes many Cuban queers leave despite the only one in four odds of making it alive to *la otra orilla* (the other shore; artificially divided since the 1960s, the two Cubas have often been called *las dos orillas*). Even today a significant number of Miami Cubans consider themselves exiles awaiting the restoration of what for many is an illusory unity, and we do not venture to contemplate the number of Cubans on the island living in "sexile" and yearning to depart toward a different type of wholeness. Politics and economic hardship, unquestionably severe, tell only part of the story. Indeed, one can legitimately ask the obvious: How many claimed political oppression—real as it was and is—as a safe way to move toward a more complete sexual personhood?[11]

It is common to assert that queer desire crosses gender, ethnic, racial, and class lines. In the queer Cuban transnational context, I say it is yearning that cuts and, paradoxically, unites the breadth of difference and experience for Cubans outside the island as well those on the island who yearn to leave, irrespective of sexual identity (explicit or occluded). Yearning is the place from which both heternormative and queer identities forge ties to forms of personhood that require fulfillment in an imaginary *elsewhere*. The identitarian slippage between being unwanted because you are queer and being unwanted because you are an antirevolutionary is fraught with uncomfortable parallels. Both are interpolated as Other—"you are not Cuban"—by a national state apparatus that, paradoxically, is replaced by its proxy in exile, a community that turns its back on Marielitos, *balseros*, *locas*, and queers, much like the Cuban state did with queers (sexual-political dissenters) and *gusanos*[12] (de-sexed, that is, "heteronormalized" political dissenters) when they were on the island. This *elsewhere* functions as a *bugarronería* of sentiment meant to displace these suspect Cubans yet again in a permanent *other* place, as if to say that irrespective of queer affiliation, gay or "straight," you are fucked by a new *bugarrón* called exile.[13] Identity as lack—"you are not Cuban"—supplants compulsory heteronormativity with a compulsory *cubanía* that makes dissenters wait in the same holding cell of abject citizenship. If this form of majoritarian subjugation did not discriminate on the identitarian basis of sexual object choice, it certainly did so once Marielitos and rafters attempted to navigate the economies of *cubanidad* in south Florida, the limited forms of belonging (economic and social) available to post-1980 Cuban arrivals. The most creative responses came from the *abjectified*; that is, those with the least to lose.[14] These were queer Cubans who negotiated exile and sexile as inclusive qualities of being, not mutually exclusive conditions of being, and they did so through telling and performative practices of freedom that understood the categories of place (where we want to be) and person (who we want to be) as necessarily mobile imaginaries founded on desires premised on the possibility of fulfillment: *being* someplace in order to *be* sometime.

It is not a stretch to concede that for Yucas Miami became an Aztlán of sorts without, of course, the strong class critique initiated by their Chicano counterparts in the western and southwestern United States.[15] Like the Mexican American Aztlán, the mythic Southwest home of the Aztec whose symbology was appropriated by Chicanos during the 1960s as a locus of an empowered identity, Miami became a way station for displaced geographies of *cubanidad*. If for Chicanos Aztlán became the mythic space where geography and memory could serve as the progenitors of a collective fiction of identity, then Miami became the way station, a necessary stop, on the road to a Cuban American identity: Miami was the space where memory became the ontological force of *cubanidad* in exile, identity as a displaced geography from which the subject can fetishize memory, and make non-belonging, or its melancholic deferral, the principal mode of quotidian experience, the essence of exile.

Hijo, we've sacrificed it all for you. . . .

Indeed, narratives of self-abnegation became one of the organizing principles for an exile consciousness that deferred and projected the parents' memory of loss and lost youth onto Yucas. At the time, Yucas were referred to as "Generation Ñ" in the south Florida magazine of the same name (a title no doubt inspired by Douglas Coupland's novel *Generation X: Tales from an Accelerated Culture* (1991) about middle-class, Anglo-American twentysomething ennui and boredom). Like the magazine, which sought to capture the market share of hip *cubanidad* in the early to mid-1990s, members of Generation Ñ could traffic in their parents' nostalgia and the memory of loss with Cohiba Cigar T-shirts; food and dance music inflected with the memory of displacement; and plastic busts of San Lázaro, Santa Barbara, and la Caridad del Cobre; not to mention the rise of a white-ified Santería for the spiritually needy, all safely marketed and consumed in the cultural spaces of Metro Dade and SoBe where, unlike the old and often reactionary Calle Ocho, for example, memory was safely depoliticized. These were spaces where politics and the real force of material loss could be safely commemorated through consumption of *cubanía* during the day before heading out to clubs like the Warsaw Ballroom, the Torpedo, Hombre, the Paragon (before the artist formerly known as Prince purchased it), and, depending on the night or one's sexual proclivities, the notorious Flamingo Park, the "after hours" of choice for SoBe *musculosos* and their admirers, including straight-laced, though not quite straight, Yucas on X (Ecstasy). (A memorable event from late 1994 comes to mind, when residents around Flamingo Park began to complain to the local authorities about the number of men going into the mangroves and police entrapment plots ensued in and out of these mangroves. Curiously, the local circuit scene came to the rescue; I remember one venue in particular where sand, shrubs, plants, Astroturf, and bleachers were set up to simulate Flamingo Park in the safety of police-free interiors. In other words, even promiscuity became safely depoliticized.)

One of the worst features of this type of *cubanidad*—that is, *cubanidad* as nostalgic commodity disengaged from political work—is that while our generational counterparts in Cuba were busy producing knowledge of and about *las dos orillas*, the intellectual conditions of possibility for thinking and theorizing new approaches to *cubanidad* in institutionalized venues such as the U.S. academy became impoverished precisely when they were needed the most. No longer heirs to an intellectual will to power, like the first generation of Cuban-born, U.S.-trained academics, Cuban, Cuban American, and Cuban intellectual sympathizers paradoxically left a good part of the generational, cultural, and literary theorizing to those trained in Cuba. This is not categorically wrong, of course; you do not have to be trained in a specific way or place to establish a viable intellectual project. But it is wrong to depoliticize a field of inquiry from the place where the project stands to lose the most if left to fester in a reactionary environment, an environment where the political dialogue for some still centers on imagining what will happen when Castro dies.

Such impoverished imaginings are what Iván de la Nuez laments in one of the few sustained critical reflections on *cubanidad* in and out of Cuba, *La balsa perpetua: soledad y conexiones de la cultura cubana* (1998).[16] For de la Nuez, the rafter experience is ultimately emblematic of the Cuban condition, which for him is tantamount to an identity in search of a project. That is, there is no sustained critique of *cubanidad* in the public sphere, because the public identities negotiated are mere reflections or caricatures of a stunted project for both the left—of which there isn't much to speak of—and the right. In other words, for de la Nuez, if the *razón de ser* (raison d'être) of the right is disidentifying with Communism as it is popularly understood, then the left has been too busy justifying why it is neither Communist nor socialist. Referring to the 1990s, he notes with aplomb (de la Nuez 1998: 140, emphasis in the original):

> *Uno de los aspectos más interesantes de Miami es la cantidad de personajes de la ciudad que han sido formados en un régimen comunista (el cubano) y que hoy forman parte del grupo de notables de la ciudad.*

Pintores de renombre, empresarios, académicos, voceros radiofónicos, propietarios de clubes nocturnos, estrellas de la música y un largo etcétera. Todo esto hace de Miami una ciudad poscomunista, una afirmación que horrorizaría a la ultraderecha cubana o al propio canon wasp que retorna con toda su fuerza en Estados Unidos.

(One of the most interesting aspects of Miami is the number of characters from the city who have been formed in a Communist regime [the Cuban one] and who today form part of the city's group of notables. Painters of renown, entrepreneurs, academics, disc jockeys, nightclub owners, music stars, and a long etcetera. All of this makes Miami a *post-Communist* city, an affirmation that would horrify the Cuban far right or the very WASP canon that has returned with all its strength in the United States.)

De la Nuez goes on to note that identitarian projects are temporally dialogic in nature as they seek a political future, not the righting of a political past; that is, they involve a critical dialogue with the *past* in the *present* in the hope of a more democratic *future*.

One of de la Nuez's few conceptual blind spots is his inability to see beyond Habermasian modalities of counterpublics; in other words, he comes dangerously close to saying that viable political work can only be undertaken in the public sphere. Indeed, what he considers "the lost Cuban American generation of the nineties" did much of its political lifesaving and life-altering work in the streets, parks, and circuit venues of places such as SoBe. When Lincoln Road was home to productive art studios, when there was no Gap, no Pottery Barn, when the suburban crowd still hadn't found its way across the causeway, the political vanguard of activism was undertaken by the likes of Locas al Rescate. Whether it was condom distribution or safe sex education, *bugarrones* with desires in Flamingo Park but wives in la Saogüecera (Little Havana in southwest Miami), queer community workers tried to educate and create conditions of possibility for recent and not so recent arrivals to survive the demagoguery of a community that welcomed them in theory but derided them in practice.

Ethnographies of Queer *Cubanidad*

In the hotter than usual summer of 1994, Locas al Rescate was headed by la Señorita Tini; you could call her Mar if you knew her well. An organic intellectual if there ever was one, Mar Tini, or Dry Martini when she was not in drag, unofficially founded the SoBe group before the height of the public discourse about Hermanos al Rescate's downed aircraft.[17] Drag for la Señorita Tini consisted of more than gender mischief enacted by a person of color. It registered how humor could disarm political forms of domination by transgressing gender systems operative within and outside of the Cuban *left* versus *right* Manichean dichotomy and whose common denominator was the maintenance of mutually sustaining gender orthodoxy. This disarming humor, evident in the group's name and performances, created practices of freedom vis-à-vis the possibility for cultural critique facilitated by drag through what José Esteban Muñoz has called the politics of *choteo*. Following Cuban philosopher Jorge Mañach's analysis of Cuban cultural identity in his *Indagación del choteo* (1928), Muñoz notes that *choteo* "signifies upon a range of activities that include tearing, talking, throwing, maligning, spying, and playing" (Muñoz 1999: 135). In addition, *choteo* can be understood as "a style of colonial mimicry that is simultaneously a form of resemblance and menace" (p. 136).[18] The practitioner of *choteo* is a *choteador* who practices a "strategy of self-enactment that helps a colonized or otherwise dispossessed subject enact a self through a critique of normative culture" (p. 136). Drag—an unlikely Trojan horse—offered both entry and a captive audience for Tini's particular brand of *choteo*, which signaled and pointed to a deadly serious *signified* (the abjectified *balsero*) mediated by a parodic and ultimately disarming *signifier* (drag). Her "rescues" were, after all, enacted in the accouterments of a feminine sublime cum *chusma de los solares de la Habana*, the class marked "trash" of the deteriorated neighborhoods of Havana.

Mar Tini left Cuba to reconquer a lost love, a lover who had left her in Cuba to be with his exiled wife in Miami. When she arrived in Miami after the Mariel boat exodus, and by way of Iowa—"una larga historia" (a long story)—Mar Tini's lover shunned her and she was intermittently homeless until she began to perform and stage "happenings." She had a beautiful voice and, like the established black SoBe drag performer of the time, Kitty Meow, she developed quite a following. On a lark, she began appearing in the SoBe club scene in the early 1990s with several "sisters" who would rile the crowd until they had everyone screaming "Locas al rescate!" The parody initiated an unwitting dialogue with a broader and more serious problematic that did not get lost in the performance. The *locas*' "rescue missions" initially consisted of catcalls ranging from "¡Ponte más ropa niño, así no vas encontrar hombre respetable!" (Put on some more clothes, boy; there's no way you're going to find a respectable man dressed like that!), to the more charming, "¡Morronga sí, Castro no!" (Yes to cock, no to Castro!). Yet it was not difficult to sense that the performance of ethnic essence interweaved with the camp *choteo* was a safe way to displace a broader problematic. Mar Tini could always point out the "Cubanitos malos"—the bad little Cubans, club bunnies who acted "como si fueran americanitos" (as if they were white) and supposedly spoke no Spanish but got every joke she said in Cuban. "Me hago la muerta para ver el entierro y ya te vi haciéndote pasar, maricón!" (I play dead to witness the wake and I saw you trying to pass, faggot!). It was part of her shtick, public humor as a safe way to rage.

Mar Tini held court and power over the caricatures of masculinity before her: overly muscular circuit bunnies whose exoskeletons—like AIDS-era armor—were often manufactured by steroids and an intense need to feel protected, exempt from the various deaths surrounding SoBe's astounding HIV rates.[19] It was obvious that many of the bodies before her wanted to exist in a state of pure desire. They wanted to be contemplated and wanted without the appearance of reciprocation; they wanted to exist in a state of desire that holds currency in the elusive empire of signs that was the club circuit of SoBe (like many other circuit spaces). Until, of course, drugs, drink, or boredom transported the same bodies that refused human affinity in the circuit to the realm of imperfect forms, their shadows cast in the modern-day cavelike alleys of SoBe and the bucolic but dark mangroves of Flamingo Park. The bodies of those Lycra-clad *musculosos* feared la Señorita Tini because her armor was her tongue and her mind, commodities carelessly squandered when one chooses to live exclusively in the I/eye of the mirror like so many of us from my generation have done in an attempt to stave off various deaths, both literal and emotional, presaged by the specter of HIV and the concomitant lack of personal meaning in the face of such profound loss. Mar Tini was aware of the conceits of survival (denial of death included) and reminded us through performance of our own performances of life in denial of death.

Mar Tini was reputed to have had a falling out with a promoter and so she began to stage her happenings in guerrilla fashion. She would still appear at circuit parties, unbeknownst to promoters or club owners. This was the case the night she made local news after an incident during one of the Warsaw Ballroom's foam parties. (Foam parties were all the rage some years ago. From the corners of a club floor foam would literally be pumped onto the dance area, making people remove wet clothing and often disappear into the foam. All of this added to the already sexually charged environment created by the space itself, the music, and, often, recreational drugs.) In the middle of the carnivalesque atmosphere, I remember her emerging from a corner as if rising from the foam. She was dressed in a long, stiff blue cape and a neon white gown with what looked like a nun's habit, and atop her head nested a spectacular and miraculously steady crown. As people began to cede way, it was clear that everyone thought she was performing, and indeed she was, but extra-officially and for reasons made unusual only in retrospect. When she centered herself on the dance floor it was clear she had half-stilts on, she was so tall. Three shirtless rafters appeared from behind her cape and began to dance around her with plastic oars like frantic sailors. I do not know if the irony was lost on everyone else, but dressed as she was as la Caridad del Cobre it became clear that this performance of ethnic drag was the closest many in the room would get to having a religious experience. When security arrived everyone thought they were part of the act until she fell off her stilts and onto the stage. She was duly kicked out by the bouncers, but a slew of foamed circuit aficionados followed and began to clap and whistle outside the Warsaw (a tribute usually reserved for the DJs, revered as they were—and are—as the high priests of modern circuit paganism). Suddenly, it seemed that everyone waiting in line to get in began to follow her and the rowers up Collins Ave. shouting, "Morronga sí, Castro no!" The marvelous curiosity begged a logical enough question: How could a Marielito and three rafters steal the show with the accoutrements of a *cubanidad* not quite lost on the spectators?

I remember my surprise that summer at hearing the most apolitical types at places like the ironically named News Café on Ocean Drive talk about Cuba, Hermanos al Rescate, rafters—those rescued at the circuit parties, those rescued at sea—and those who did not make the crossing. "Este es mi hijo" (This is my son), said la Señorita Tini, showing me the photograph of a son lost at sea. "No quiso esperar y nunca llegó. Su madre ahora me odia más que nunca" (He didn't want to wait and never arrived. His mother hates me now more than ever), she says as she looks up to meet my eyes, "y con razón" (and with good reason).

You wanted to ask things you had no right to ask.

The Affective Life of Locas

In my mind's eye, la Señorita Tini's club rescue mission as la Caridad del Cobre might have been nothing more than an instance of humorous and gender-bending ethnic drag, a curiosity to recall and relate from a summer of excess and reckoning more than ten years past. But, you see, my mother's name is Caridad, named after Our Lady of Charity, patroness of Cuba, and she took me to the shrine of the Virgin in the town of El Cobre when I was almost four. It was a particularly long trip from Bolondrón in the province of Matanzas to El Cobre in the province of Santiago de Cuba. It was a costly trip, one forever etched in my mind and undertaken just before my mother was sent to *la granja*, an internment camp for political dissenters who did time before their official expulsion from Cuba. It was then that I first heard about the legend of the Virgin who had appeared to three fishermen, "los tres Juanes," in the Bay of Nipe on the northeastern tip of Cuba and rescued them from a terrible storm. Historian María Elena Díaz (2000: 1) notes that "these fishermen represent the trinity of races [black, white, and mulatto] constituting the Cuban nation (excluding the usually excluded Chinese). Over the four centuries of the shrine's existence, various sectors of the population have reportedly invoked, contested, and reinvented this Marian tradition. Many forms of community and social identity, both religious and secular, as well as multiple—and at times conflicting—political agendas have been, and still are, formulated through this powerful story of the past."[20] The Virgin has been variously reimagined, as Díaz notes in her study, including at the hermitage in Miami, which has become "a diasporic space [for] Cubans in exile, one often charged with strong political meanings regarding the present and the past" (p. 20).

I was dancing to a house infusion remix of the already dated Dead or Alive anthem "Something in My House" when I saw la Señorita Tini as the Virgin in the Warsaw and I thought about my mother, the trip to El Cobre, my father's long exile, and my mother's internment at *la granja*.

> *The Warsaw was not the place for addled memories or affective irony— that disturbing perception of inconsistency, in which an apparently innocuous event is undermined by its content—but the Lady of Charity was there to remind you just who you were and why you were where you were. Your mother tells you that on the trip to El Cobre you told anyone who would listen that she was going to save "los tres juanes."*

There are things about my mother's internment that I want to ask, but she says there is nothing to say. I want to know why my mother could not have children after that year and a half of internment and why, according to my paternal grandmother, Rosario Guillermo de Lima, my mother refused to speak for almost a year after the experience. As I have pieced the dates together, she became *yerma* (barren) after her internment in *la granja*, an internment which also made her mute. Yet she speaks to me with her eyes; perhaps only because I need her to, but she speaks to me. I have only a single picture of my mother from this period. It was taken soon after we arrived in Spain, somewhere between twelve and eighteen months after *la granja*. There is no communal history relating to these internment camps where my mother labored up until 1971.[21] There is no history of this for me save a photograph that speaks to me because I need it to tell me things that can help explain my own piece of a broader transnational haunting.

Reckonings: After Turning Our Backs on "Pepito Pérez"

The Lady of Charity functions as the ambulatory protector of Cubans. Whether in Cuba, Miami, at sea—or elsewhere in the emotional imaginary of the heart—she hovers and oversees as witness. Like Freud's "familiar stranger," she lingers and demands a commerce of feeling that requires her interlocutors to make their relation to her ghostly being explicit. We are complicit with her hauntings. Like the Statue of Liberty, the Virgin of Charity is symbol, beacon, and icon. She is the appropriated Greek Themis who stands in for Cuban justice, but the Virgin—like her younger Ellis Island counterpart who also floats on water—does not don a blindfold. Justice requires vigilance, and invoking the Virgin for many Cubans is about invoking the mind's eye to redirect our focus to the evidence before us. She cannot rescue everyone because she cannot be everywhere at once, yet her sight is unmarred as the perpetual witness of *cubanía*'s transnational plight; everywhere she leaves traces of the reckoning to be undertaken. So we witness. We help her intercede—even if unwittingly—when we pause to look at the evidence of loss before us, because she will not leave until we have done our share of reckoning.

All empty *balsas* are haunted. The ghost rafts appear on beaches, in inlets, and in coves from the Florida Keys up to the Miami peninsula and beyond. They are encountered by beachcombers, cruise ships, and Coast Guard cutters and appear in meteorological photographs taken from weather boats and imaging satellites. Ghost rafts deliver a message from a host of Pepitos and Pepitas Pérez.[22] Like the material detritus of lost hope—a lost wedding ring or the frayed photograph of a beloved—these rafts tell a story of prior actions and motivations. Ghost rafts are the forensic artifacts of a failed transnational will to power. Like someone else's love letter mistakenly delivered to us, they arrive from an unidentifiable agent who tells a story of intense yearning and intentions stifled by circumstance. Since we are the unwitting addressee, we can ignore the message. After all, it is often cryptic, and the writing on the raft—the imaginary wall of Cuban (trans)national reckoning—is not always clear or legible. Besides, the living cannot possibly commune with the dead, much less with their lost objects, the things the dead carried on their journey, the raft that carried them to their fate, the monumental loss left for the grieving.

If you arrived by the port of Mariel in 1980, one of your options was to leave Cuba in a frock, as Reinaldo Arenas claims to have done in his autobiography, in the hopes of being duly dismissed as a transvestite transnational. But when you leave on a raft there are no such options and the odds are against you. That means that more rafts than people make it to south Florida shores. Most striking about ghost rafts is their unanchored referents: the identities of the dead. To codify the experience of identity for those lost at sea, which the ghost rafts so tenderly but weakly point to, requires a willingness to grant the aura of personhood to a postmortem Cuban identity. I do not mean a literal identification of a John or Jane Doe, a Pepito or Pepita Pérez, in a gesture of utopian closure (important though unrealistic as it may be), but rather an understanding of how the rites of death relate to the ongoing social life of a community. If death rites are concerned with issues relating to a community's identity, to the social continuity of that community through rememberings, then we need to understand why we have no mourning rites for ghost rafts.

What is it about the experience of Cuban transnationalism that allows us to excise a part of our body politic from our symbolic cultural imaginary? What is it about being on land and alive that allows us to send the ghost rafts' referents—the very materiality of the dead *balseros*—to an internment space whose borders and confines are rock, reef, and salt water?

The Cuban transnational is queerly *abjectified* in the holding cell of Cuban affiliation unless political affinities are articulated, performed, and enacted before a broader body politic. Cuban transnationalism is therefore exemplary to the degree that it requires a stateless citizenship to confer affiliation and procure inclusion onto the stateless body politic, the community's social imaginary. This stateless citizenship could be said to kill the *balsero* subject again after death because it requires defined allegiances to state-sanctioned modes of being, a being at home in relation to the Cuban nation—however conceived— that has no place for the dead because it presumes there can be no *cubanidad* for the stateless transnational after death. This hegemonic and stateless citizenship functions nonetheless as a state technology that disengages yearning from the political work the dead crave; it wrests yearning from rigor mortised hands and places it squarely in the land of the living as a quality of being alive. Yet the interstices of Cuban transnationalism are littered with the detritus of yearning offered to us by dead *balseros* who are in a perpetual state of being dead, a permanent homelessness. Fear of the dissolution of the Cuban state as it was understood to exist prior to 1959 has created a longing for a lived experience of *cubanidad* that cannot apprehend the postmortem forms of citizenship it has created. The yearned-for restoration of that deadly and illusory pre-1959 unity has created deaths it has yet to account for, deaths that will continue to haunt *cubanía*'s house of meaning. These deaths, enticements of various sorts to leave the island and therefore win over *la otra orilla*, were sanctioned killings in a war of wills to define the very being of *cubanidad*. There is, therefore, great political benefit in conjoining with the yearning of the dead for more complete forms of personhood. The dead talk, walk, and sit at *cubanía*'s table when we reanimate the forms of belonging that queer practices of freedom challenge us to imagine outside the orthodoxy of feeling Cuban, the *bugarronería* of sentiment to which I alluded earlier. The incorporation of abject *cubanidad* into the Cuban and Cuban American body politic, from the socially dead queer to the materially dead *balsero*, opens up fields of feelings that position the meaning of Cuban affiliation within our touch.

The survival of the dead's objects that wash ashore or are found at sea are ironic proxies for human loss, but they are the links between our being alive and their being dead, and they bind us to imagining *cubanía* anew. There is as yet no vocabulary of feeling that can explain Cuba's Sargasso Sea of ghost rafts. But unlike the thick seaweed that traps ships and people in the center of the

Gulf Stream's placid waters, the ghost rafts are delivered ashore for our contemplation, the "human latitudes"[23] of a queer and incomparable irony.

Mi hijo, lo sacrificamos todo por ti. . . .

If our parents' ultimate sacrifice for my generation of Cuban transnationals was their lives as they knew it, then our sacrifice here—alive and on land—should be the queer burden of memory: the precious dividends of a loss less tortured by an *other* haunting, a queerer sense of the abject commemorated, remembered into the transnational body politic imagined.

Imagining Closure

I began with the systematic compulsions and hauntings that drive us to *be* and to *do*, an ontology of action occasioned by transnational displacements and the condition of being alive that call us to document *cubanidad* in the academy—despite limited remuneration and sometimes incomparable sacrifices—in order to witness and recover our histories, and ourselves, as we rummage through the cultural found objects that clamor for attention, the heart of queer affiliations in the face of cultural reductionism and historical amnesia. Citing Raymond Williams, Gordon unabashedly invokes the generative tensions to be found in work that strives to be transformative, "not feeling against thought, but thought as felt and feeling as thought: practical consciousness of a present kind, in a living and interrelating continuity" (Gordon 1997: 198).

Socially and politically, queer Cuban rafters and Marielitos in SoBe could be said to be as dead as the rafters lost at sea were it not for their active engagement with the community writ large. When queer Cuban rafters and the Marielitos who comprised Locas bought the memory of lost rafters to the fore by keeping live rafters (those who made it to south Florida alive) literally living through safe-sex education (for both the queer identified and straight identified subjects) and in the social imaginary of the community through performances of *cubanidad*, then we can understand how freedom for Locas was an ethical and loving call to social praxis. La Señorita Tini's public evocation of refashioned and parodied Cuban identities formulated a personal engagement for me with communal memory that commemorated forms of non-belonging (processes of abjectification, if you will) that are integral to understanding Cuban transnationalism. Her performances of Cuban transnational memory inaugurated forms of cultural recovery through remembrance rather than excision, a practice of freedom through a call to social praxis. Locas al Rescate's spatial and performative takeovers amidst the foam, and in the parks and other recessed corners of desire, produced practices of freedom in spaces where endangered knowledge was unrepresentable to many: the park, the bar, the beach, the cove, the bushes, or the bedroom, all queer spaces from which to interrogate *cubanidad*'s various hauntings in all their transnational complexity and contradictory imaginings. Queer haunting is the engagement with emotion, the affective density of lived experience, an affirmation of a complex personhood too long denied. The Locas' claiming of space denied (club space, park space, love space, seascapes), the appropriation through trespass of cordoned geographies, enacted practices of freedom through the evocation of loss with the forms of *being* that are at stake when we ignore the rafter ashore, the empty raft, the complexity of yearning across borders of the state and the heart, the complexity of estrangement and abjection that makes "queer" both a noun and a transitive verb in search of its object.

> *It could begin with the memory of a trip to El Cobre, a palimpsest suffused with your parent's memories supplanting those you believe to be your own, the grafted accounts of loss and sacrifice,* "Mi hijo, lo sacrificamos todo por ti," *the mantra you woke up to so many times in graduate school after your father died, the one you hear every time you recall your mother's face when she saw you kissing that boy in Hialeah when you thought no one was looking. You were old enough then to remember her eyes watery, her lips pursed with incomprehension. It is a memory that belies Caridad's own logic of self-sacrifice through exile, the very justification that provided the emotional fuel for staving off displacement, divorce, your father's death, illness, and more. It is an image you also believe prompted her slow retreat into memory, you and that one boy you loved at sixteen, the haze of nostalgia and loss clouding her features until she is no longer a young woman and you are no longer that semblance of the self she used to know. You, her only child.*

The queer burden of refashioning Cuba's transnational memories is a grave but necessary act of personal reckoning.

Notes

A version of this chapter was presented at Florida International University's Fifth Cuban Research Institute Conference on Cuban and Cuban American Studies (October 29–31, 2003) in the panel "Trans-Disciplinary Dislocations, Trans-Cultural Studies: Re-Situating Cuban American Studies in the Contemporary U.S. Academy." The panel members were Ricardo Ortiz, who organized and moderated the session, José Esteban Muñoz, Licia Fiol-Matta, and myself. I would like to thank my fellow presenters, especially Ricardo, and the audience members who provided wonderful insight into our respective projects. My special thanks to Ruth Behar for her insightful comments on my talk. Damián Fernández encouraged me to develop the presentation into its present incarnation; I thank him for his careful reading and thoughtful suggestions. My colleague Azade

Seyhan's thoughtful comments were instructive, as were the anonymous readers' comments.

1. My use of the term "queer" is necessarily limiting as I focus on very specific interpolations of queer identities; specifically, Cuban American drag performers in South Beach and my own engagement within this community as both witness and participant. With this caveat in mind I would, nonetheless, like to follow Alexander Doty's suggestive and critically strategic use of the term "queer" "to mark a flexible space for the expression of all aspects of non- (anti-, contra-) straight cultural production and reception" (Doty 1993: 3). It is also important to note the significant contributions of critics working on Latin American, Latina, and Latino queer studies, especially Emilio Bejel, Licia Fiol-Matta, José Esteban Muñoz, José Quiroga, Juana Rodríguez, and many others. With regard to "transnationalism," I proffer the anthropological definition offered by Linda Basch and colleagues "as the process by which immigrants forge and sustain multistranded social relations that link together their societies of origin and settlement. We call these processes transnationalism to emphasize that many immigrants today build social fields that cross geographic, cultural, and political borders" (Basch, Glick Schiller, and Szanton Blanc 1994: 7). The translations that follow throughout the chapter are my own.

2. In referring to his work in *The Care of the Self*, Michel Foucault summarized the ethical cornerstone of his critique of normative forms of sexual subjection and the instrumentality of power by rhetorically positioning an answer within a question: "For what is morality, if not the practice of liberty, the deliberate practice of freedom? . . . Liberty is the ontological condition of ethics. But ethics is the deliberate form assumed by liberty" (cited in Bernauer and Rasmussen 1994: 4). Foucault's "practice of freedom" as the principled ethic of the care of the self cum others was appropriated by Simon Watney in his important collection of essays, *Practices of Freedom: Selected Writings on HIV/AIDS* (1994). For a discussion of practices of freedom as an "ethic of the care of the self" in relation to Latino performance studies see Muñoz (1999); for an example in Latino poetry see Lima (2001).

3. Marielitos are Cubans who left the island in the port of Mariel boat exodus of 1980. After Cubans seeking political asylum stormed the Peruvian Embassy in Havana, Castro purportedly purged his jails and allowed prisoners to leave the country as political dissidents. For a discussion of *balseros* as an orientalized commodity, see León (1997).

4. In one of the few sustained critiques of the Cuban diaspora, de la Nuez (1998) considers the *balsa*, or raft, the foundational metaphor for *cubanidad* (Cubanness) as experienced in exile and on the island.

5. For an exemplary exception see Fernández (2000).

6. See Clifford (1992); Gupta and Ferguson (1992).

7. Aside from the literal translation I have provided, "Mi hijo" is a term employed not just by parents but by elders to signify affection toward an addressee who is implored to understand the interpolated main clause or phrase. A less literal but more accurate translation would read, "Son, please understand that. . . ."

8. As of 1994, the United States has had a "wet foot–dry foot" policy. Cubans who make it to shore (with dry feet) are permitted to apply for asylum, while those inter-

dicted (with wet feet) are returned to Cuba. In a curious interpretation of policy in the summer of 1999, the Coast Guard was captured on camera using pepper spray and force to keep Cuban rafters from drying their feet.

9. Gordon wishes to expand what she sees as an important though unfinished assertion about affective engagement with the past in *The Dialectic of Enlightenment*: "Despairing at the loss of historical perspective, at our 'disturbed relationship with the dead—forgotten and embalmed,' they [Horkheimer and Adorno] believed we needed some kind of theory of ghosts, or at least a way of both mourning modernity's 'wound in civilization' and eliminating the destructive forces that open it up over and over again: 'Only the conscious horror of destruction creates the correct relationship with the dead: unity with them because we, like them, are the victims of the same condition and the same disappointed hope'" (Gordon 1997: 19–20).

10. Not surprisingly, it was during this period (1993) that Miami Cuban American Pedro Zamora became a household name. Appearing on the MTV reality series "The Real World," Zamora brought to the living rooms of millions the real life of a Cuban American from Miami who was living with AIDS. José Esteban Muñoz notes that upon Zamora's death in 1994 the *Wall Street Journal* ran a cover story featuring a letter that a South Carolina woman wrote Zamora, one among the "thousands he received per week." In it she explained how she was transformed: "I never thought anyone could change my opinion of homosexuals and AIDS. Because of you I saw the human side of something that once seemed so unreal to me" (Muñoz 1999: 143). Zamora also appeared on many news programs and talk shows, including "Oprah." President Bill Clinton also lauded Zamora's bravery in speaking out about AIDS prevention and self-esteem.

11. For Benigno Sánchez-Eppler, Reinaldo Arenas is an exemplar of this queer sexual and political transnationalism for he "provide[s] a very pointed example of how sexuality makes people move and how moving affects the practices of the representation of sexuality and the investment in some sort of return" (Sánchez-Eppler 2000: 154). Arenas' cultural, political, and highly personal work was made iconic through print and film in a transnational network of images. Though he was only able to die once, Arenas will likely live and die many times over in Julian Schnabel's version of his life in *Before Night Falls* (2000). Indeed, his iconic status via celluloid will likely safeguard his longevity, his many afterlives, long after the death of the political regime he censured with profound vitriol. He would likely appreciate the irony of living as a character in the perpetual *medias res* of *cubanidad*. This longevity is small consolation, though, since Arenas found neither what he would consider political nor sexual freedom in the United States, as he so acerbically noted in his autobiography.

12. *Gusanos* (worms) is the derisive term used in Cuba to describe defectors and political dissidents.

13. *Bugarrón* is a curious term from the Cuban sexual vernacular that refers to the active partner in homosexual anal sex. The active partner is understood to be heterosexual not by virtue of his sexual object choice, but rather by virtue of his dominant intrusion and "taking" of the body of another male. Only the penetrated male is labeled *loca*. Within this cultural imaginary the *bugarrón* is able to maintain his (hetero)sexual

subject integrity. In the Mexican context, as described by the late Nobel Prize winning Octavio Paz, the space and sociocultural position of that which is feminized is a priori "screwed."

14. Arnaldo Cruz-Malavé's brilliant reading of Puerto Rican literature as a failed Bildungsroman leads him to conclude that "Puerto Rican canonical texts have not ruled through potency but through impotence. . . . Puerto Rican canonical texts have rallied us and bound us through failure and impotence" (Cruz-Malavé 1995: 140). In referring to René Marquéz's story "En la popa hay un cuerpo reclinado," he notes that this impotence in literature creates an "abject" subjectivity that is incapable of sustaining the hierarchies of heteronormative paternalism. I am similarly interested in invoking an "abject" *cubanidad* that is discarded from the fictions of national identity on and off of the island. Unlike Cruz-Malavé, however, in this chapter I am interested in understanding how *cubanidad* is wrested from the hegemonic center and deployed in subversive practices of freedom.

15. De la Nuez sees this quite differently. He notes, "Si los chicanos reivindican su reconquista del Oeste americano con argumento de que en esa región se encontraba la mítica Aztlán, en Miami no ocurre nada parecido: no se busca, por allí, reconquistar el espacio sino un tiempo: el de la Eterna Juventud, ya perseguido en Florida por Ponce de León hace unos quinientos años" (If Chicanos vindicated their reconquest of the American West with the argument that in that region resided the mythical Aztlán, in Miami nothing of the sort occurs: the search there is about not the reconquest of space but of time: the search for eternal youth, pursued over five hundred years by Ponce de León; de la Nuez 1998: 138). Yet there was never an actual fixed geographic location for Aztlán (despite some novel anthropological suggestions to the contrary). Foremost, Aztlán resided in the collective imagination of a people in search of a collective space from which to be as economically and humanly free as possible. Miami, similarly, was imagined as the metaphorical place where the pursuit of sexual freedom could be as attainable as the more common pursuit of economic freedom.

16. For an important collection of essays that address various modalities and expressions of Cuban identitarian strategies see Cámara Betancourt and Fernández 2000.

17. The antecedents related to Hermanos al Rescate were related to Cuba's Special Period. What was left of the Cuban economy bottomed out and *balseros*—those who survived the treacherous waters—began to arrive on U.S. soil, all ostensibly to seek political asylum. The problem intensified when Haitian rafters who did the same were denied entry. This prompted the Clinton administration to sign an immigration accord with Cuba, and beginning in 1995 Cubans were no longer allowed what were understood to be special privileges. In 1996 Cuban authorities claimed that Hermanos al Rescate had violated Cuban airspace by going beyond the twenty-fourth parallel, prompting the downing of two of Hermanos' small planes by the Cuban Air Force. The incident received international attention. In another important aside, the documentary *Estado del tiempo* (1994) charting the *balsero* experience received considerable criticism for not making a clear distinction between political and economic exile. This fact was not lost on community activists who dealt with these populations on a day-to-day basis. Indeed, sexual migration—leaving to love—does not appear in the film or in most

of the social science literature relating to *balseros* because the default identity is usually that of the heterosexual political defector.

18. For the African etymological roots of *choteo* see Cuban anthropologist Fernando Ortiz's *Glosario de afronegrismos* (1924). He associates the term with Lucumí or Yoruba etymology (cited in Muñoz 1999: 135). Muñoz expands upon Mañach's understanding of it for strategic purposes. Mañach was primarily concerned with resemantizing the term in order to cast it in a developmental narrative of national progress toward a more refined cultural maturity, that is, a Cuban modernity: "A medida que nos hacemos más ricos y más refinados . . . acrecentamos nuestro sentido de la jerarquía y disminuimos, por consiguiente, las condiciones de la vida del choteo" (As we become richer and more refined . . . we increase our sense of hierarchies and consequently diminish the conditions of life as *choteo*; Mañach 1928: 91). We can better understand Mañach if we recall that he was a positivist disciple of Spanish essayist and philosopher José Ortega y Gassett. Similarly, Ortega was a disciple of Husserl, as was his colleague Martin Heidegger. Ortega brought phenomenology to the Spanish-speaking world with translations of his German "maestros" in Spain's *Revista de Occidente*, making the Hispanic world one of the first to sample Husserl's and later Heidegger's writings.

19. In May 1995, the queer publication *Out* featured a story by Miami-based freelance writer Glenn Albin, "To Live and Die in South Beach." The piece noted that HIV-positive men in their thirties and beyond were moving to Miami to "retire," creating a new type of viral retiree. Though women and people of color were conspicuously absent from the piece, its disco graveyard theme permeated the talk of the beach and created a heightened sense of sex-negativity.

20. Díaz's study, though meticulously historical, is explicitly and intimately tied to personal history and memory: "My interest in Cuba laid dormant for many years and then was triggered with force in 1980. It happened during my return trip as an adult after twenty years of absence from the mythical country I had left as a small child. Thereafter the imagined ties were gradually rewoven in absentia. Ultimately the desire to take a more active part in the island's history materialized in the gesture of writing a slice of its history from afar" (Díaz 2000: xi).

21. The infamous Unidades Militares de Ayuda a la Producción (Military Units to Help Production), forced work camps for dissenters of all stripes, were suspended in 1967, but similar internment camps still exist. Curiously, the word "concentration" used in the context of forcible internment (that is, "concentration camp") was first used during the final Cuban war of independence (1895–1898) by Spanish military governor Valeriano Weyler, known as "The Butcher" (Ferrer 1999: 152). Weyler's policy of *reconcentración* (to "reconcentrate" through displacement) resulted in the mass internment of rural populations in the suburban areas of large cities in an attempt to quell the Cuban independence movement.

22. "Pepito Pérez" was a fictional character fabricated by the U.S.-supported exiled Cuban right to convince Cubans on the island that they should leave. This was accomplished through various information outlets, mostly radio, where a fictional Pepito Pérez was interviewed, saying how only a few days after arriving in the United States, he was already working in a fictional company and making several thousand dollars a

month. The Pepito Pérez myth has had many incarnations and has traveled the airwaves far enough into the Cuban popular imaginary to serve purposes in both the public and private spheres. As a child, I remember being told that a roomful of toys was waiting for me upon my arrival in the United States, but only if I behaved. That promise was the junior version of the Pepito Pérez myth and—like most forms of control or coercion—kept children yearning in affective abeyance much like the adults who were seduced by the mythic lure of the Pepito Pérez fiction.

23. Early Spanish explorers often reported finding themselves in stagnant water for weeks in the Sargasso Sea, popularly known as the Bermuda Triangle (the body of water roughly bordered by the triangulation between Puerto Rico, Bermuda, and Florida). To save drinking water and free their ships from the thick sargassum, they were forced to throw their horses overboard. Hence, the area is known as the horse latitudes.

Bibliography

Albin, Glenn. 1995. "To Live and Die in South Beach." *Out* (May): 72–77, 125–28.

Aparacico, Frances R., and Susana Chávez-Silverman, eds. 1997. *Tropicalizations: Transcultural Representations of Latinidad*. Hanover: University Press of New England.

Arenas, Reinaldo. 1992. *Antes que anochezca: autobiografía*. Barcelona: Editorial Tusquets.

Basch, Linda, Nina Glick Schiller, and Cristina Szanton Blanc. 1994. *Nations Unbound: Transnational Projects, Postcolonial Predicaments and Deterritorialized Nation-States*. Amsterdam: Gordon and Breach.

Bernauer, James, and David Rasmussen, eds. 1994. *The Final Foucault*. Cambridge, Mass.: MIT Press.

Bernaza, Luis Felipe, director. 1994. *Estado del tiempo/Changing Tides*. New York: Cinema Guild. Motion picture.

Bosch, Carles, and Josep M. Domènech, directors. 2002. *Balseros*. Spain: Bausan Films S.L. y Televisió de Catalunya/Seventh Art Releasing and HBO/Cinemax Documentary Films. Motion picture.

Cámara Betancourt, Madeline, and Damián J. Fernández. 2000. *Cuba, the Elusive Nation: Interpretations of a National Identity*. Gainesville: University Press of Florida.

Clifford, James. 1992. "Traveling Cultures." In *Cultural Studies*, edited by Lawrence Grossberg, Cary Nelson, and Paula A. Treichler. New York: Routledge.

Coupland, Douglas. 1991. *Generation X: Tales for an Accelerated Culture*. New York: St. Martin's Press.

Cruz-Malavé, Arnaldo. 1995. "Toward an Art of Transvestism: Colonialism and Homosexuality in Puerto Rican Literature." In *¿Entiendes?: Queer Readings, Hispanic Writings*, edited by Emilie L. Bergmann and Paul Julian Smith, 137–67. Durham: Duke University Press.

de la Nuez, Iván. 1998. *La balsa perpetua: soledad y conexiones de la cultura cubana*. Barcelona, Spain: Editorial Casiopea.

Díaz, María Elena. 2000. *The Virgin, the King and the Royal Slaves of El Cobre: Nego-

tiating Freedom in Colonial Cuba, 1670–1780. Stanford, Calif.: Stanford University Press.

Doty, Alexander. 1993. *Making Things Perfectly Queer: Interpreting Mass Culture.* Minneapolis: University of Minnesota Press.

Fernández, Damián J. 2000. *Cuba and the Politics of Passion.* Austin: University of Texas Press.

Ferrer, Ada. 1999. *Insurgent Cuba: Race, Nation, and Revolution, 1868–1898.* Chapel Hill: University of North Carolina Press.

Foucault, Michel. 1986. *The Care of the Self,* translated by Robert Hurley. New York: Pantheon Books.

Fraxedas, J. Joaquín. 1993. *The Lonely Crossing of Juan Cabrera.* New York: St. Martin's Press.

García Canclini, Nestor. 1995. *Hybrid Cultures: Strategies for Entering and Leaving Modernity,* translated by Christopher L. Chiappari and Silvia L. López. Minneapolis: University of Minnesota Press.

Glick Schiller, Nina, Linda Basch, and Cristina Blanc-Szanton. 1992. *Towards a Transnational Perspective on Migration: Race, Class, Ethnicity and Nationalism Reconsidered.* New York: New York Academy of Science.

Gordon, Avery F. 1997. *Ghostly Matters: Haunting and the Sociological Imagination.* Minneapolis: University of Minnesota Press.

Gupta, Akhil, and James Ferguson. 1992. "Beyond 'Culture': Space, Identity, and Politics of Difference." *Cultural Anthropology* 7: 6–23.

Habermas, Jürgen. 1989. *The Structural Transformation of the Public Sphere: An Inquiry into the Category of Bourgeois Society,* translated by Thomas Burger and Frederick Lawrence.

Horkheimer, Max, and Theodor Adorno. 1944. *The Dialectic of Enlightenment,* translated by John Cumming. New York: Continuum. Reprint, 1987.

León, Juan. 1997. "Tropical Overexposure: Miami's 'Sophisticated Tropics' and the *Balsero.*" In *Tropicalizations: Transcultural Representations of Latinidad,* edited by Frances R. Aparacico and Susana Chávez-Silverman, 213–28. Hanover: University Press of New England.

Lima, Lázaro. 2001. "Haunting the *Corpus Delicti*: Rafael Campo's *What the Body Told* and Wallace Stevens' (Modernist) Body." *The Wallace Stevens Journal* 25, no. 2: 220–32.

Mañach, Jorge. 1928. *La crisis de la alta cultura cubana. Indagación del choteo.* Reprint, Miami: Ediciones Universal, 1991.

Muñoz, José Esteban. 1999. *Disidentifications: Queers of Color and the Performance of Politics.* Minneapolis: University of Minnesota Press.

Ortiz, Fernando. 1924. *Glosario de afronegrismos.* Reprint, Havana: Editorial de Ciencias Sociales, 1994.

Sánchez-Eppler, Benigno. 2000. "Reinaldo Arenas, Re-writer Revenant, and the Repatriation of Cuban Homoerotic Desire." In *Queer Diasporas,* edited by Cindy Patton and Benigno Sánchez-Eppler. Durham: Duke University Press.

Sayles, John. 1991. *Los Gusanos: A Novel.* New York: Harper Collins.

Schnabel, Julian, director. 2000. *Before Night Falls*. Fineline Features/Grandview Pictures. Motion picture.

Watney, Simon. 1994. *Practices of Freedom: Selected Writings on HIV/AIDS*. Durham: Duke University Press.

6

Cosmopolitan, International, Transnational

Locating Cuban Music

Susan Thomas

Malos tiempos estos para la pureza. (These are bad times for purity.)
—Enrique Del Risco, "Todo depende" (2003)

With all the recent interest in the transnational flow of people, culture, and commodities, musicologists often find themselves a bit perplexed by all the hoopla. Even the most traditional texts on music history are filled with discussions of the migration of composers and performers; the appropriation of dance rhythms, performance traditions, and instruments from other lands; the often contentious negotiation of identity through the clashing of styles; and the effects of international political, philosophical, and economic changes on music and music making. Music might be considered one of the cultural forms most obviously and overtly reflective of cross-cultural and transnational contact for, as Cristóbal Díaz Ayala reminds us, music crosses borders freely, entering as artistic "contraband" in the memories of travelers (Díaz Ayala 1997: 21).

A study that purports to focus on musical transnationalism might thus appear to be yet another academic reinvention of the wheel. This is particularly so when the subject of such an enterprise is Cuba, for the island and its people have been situated on the transnational crossroads since the fifteenth century, as Damián Fernández points out in the introduction to this volume, and Cuban music making has been a multicultural enterprise since the early days of colonialism. However, recent events also strongly suggest that there is something new afoot in contemporary Cuban music and in the manner in which it is being produced. Thus, while it cannot be stated that transnational processes in Cuban music are an entirely new phenomenon, it also seems far too expedient merely to say that they are the continuation of what has become a centuries-long practice of internationalized Cuban musical production and reception.

This chapter examines the historically international profile of Cuban music and music making. While Cuban music has long participated in a crossing of cultural, ethnic, and national boundaries, the manner in which this participation has occurred has been far from homogenous. Differentiating the varying ways that Cuba has contributed to and participated in global musical culture is useful in developing a more nuanced understanding of Cuban music history. It is useful therefore to separate discussion of Cuban music into three categories: cosmopolitanism, internationalism, and transnationalism. A major goal of this approach is to counteract the increasingly prevalent narratives of purity and authenticity that have been developed both by the nostalgia-seekers of the West and by the socialist state apparatus on the island, which has strived to recast Cuban musical patrimony as a product of an insular, and increasingly defensive, nationalist project.

Cuban Cosmopolitanism

The eagerness and flexibility with which Cuban musicians have historically accepted and appropriated sounds and musical styles from all over the world is a defining factor in Cuban music history. Indeed, cultural cosmopolitanism was seen as such an integral part of Cuban musical identity that the concept itself was nationalized in Fernando Ortiz's use of the term "transculturation" (Ortiz 1973). Ortiz, who developed the term to describe the synthesis of African and Spanish music and culture, showed that disparate musical elements did not simply coexist on the island in a diverse potpourri of international sounds. Rather, new sounds and elements were absorbed, translated, and redefined within *local* culture, giving Cuban cosmopolitan tendencies a unique characteristic.

From the blending of various African ethnic styles in colonial-era *cabildos* to the ready appropriation of French piano technique and North American big-band lineups in later times, it is difficult if not impossible to locate musical genres in Cuba that have *not* been affected by transcultural cosmopolitanism. Examples include works as varied as the compositions of Baroque composer Esteban Salas (1725–1803); genres such as the *contradanza, danza,* and *habanera*; the Afro-Cubanist movement; the *zarzuela*; *son* ensembles; Afro-Cuban jazz; and the "rumba- fication" of North American pop songs. While a comprehensive study of the appropriation and transformation of outside musical material would be impossible here, a study of two genres, the *contradanza* and the *zarzuela*, will serve as case studies to show how cosmopolitanism has functioned as part of Cuban musical culture.

The *contradanza*, originally a type of circle dance, has a lineage that traces back to the British Isles. From there the genre moved to France and later to the French Caribbean. The French planters who fled Haiti following the 1791 revolution brought the dance with them to Cuba, where local musicians quickly transformed and Cubanized it, leading to offshoots such as the *guajira*, *clave*, *criolla*, *danza*, *danzón*, and *habanera* (Carpentier 2001: 147; León 1987: 207–48). The *contradanza* does not only represent the transformation of a French-Haitian dance form into an icon of national music, however. *Contradanza* composers such as Manuel Saumell (1817–1870) and Ignacio Cervantes (1847–1905) also participated in a lively musical dialogue with Europe and the rest of the Americas. Continental influence was fundamental in the musical training of both composers; Saumell studied in Cuba under a Parisian, while Cervantes' contact was more direct—he studied at the Paris Conservatory (Carpentier 2001: 186, 204). Their musical output became part of an international musical discourse of nationally stylized small forms and salon music, along with works by composers such as Frederic Chopin and Franz Liszt. Nineteenth-century Cuban composition also significantly influenced Louis Moreau Gottschalk, a New Orleans–based composer who helped to bring the rhythms of the *habanera*, *contradanza*, and *guaracha* across the Caribbean basin to the United States, introducing North American audiences to what would later be termed the "Latin Tinge."

In the nineteenth century, Cuban audiences frequented performances of Spanish *zarzuela*, light opera with spoken dialogue. *Zarzuela* compositions were imported from Spain or occasionally composed by Cuban musicians in the Spanish style. By the early twentieth century, however, Cuban composers and librettists created their own nationalized form in response to Spanish trends that favored shorter, more economical works and comedic strategies based on ethnic caricature. The Cuban version used these elements to incorporate the comic personality types found in local *teatro vernáculo*, placing the characters of the *mulata*, *gallego*, and *negrito* at the center of plots. While Cuban *zarzuelas* generally followed Spanish convention regarding the placement of musical numbers such as *romanzas*, duos, and ensembles, the music produced was undeniably local in character. Featuring *guarachas*, tango-congos, *sones*, rumbas, *pregones*, and other genres, the *zarzuela* became one of the primary showcases for the Afro-Cubanist movement (Moore 1997: 138–41; Thomas 2002).

The facility with which Cuban musicians and audiences have embraced and transformed international musical genres has not always been viewed favorably by music historians, who often discount such fusions and borrowings as a sign of colonial or postcolonial cultural hegemony. This discourse tends to favor musical forms that fit a particular description of popular music and discounts as inauthentic musical forms that through their style, performance practice, or transmission exhibit an overt debt to North American or European culture. Notated music fares particularly badly in this type of criticism, as it is often viewed as evidence of elitism. Yet such criticism may itself be a form of hegemonic pressure, as it does not seem to reflect Cubans' views of their own musical practices. A survey of prerevolutionary publications, among them *Pro-Arte Musical*, *Bohemia*, and *Musicalia*, as well as the more recent work of Cuban musicologists such as Leonardo Acosta, Radamés Giro, and Cristóbal Díaz Ayala, makes it clear that Cuban musicians and Cubans in general have continued to see themselves as part of a larger cultural and musical framework that includes the rest of Latin America, the United States, and Europe, and that they have not felt that their familiarity with or appropriation of musical material as a result of this contact in any way diminishes their Cubanness.

That Cuban musicians have no problem reconciling musical styles from elsewhere with their sense of *cubanidad*, or Cubanness, is equally clear today. Contemporary musicians, who have incorporated the sounds of hip-hop, acid jazz, Argentine rock, reggae, and grunge into their music, likewise insist that the result remains intrinsically Cuban and is reflective of the contemporary Cuban experience. Luis Barbería (1997), a singer-songwriter currently living in Spain, is frank about his appropriation and transformation of North American hip-hop when he raps:

> Ya sé que no soy del Bronx
> que soy un negro bien cubano y tengo otro sabor
> pero para varear quiero rapear nuevo, me siento nuevo
> deja este barullo
> que te quiero ver moviendo el culo

> I already know that I'm not from the Bronx
> that I'm a black who's really Cuban and that I have another flavor
> But for variety I want to rap in a new way, I feel new
> Let it go already
> I want to see you move your ass

He goes on to defend not only his right to rap, but the authenticity of his music as Cuban expression, in a language rich with vernacular slang:

> Mi rap sale de un solar
> de guapería, sabrosura y de qué bolá
> de mucho aguaje, gente que no cree en nada
> sólo en la mano de Orula y el camino de Elegguá

> My rap comes from a *solar*
> Of toughness, flavor, and what's up
> Of a lot of attitude, people that don't believe in anything
> Just in the hand of Orula and the path of Elegguá

Cuban Music Goes International

Perhaps one of the most important points of departure in the work of Fernando Ortiz and his theory of transculturation is that he did not merely document the appropriation and assimilation of disparate cultural and material elements into a new, distinct culture. He went on to show that these Cuban cultural products later returned to Europe, transforming European life. Had Ortiz lived long enough to witness it, he would have seen this process, which writers María Teresa Linares and Faustino Núñez (1998) have termed *la ida y la vuelta,* occur not only in the relationship between Cuba and Europe, but also in situations as diverse as the international crazes for the rumba and the mambo, the Cubanization of North American jazz, the appropriation and assimilation of Cuban rhythms into African music, and the popularity of *timba* and *rueda de casino* dancing in Russia.

The phenomenon sparked by the *Buena Vista Social Club* recording (1997) and documentary (1999) is perhaps the most poignant example of the international reach of Cuban music and musicians in recent years. Billed as a sort of "rescue operation" of traditional Cuban music by North American musician Ry Cooder and German filmmaker Wim Wenders (the mythology surrounding the project's origins is certainly open to debate), the project featured the work of venerable older Cuban musicians. The international impact of *Buena Vista Social Club* is undeniable, with many of the artists going on to launch solo recordings and concerts of the collective selling out in cities in Europe, Asia, and the Americas. While the recording was marketed as "authentically" Cuban, the album's content is a testament to cosmopolitanism, with *sones* sidling up alongside *boleros,* the sensibilities of North American jazz tingeing the *feeling* performances of Omara Portuondo, and traditional Cuban instrumentation joined by Ry Cooder on slide guitar and his son Joaquín on Middle Eastern *dumbek.*

For all its impact, *Buena Vista* was not a new phenomenon. Like musical cosmopolitanism, the internationalization of Cuban music has a long history. Already in the nineteenth century, the musical fruits of transculturation enjoyed a vibrant dialogue with the Continent, with genres such as the *contradanza* participating in a lively international musical exchange. Yet the work of composers such as Saumell, Cervantes, Nicolás Ruíz Espadero, and their contemporaries did not journey abroad only in the "memories of travelers." The nineteenth century also saw the increasing movement of Cuban musicians abroad, a movement which would increase in the thirty-year struggle for independence from 1868 to 1898, as musicians sought greater economic and political stability away from the island. During the 1868 war, for example, Cuban musical comedians known as *bufos* (an adaptation of the comedy brought to Havana by the Bufos Madrileños) fled the violence and censorship of the island

for Mexico, where they presented Mexican audiences with a picaresque caricature of Cuban popular theater and introduced musical genres such as the
danzón, *clave*, and *bolero* (Díaz Ayala 1997).

It became increasingly common for individual musicians to spend lengthy
periods of their lives away from the island. Violinist/composer José White
(1836–1918), for example, thrilled European audiences with his virtuosity.
Praised by the press and admired by composers as diverse as Rossini, Saint-
Saëns, and Gottschalk (Faivre d'Arcier 1997), White brought his celebrated
habanera, "La bella cubana," to Continental audiences just as composers began to challenge the monolithic grandiosity of large-scale musical compositions such as the symphony and the sonata with smaller forms intended for
solo or chamber performance. Such forms were often based on vernacular
dance music and reflected the growing sense of regional nationalism spreading
across Europe. White was not the only Cuban integrated into the European
musical scene. Composer/pianist José Manuel "Lico" Jiménez, noted in Cuban
music history texts as the first composer to cultivate the *Lied* in Cuba, also
spent lengthy periods of his life in Europe, mainly in Germany. Jiménez was a
student of both Reinecke and Moscheles, and his piano skills were lauded by
Wagner and Liszt, with whom he had personal contact (Orovio 1981: 255).
Although he returned briefly to Cuba, Jiménez became professor of piano and
composition at the Hamburg Conservatory, and died in Hamburg.

The practice of Cuban musicians spending long periods of time away from
the island did not end in 1898 with the cessation of armed conflict. The early
years of the Cuban republic saw the continuation and the amplification of the
waves of Cuban performers and composers traveling abroad. During the re-
publican period, political instability and economic necessity caused musicians
to seek their fortunes elsewhere, particularly in Mexico, Argentina, Spain,
France, and the United States. Indeed, success abroad was a determining factor
in the careers of some of Cuba's most hallowed musicians, including Ernesto
Lecuona (1895–1963), Moisés Simons (1889–1945), Rita Montaner (1900–
1958), and Ignacio Villa "Bola de Nieve" (1911–1971).

The Transnational Experience of Cuban Music

In the more than four decades following the Cuban Revolution, the island has
often been portrayed as isolated and cut off from the cultural changes happening elsewhere in the world, particularly in North America. Even before the
government opened the doors to international tourism and foreign investment,
however, Cuban music continued to undergo the processes of cosmopolitanism
and internationalization. Nevertheless, since the early 1990s, the *practice* of
Cuban music making has changed. The dramatic relocation of large numbers
of musicians abroad; changing perceptions of the role of those living in the

Cuban diaspora; advances in communication such as the Internet, e-mail, and instant messaging; plus technological advances in recording and digital mastering have greatly altered the ways Cuban music is imagined, realized, marketed, and consumed. These changes are affected by migration, politics, global economics, and an evolving perception among Cubans abroad and on the island of the meanings—and the location—of Cubanness, emigration, and exile.

Cuban music has become an increasingly transnational enterprise. This process is evident in a variety of phenomena: the export of *timba* music and *rueda de casino* dancing in the wake of the *boom de la salsa* of the 1990s; the presence of North American hip-hop artists at Cuban rap festivals or the Cuban rap group Obsesión's recent tour with U.S. hip-hop group The Roots; the success of folkloric ensembles such as Afrocuba de Matanzas in the United States and Europe; and the international popularity of the Paris-based hip-hop group Orishas, with their French-tinged reflections on life on the island and the blurred margins of emigration.

Contemporary Cuban singer-songwriters make an excellent case study for examining the transnational flow of musical ideas, musicians, and material culture over the last twenty years, as they have, perhaps more than representatives of any other musical genre, left the island in disproportionate numbers and settled in a variety of locations. Their case is particularly rich because it illustrates the importance of international musical dialogue in the years prior to the Special Period. They have developed and maintained both professional and personal ties between their new location and the island and among each other. The extent to which transnational musical collaboration and exchange occurs between members of this group living in cities such as Madrid, New York, Miami, Paris, and Mexico City, as well as with musicians and musical institutions in Cuba, is remarkable.

Singer-songwriter Kelvis Ochoa's song "Cuando salí de la Habana" on the album *Habana Abierta: 24 Horas* (1999) expresses the growing diasporic reality of 1990s Cuba, as young people have begun to leave the economically ravished island in droves via defections, marriages, university programs, and rubber rafts. Ochoa's lyrics suggest a sentiment common among many Cuban artists that the center of cultural production, of creative innovation, is no longer the Cuban capital. Instead, there has been a growing recognition that the "center" has moved outward to encompass a number of urban locations, including Madrid, Paris, New York, and Mexico City.

Cuando salí de la Habana

Kelvis Ochoa

Bajando con equipaje me ví
Picando media mañana

La radio aflojando salsa otra vez
Desde frente a mi ventana

Las cosas que he visto en esa ciudad
(pero la vida que se derrama)
Piñol fraseando canciones de ayer
Una bronca de dos fianas
Besito a mi padre
Lloraba Mamá
Sentía que me estrujaba
De pronto el gorrión[1] que sentía al partir
Chocaba con una calada[2]
Teniendo yo que decir

Hace calor en la Habana, mi hermana
Hace calor en la Habana
Hace calor en la Habana mi hermana
Cuéntame de Madrid

Madrid con su intensa Puerta del Sol
(Montera, luego La Palma)
Armando una bulla en el Suristán
Vanito se huracanaba
Pasamos el veranito (so-so)
Octubre se obstinaba
Flotando en el aire, aquel frío picó
el gorrión que otra vez se chocaba
Teniendo yo que decir

Hace calor en la Habana, mi hermana
· · ·

Y sé muy bien lo que necesito
No quiero que me digan que debo hacer
Poco me importa si es un ratico
Así mientras me dure aprovecharé
Fui friki, donante, mecánico y hasta chofer
Fui ruso ignorante,
llevando en la piel de existir
Como un divino reptil

Hace calor en la Habana, mi hermana
· · ·

Que quiero un cachito pa' vivir

(Coming down with luggage I saw myself
whiling away half the morning
The radio let loose salsa again
in front of my window

The things that I've seen in that city
(but the life that is wasted)
Piñol phrasing songs from yesterday
A fight between two cops
A kiss to my father
Mama cried
I felt that I was being crushed
Soon the swallow (nostalgia) that was about to leave
Crashed with a dive
I, having to say

It's hot in Havana, sister
It's hot in Havana
It's hot in Havana, sister
Tell me about Madrid

Madrid with its intense Puerta del Sol
(Montera, later La Palma)
Making a racket in the Suristan
Vanito was a hurricane
We passed the summer (so-so)
October got stubborn
Floating in the air, the cold struck
The swallow (nostalgia) that once again crashed
I, having to say

It's hot in Havana, sister
. . .

I know very well what I need
I don't want anyone to tell me what I should do
It doesn't matter if it's only a little while
While it lasts, I'll take advantage of it
I was a freak, donor, mechanic. And even a chauffeur
I was an ignorant Russian
Existing in my skin

Like a divine reptile

It's hot in Havana, sister
. . .
I want a space in order to live)

The song's instrumental introduction is taken from a Russian cartoon that played on Cuban television in the 1970s. The title, "Cuando salí de la Habana," is a reference to the children's song "Cuando salí de la Habana de nadie me despedí," whose lyrics were:

Cuando salí de la Habana
de nadie me despedí
solo de un perrito chino
que venía detrás de mí

Como el perrito era chino
un señor me lo compró
por un poco de dinero
y unas botas de charol

Las botas se me rompieron el dinero se acabó
ay perrito de mi vida,
ay perrito de mi amor.

(When I left Havana
I didn't say goodbye to anybody
Just to a little Chinese dog
That went along behind me

Since the little dog was Chinese
A man bought it from me
For a little bit of money
And some patent leather boots

The boots got broken, the money ran out
Oh, little dog of my life
Oh, little dog, my love.)

These two sources create an atmosphere of loss and regret in the very first bars of the song.

By setting the most serious part of the lyrics—the bridge section that begins "yo sé bien lo que necesito"—over *palmas* percussion, Ochoa references a trope for melancholy and nostalgia from his new home—the "deep song" of the flamenco tradition. The gesture is at once both obvious and profound. It refers to Ochoa's relocation to Madrid by calling up the most commonly referenced trope for Spanishness, *gitano* music, a music that, not unlike Afro-Cuban music, has served as a symbol of nationalism at the same time as the people and culture that produce it are disenfranchised.

The intertextuality of "Cuando salí de la Habana" makes it intensely Caribbean, yet the appropriation of Russian melody, Spanish rhythm, and the sonorities of North American rock mark it as highly international. Indeed, the sense one gets from reading recent journalism (particularly the spate of print and online articles that heralded Habana Abierta's visit to Miami on October 3–4, 2003) is that Cuban culture has suddenly "become" international. As I made clear earlier in this chapter, however, Cuban popular music has always appropriated and recrafted foreign musical styles. Even in the relatively closed years following the revolution, Cuba continued to be a musical crossroads, although on a much more muted scale. Merchant marines would bring home records, diplomats who traveled to Soviet-bloc countries returned with pirated copies of British pop, and Cuban musicians who participated in song festivals in Brazil and Chile returned with a diversity of American sounds.

As the previous discussion of internationalism illustrates, the practice of Cuban musicians choosing to pursue their careers abroad is hardly unique to postrevolutionary musicians or to Ochoa's generation in particular. Nevertheless, the sheer number of émigrés among the most recent generation of singer-songwriters is remarkable. Most notable among this group are David Torrens in Mexico City; the members of Orishas in Paris; Adrian Morales in Barcelona; Descemer Bueno in New York; and, in Madrid alone, Athanai, Luis Barbería, Vanito Caballero Brown, Nilo Castillo, Gema Corredera, Julio Fowler, Alejandro Frómeta, Alejandro Gutiérrez, Boris Larramendi, José Luis Medina, Kelvis Ochoa, Raúl Torres, Pavel Urkiza, Pepe del Valle, Andy Villalón, and a number of percussionists, guitarists, pianists, and bass players, many of whom traveled to Europe as backup musicians for song festivals and stayed there (one of the most high-profile examples is the entire band and technical team of Carlos Varela, who stayed behind after a Spanish tour in the 1990s).

To understand how so many musicians representing the same generation and similar aesthetics and philosophies came to be located in Madrid and elsewhere, it is necessary to look at the historical moment when their musical style emerged. In the late 1980s, Cuban singer-songwriters, poets, and comedians met at informal gatherings known as *peñas*. These young musicians represented a new generation that grew up watching their parents and older siblings listen to forbidden copies of the Beatles and British pop and witnessing a series of unforgettable musical events. One of those events was the 1983 visit to Cuba by Venezuelan *salsero* Oscar D' León. León's Cuban appearance was a smashing success that helped legitimize Afro-Cuban dance music on the island and was a critical antecedent to the 1990s *boom de la salsa*. An even more direct influence on these musicians was the 1987 concert by Argentine rock musician Fito Paez in Havana's Karl Marx Theater. Paez and his left-leaning *rock en español* energized a generation of Cuban musicians who had grown up under the influence of socially conscious singer-songwriters such as Pablo Milanés and Silvio Rodríguez. The music created by these musicians at *peñas* such as the one held on the corner of 13th and 8th streets in the Vedado section of Havana went far beyond the simpler, anti-virtuosic "man-with-guitar" style made popular and later institutionalized by the musicians of the *nueva trova* movement. The young musicians strove to be international, appropriating the styles of British and Argentine rock, the harmonic and rhythmic experimentation of Brazilian music, and the "flo" of North American rap. The emerging music was intrinsically Cuban as well as cosmopolitan, and song lyrics exploited the local, using vernacular speech to describe the problems of everyday life after three decades of Cuban socialism.

Enrique del Risco, a young Cuban writer who read his poetry and humor at the *peña* on 13th and 8th and who now lives in New York, has written extensively on the subject of the Cuban diaspora. His writings have taken him more than once to the music his former *socios* are making in Madrid. Del Risco has become in many ways a Carpentier for his generation. His chronicles in online journals such as *Encuentro* and *Cuba Nuestra* comment on contemporary literature, art, music, and politics, and he examines international cultural movements through a uniquely Cuban lens. Del Risco (2002) writes of the musicians of Habana Abierta, "I don't know whether to call them a 'generation,' this group of friends of similar age, experience, influences, aesthetic creeds, vital conception, and artistic intentions. Nor does it matter. In any case, the group that began to come together at the crossing of 13th and 8th streets in the Vedado and that together and separately has recorded nearly a dozen records has been the most subversive thing that has happened to Cuban popular music in a long time."

Not only was the music coming out of Havana's *peñas* among the most progressive compositions of the time (Arsenio Rodríguez, 2003, writing from Barcelona, recalls 13th and 8th as "the little Seattle of Cuban music in the 1990s"), its socially critical message and international (read "capitalist") sound made it anathema to Cuban institutions. Whereas the *nueva trova* movement extolled the virtues of the revolution and the promises of socialism, the younger singer-songwriters followed the path pioneered by rock-*trovador* Carlos Varela and used their music to criticize the problems they saw around them. José Luis Medina in "Ritmo sabroso" sang of the revolution's failures in dealing with crime, corruption, and domestic and sexual violence. Pepe del Valle, in "Con tanta presión," lamented the lack of space and opportunities for Cuba's young people to develop themselves.

Supportive critics from the *nueva trova* movement came up with the label *novísima trova* to describe the new music—an attempt, perhaps, to portray the music as socially conscious rather than politically critical. But the combination of social criticism with an unorthodox musical style kept the musicians of 13th and 8th and other *peñas* from enjoying professional careers. They lacked institutional support and, aside from the efforts of a few daring individuals, most notably Juanito Camacho of Radio Ciudad de la Habana, they were not promoted on the radio or television. Given this reality, *la generación de los topos* (the generation of the moles, or the underground generation) might have been a better name for Cuba's young singer-songwriters than the more institutional and upbeat *novísima trova*. Faced with so few professional opportunities, it is not surprising that nearly all of the musicians who participated in this movement have left the island.

On his recent album *Siete* (2003), Carlos Varela tells us that the reality of Cubans over the last twenty years has been divided between "*el quédate o vete*" (stay or go).[3] The gradual opening of Cuba to the outside in recent years has slowly increased options for Cubans wishing to leave the island, either permanently or temporarily. Yet the reality facing Cuba—and Cuban musicians—today is far more complicated than the binary choice in Varela's lyrics. Varela himself knows this reality all too well, for he and his musicians are among the Cuban groups that *entran y salen* (come and go) the most. Cuban musicians, along with visual artists, occupy a unique position within Cuban society because they are able to acquire exit visas for travel abroad, allowing them to spend long periods of time off the island and earn hard currency. Their economic and social status and their relative mobility compared to average Cubans have given them a distinct status in Cuban society. As visual artist Alexis Esquivel Bermúdez told me, "We're like little foreigners."

Cuban musicians traveling abroad maintain close ties with musicians who have left the island, often engaging in impromptu concerts or jam sessions with Cuban émigrés and even inviting their former colleagues up on stage during formal performances. At a concert in Madrid in July 2003, for example, Carlos Varela and his band were joined onstage by Kelvis Ochoa and Athanai, and present in the house were all the previous members of Varela's band who had stayed behind after a Spanish tour in the late 1990s.

For those musicians who have chosen to relocate to other countries, however, the adjustment to music capitalism has not been easy. The generation's eclectic musical style (neither *trova* nor rock nor salsa) has made it difficult for them to attract the attention of record labels. Furthermore, the craze for Cuban music that swept Europe and the United States in the late 1990s showed a distinct preference for perceived "authentic" Cuban sounds, preferably those from before 1950, as exemplified by the Buena Vista Social Club phenomenon. The musicians also found that the vernacular quality of their work—their references to Cuban social reality—went over the heads of non-Cuban listeners, and that the harmonic and rhythmic intricacy they prized overwhelmed audiences who preferred a cleaner—and more pop-like—palette. As Pepe del Valle put it, "They listen to your music and they say to you, 'Qué bien, qué bonito, qué original,' but they miss a lot and really they don't understand" (Matos 2001).

The new realities have directly affected the musicians' creative processes. The sudden need to take mass-market appeal into account has caused some musicians, including Luis Barbería and Jose Luis Medina, to look for even more international models. Barbería's 2002 album, for example, draws its influences from North American funk and soul, using his low baritone voice (unusual in Cuban popular music) to create a sort of Cuban version of Barry White. In contrast, many other musicians' recent work shows evidence of an increasing "Cubanness," highlighting in particular the older, traditional Cuban rhythms now popular off the island. The best-known example of this is, of course, the Paris-based Orishas' sampling of "Chan-Chan" (Orishas 2000). Compay Segundo's well-known harmonic progression was also the basis for a composition by rapper Nilo Castillo and was popular with Madrid audiences well before the Orishas' debut album received international acclaim. Julio Fowler's and Boris Larramendi's recent solo albums show evidence of this trend, and Kelvis Ochoa, who cut his teeth in Havana in the early 1990s in the rock group Kelvis y los 4 Gatos, has abandoned the rock-and-pop-influenced music of his early career for a style that leans heavily on Cuban genres such as *son*, *conga*, *guaguanco*, and the *sucu-sucu* of his native Isle of Youth.

One of the most remarkable things about the way contemporary Cuban music is created, produced, and consumed is the level of interaction between Cuban musicians in various countries and those who remain on the island. Their transnational communication and collaboration show the extent to which Cuban culture, once thought to exist in isolation, is being constructed constantly on a global scale. Clearly, the politics of diaspora have changed. E-mail has made contact with friends and colleagues who live in many different countries commonplace. Unlike the generation of expatriate musicians that preceded them, many musicians who live abroad now return home to the island on a regular basis, both to visit family and, increasingly, to collaborate professionally. The most striking example of this phenomenon occurred in January 2003, when the members of Habana Abierta (now based in Madrid) played together on the island for the first time in more than seven years.[4] At the invitation of the Ministry of Culture, the band filled the Salón Rosado of the Tropical (the storied seat of Los Van Van) to capacity without any official publicity. Accounts vary, but the unpublicized concert is said to have attracted somewhere between eight and ten thousand people. The show itself seemed less a performance by Habana Abierta than a reunion of nearly every fusion-friendly musician who was in Havana at the time: The band was joined on stage by Gerardo Alfonso, Paul Menéndez, David Torrens (visiting from Mexico), Robertico Carcassés, Yusa, Athanai (visiting from Spain), and a number of participants from the infamous *farándula* of 13th and 8th.

A good example of the kind of transnational collaborations taking place between Cuban musicians today is Gema and Pavel's 2003 album, *Art Bembé*, a double disc collection that also includes a book of visual art, essays, and poetry by Cubans living in Havana, New York, and Madrid. The statement on the album's cover, "Interactivo: Madrid, Nueva York, la Habana," is an early indication of the transnational character of the project and refers to the fact that tracks were recorded in all three locations. Many musicians collaborated on the project, including Yusa, Robertico Carcassés, Freehole Negro, Haydee Milanés (the daughter of Pablo Milanés), Juan Carlos Formell, and Francis del Rio, all currently living in Cuba; New York-based Descemer Bueno, Roman Díaz, Junior Terry, and Ahmed Barroso; and from Madrid, Fernando Fabier, Alberto Fabián, Gladys Silot, Carlos Puig, and Manuel Machado. The album itself is a testament to Cuban hybridity, mixing the sounds of Afro-Cuban religious chants, *boleros*, and *guaguancos* with funk, flamenco, soul, hip-hop, and borrowed sounds from the Madrid subway and Havana sidewalks.

Art Bembé is not an anomaly. Pavel Urkiza has produced, arranged, and provided artistic support for a number of Cuban albums, including Yusa's 2002 self-titled album featuring the participation of musicians living both on and off the island. Kelvis Ochoa spent nearly half of 2003 touring and performing in Cuba, where he was named "personality of the year" and his music is played frequently on the radio. His forthcoming album also includes tracks recorded in three countries. Like Urkiza, he collaborates with members of Interactivo, a Havana-based collective headed by pianist Robertico Carcassés that is known for bringing jazz, *trova*, *feeling*, and hip-hop musicians together.

Press accounts of the "new" Cuban music being "discovered" in Madrid, Havana, and other cities cite the musicians' international exposure and cosmopolitanism as evidence of a sea change in Cuban musicianship. A look at the history of these musicians shows that their individual styles are the result of nearly twenty years of musical practice. It is the music industry and cultural institutions that have been slow to recognize the artistic possibilities of this type of musical fusion, not the musicians. Yet clearly something new is being produced in places like Madrid. It can perhaps best be described as a new vision of *cubanidad*, a reinterpretation of Benítez-Rojo's "certain way" (Benítez-Rojo 1989). Perhaps these musicians, who have stressed collaboration, openness to change, and group solidarity, will follow other Cuban *trovadores* in providing a progressive social vision as Cuba and Cubans head into increasingly fractured and uncertain times.

Notes

1. *Gorrión*: literally, "swallow," colloquially, "nostalgia."
2. *Chocaba con una calada*: colloquially, "was smoking marijuana."
3. These words appear in the lyrics to "Siete," the title song of Varela's 2003 album.
4. The concert was the subject of a documentary, *Habana Abierta* (2003), directed by Jorge Perrugoría and Arturo Sotto.

Bibliography

Benítez-Rojo, Antonio. 1989. *La isla que se repite: El Caribe y la perspectiva posmoderna*. Hanover, N.H.: Ediciones del Norte.

Carpentier, Alejo. 2001. *Music in Cuba*. Edited and with an introduction by Timothy Brennan; translated by Alan West-Durán. Minneapolis: University of Minnesota Press.

Del Risco, Enrique. 2002. "El ultimo exilio o nuevas posibilidades de lo cubano." *Cuba Nuestra* (8 January). <http://cubanuestra.nu/web/article.asp?artID=63>.

———. 2003. "Todo depende." In booklet accompanying the two-CD set *Art Bembé*, by Gema and Pavel. Madrid: Peer Music.

Díaz Ayala, Cristóbal. 1997. *Cuando salí de la Habana: 1898–1997: cien años de música cubana por el mundo*. San Juan, Puerto Rico: Fundación Musicalia.

Faivre d'Arcier, Sabine. 1997. *José White y su tiempo*. Havana: Editorial Letras Cubanas.

León, Argeliers. 1987. *Del canto y el tiempo*. Havana: Editorial Pueblo y Educación.

Linares, María Teresa, and Faustino Núñez. 1998. "The Arrival and the Return." In *La música entre Cuba y España*. Madrid: Fundación Autor.

Matos, Denys. 2001. "Interview with Pepe del Valle." <http://arch.cubaencuentro.com/rawtext/enclave/2001/04/16/1950.html>.

Moore, Robin. 1997. *Nationalizing Blackness: Afrocubanismo and Artistic Revolution in Havana, 1920–1940*. Pittsburgh: Pittsburgh University Press.

Orovio, Helio. 1981. *Diccionario de la música cubana*. Havana: Editorial Letras Cubanas.

Ortiz, Fernando. 1973. *Contrapunteo cubano*. Barcelona: Editorial Ariel.

Perrugoría, Jorge, and Arturo Sotto. 2003. *Habana Abierta*. Cuba: ICAIC.

Rodríguez, Arsenio. 2003. "Divino guión: Apuntes de una reconquista: Habana Abierta y su recién finalizada gira musical en Cuba." *Encuentro en la Red* (30 January). <http://arch.cubaencuentro.com/rawtext/musica/2003/01/23/11619.html>.

Thomas, Susan. 2002. "Lo más femenino de los géneros: Gender, Race, and Representation in the Cuban Zarzuela, 1927–1944." Ph.D. diss., Brandeis University.

Wenders, Wim, director. 1999. *Buena Vista Social Club*. Road Movies Production.

Discography

Athanai. 1997. *Séptimo Cielo*. No More Discos.

Barbería, Luis. 1997. "Échate esto." *Habana Abierta*. Nube Negra Records.

———. 2002. *Luis Barbería*. Muxxic Records.

Buena Vista Social Club. 1997. *Buena Vista Social Club*. Nonesuch Records.

Castillo, Nilo (Nilo MC). 2002. *Guajiro del asfalto*. Virgin Records, Spain.

Gema y Pavel. 2003. *Art Bembé*. Peermusic Spain.

Habana Abierta. 1997. *Habana Abierta*. Nube Negra Records.

———. 1999. *24 horas*. BMG Music Spain.

Larramendi, Boris. 2002. *Yo no tengo la culpa*. BMG Music Spain.

Ochoa, Kelvis. 2001. *Kelvis*. BMG Music Spain.

Orishas. 2000. *A lo cubano*. EMI Music.

Varela, Carlos. 2003. *Siete*. Iberautor Promociones Culturales.

Yusa. 2002. *Yusa*. Tumi Music.

7

Rap's Diasporic Dialogues

Cuba's Redefinition of Blackness

Alan West-Durán

A June 2003 event held at the Apollo Theater was billed as the Hip Hop Unity Concert. It featured two groups from Cuba, Obsesión and Doble Filo, as well as The Roots, Common, Soulive w/J-Live, Kanye West, El Meswy, and Tomorrowz Weaponz, among others. With opening words by Harry Belafonte and emceed by Black Thought (Tariq Trotter) of The Roots, it seemed a perfect confluence of Afro-diasporic voices and histories—from one of the great popularizers of calypso who was an important figure in the civil rights movement to socially conscious rappers from the United States and Cuba—in a historic Harlem theater that has hosted everyone from Ella Fitzgerald and James Brown to the Black Panthers and Elijah Muhammad.

The concert seemed to exemplify Paul Gilroy's notion of the Black Atlantic, the vast African dialogue born of enslavement, diaspora, dispersion, and dispossession. The creation, continuities, and disruptions of the Black Atlantic are not merely a reaction to an unspeakable trauma, however, but an ongoing, spirited, and inventive ensemble of voices, affirmations, and counterresponses. As George Lipsitz points out,

> The flow of information and ideas among diasporic people has not been from Africa outward to Europe and the Americas, but rather has been a reciprocal self-renewing dialogue in communities characterized by upheaval and change. The story of the African diaspora is more than an aftershock of the slave trade, it is an ongoing dynamic creation. The radicalism of diasporic African culture comes not only from the contrast between African and Euro-American values, but also from the utility of exploiting diasporic choices everywhere—in Africa, as well as in Europe, the Caribbean, and the Americas. Just as American and European blacks have drawn on African traditions to contest Euro-American power rela-

tions, Africans have drawn upon cultures of opposition and strategies of signification developed by diasporic Africans as a form of struggle on the African continent. (Lipsitz 1994: 39)

Gilroy's framework sees the Black Atlantic as going beyond national (and essentialist) boundaries with words such as fractal, rhizomorphic transcultural, and transnational (Gilroy 1993: 4, 15, 19). In discussing Cuban rap as part of transnational dialogue I will argue that symbolic borders of race and nation cannot be circumscribed to the island's national territory, and that transnationalism (as it is often understood) is not merely a matter of crossing state borders, since most Cuban rappers have never left the island (Duany 2002: 37–38).

Cuba has traditionally seen its Afro-Cuban history and realities from within a nationalist framework and, therefore, has often viewed affirmations of Africanness as divisive or even unpatriotic. This is all the more remarkable since the majority of combatants in both the Ten Years' War (1868–1878) and the Spanish-Cuban-American War (1895–1898) were Afro-Cuban. In the latter war, with slavery abolished, the estimates run as high as 80 percent. What is most important is that dark-skinned Cubans played a major role in the two independence struggles, their willingness to give their blood for Cuba is undeniable, and the *mambí* (a runaway slave or one freed by his masters who then took up arms against the Spanish) is an iconic figure in Cuban history and culture. But other historical factors also come into play: the discourse of Cuba's elites (such as Arango y Parreño and Saco), the existence of a large free colored population, the nature of the independence struggle, particularly the presence and influence of *cabildos* before and after slavery, the African-Caribbean emigrations (1915–1930), European immigration (1880–1910) designed to whiten the population, and the 1912 massacre of more than five thousand Afro-Cubans.

Scholars often cite these factors along with Cuba's relaxed attitude toward miscegenation, the nonexistence of Jim Crow–type segregation, and the absence of a Spanish creole or patois to account for the lack of black nationalism or separatism on the island. Yet Marcus Garvey's Universal Negro Improvement Association (UNIA) had fifty-two chapters in Cuba, the highest of any country outside the United States, and Cuban President García Menocal actually met with Garvey in 1921. It is difficult to imagine a U.S. president meeting with Marcus Garvey. Most members of Cuba's UNIA were West Indian; that is, Jamaican, Haitian, or other English-speaking West Indians (Martin 1983: 69–71). Cubans did not respond enthusiastically to Garvey's African repatriation message, but they resonated with his calls for black pride, self-improvement, and institution building. The brutal repression of UNIA under Machado

(1928–1930) led to its demise. Still, UNIA's Cuban history and its aftermath warrant further study.

Cubans often reiterate that they all belong to the Cuban race, echoing a famous phrase by José Martí: "A Cuban is more than mulatto, black, or white." Martí's phrase was insufficient and was certainly not Cuba's definitive statement on its African roots, however. A few decades after Martí's death, the Afrocubanismo movement—with all of its appropriations, essentialisms, exoticisms, and stereotyping—was central to redefining the country's musical, artistic, and literary legacy, as well as to offering a more inclusive definition of national identity (R. Moore 1997). That the Afro-diasporic dialogue was multidirectional and transnational can be seen in Langston Hughes' influence on Nicolás Guillén (and vice-versa), Wifredo Lam's discovery (or rediscovery) of Afro-Cuban religions via Cubism and the European avant-gardes (who, in turn, were influenced by African art), and the extraordinary encounters between Machito, Mario Bauzá, Chano Pozo, and Dizzy Gillespie that led to what we now call Latin jazz.

Afrocubanismo's exploration and celebration of its African heritage was—with the exception of Nicolás Guillén and a few others—mostly led and promoted by whites such as Alejo Carpentier, Lydia Cabrera, Mariano Brull, Emilio Ballagas, and Fernando Ortiz. The voices of such people of color as journalist Gustavo Urrutia (1881–1958) and pharmacist-journalist Rómulo Lachatañeré (1909–1952) were certainly heard, but they never achieved the canonical status of their white cohorts (Fernández Robaina 1994, 2003).

Not surprisingly, out of Afrocubanismo grew Cuba's celebration of *mestizaje* or *mulataje*, often linked to Guillén's work, which I will discuss further on as I examine rappers who have taken his poetry or ideas and critically engaged them for a twenty-first-century Cuba.

Historically speaking, then, Afro-Cuban culture has long carried on a conversation that is *at least* triangular in its broadest scope. As I have written elsewhere,

> If slavery was a triangular phenomenon (Africa–The Americas–Europe), with world repercussions, the Afro-Caribbean realm also has a world scope, central to the Black Atlantic. This Black Atlantic would include Latin Jazz, Yoruba and Congolese influences in Afro-Cuban religions, Bahamian storytelling traditions, Curaçaoan funeral practices, U.S. hip-hop influences in Puerto Rico's rap scene, Trinidadian cuisine, Fanon's crucial contributions to the independence of Algeria, Senegalese musicians making a living playing Cuban dance music, Bob Marley's invitation to sing at Zimbabwe's independence celebration, Cuba's military prominence in ending apartheid in South Africa, and Wifredo Lam illustrating books by Aimé Césaire. (West-Durán 2003: xxxi)

Using a more overtly Cuban phraseology, we could say that the Afro-diasporic dialogue is part of a wider phenomenon of transculturation embedded within a transnational history (see Ortiz 1995). Generally, the term "transculturation" is used to describe the historical process of cultural change and creation under terms of subordination and resistance between European and non-European cultures. But in this case we must consider its inter-African dimensions. Slaves transported to the Caribbean came from different cultures, religions, languages, and social structures: Yoruba, Congo, Abakuá (Carabalí), Wolof, Ewe-Fon (Arará), Mina, Mandinga (Fula), Hausa, Ashanti, and Ngola, to name the most common. So simultaneous to their interaction within a coerced milieu and under severe exploitation, they were also forging an inter-African transculturation with their shipmates. This element of transculturation is frequently overlooked and, unfortunately, exceedingly difficult to study.

In examining Cuban hip-hop, the double diasporic elements of U.S. hip-hop come to the fore. Among the pioneers of U.S. rap are such performers as Afrika Bambataa, Grandmaster Flash, and Kool DJ Herc, all from Caribbean backgrounds; equally significant was the influence of Puerto Rican DJs (such as Charlie Chase) active in rap's South Bronx emergence, as well as the extraordinary *boricua* presence in the evolution of break dancing (Rock Steady Crew, The Furious Rockers, The New York City Breakers and others). Clearly, the Jamaican sound systems of the 1950s (Coxsone Dodd and Duke Reid), Prince Buster, and dub practitioners such as Big Youth, U-Roy, King Tubby, and Lee Perry, not to mention dub poets Linton Kwesi Johnson and Michael Smith, also were influential in the origins of rap. The heavy bass and percussion, the repetition of certain rhythmic elements, the rhythms and rhymes of the vocal line, and DJs grabbing the mike to whip up a crowd are all traits of a dynamic and powerful transnational Caribbean and Afro-diasporic dialogue (see Hebdige 1987: 136–48; Potter 1995: 36–40).

This Afro-diasporic conversation with a transnational scope (African American, Jamaican, Puerto Rican) found a kindred voice in Cuba's black musical scene. The island's Afro-musical traditions are deep-rooted. Cuban rappers have drawn on Yoruba chants, *rumba*, mambo, *son*, and the *guaracha* to fashion their own, original Cuban rap. The Spanish language also lends itself to rapping, with its ingenious word play and heavy emphasis on rhyme. Non-rappers are eager to use rap as part of their music, as can be seen in recent recordings by Cachaíto López, Celia Cruz, Omar Sosa, Orlando "Maraca" Valle, even the Orquesta Aragón.

Cuba's rap scene is firmly established, with more than five hundred groups (according to rapper-producer Pablo Herrera) and thousands attending the island's annual festival in mid-August in Alamar and other locations. The more recent festivals have featured roundtable discussions on Cuban, U.S., Latin American, and European hip-hop. The Cuban authorities initially regarded the rap scene with a degree of disapproval, but have since designated an official (until December 2004, Ariel Fernández) to oversee it at the Ministry of Culture. In August 2003, the Ministry of Culture launched Cuba's first hip-hop magazine, *Movimiento*, an interesting mix of interviews with artists, song lyrics, analytic-theoretical essays, comics, and a history of rap written by Kurtis Blow. Nevertheless, the venues for the main concerts at the 2003 rap festival were in two distant locales, Alamar and the Salón Rosado at the Tropical. The first is twenty-five minutes east of Havana, the second in the extreme western part of the city. Given the transportation problems in Cuba, distance represents a major obstacle for most Cubans. The other venue was the Café Cantante, a much better location, but one that barely has room for a couple of hundred people. Also, at the concerts and roundtable sessions, which lasted two full days, group members themselves were hawking compact discs in the hallways. These points indicate that while the Cuban state has accepted hip-hop, some logistical, financial, and creative issues remain unresolved. The logistical limitations seem to indicate acceptance with an undercurrent of containment, which seems ironic given the name of the magazine (*Movement*) the government sponsors and publishes.[1]

My intent in this chapter is not to give a history of Cuban rap,[2] but instead to invoke the concepts of a proliferating and creative Afro-diasporic (Black Atlantic, transnational) dialogue in arguing that Cuba is involved in a redefinition of its traditional views of blackness via a "hybrid essentialism" that denies a pure or monolithic concept of identity but puts forth certain ideas of Cubanness and Africanness that are grounded geographically, culturally, and spiritually in the island.

As previously mentioned, Cuba's Afrocubanismo movement offers a mixed-race identity for the Cuban nation, a kind of cultural *mulataje* that gives Cuba its unique identity. Implicit in this definition is that through continued race mixing, the island will become lighter, not darker. Miscegenation was (and still often is) seen as a whitening process.

Along with Damas, Césaire, Senghor, Palés Matos, and Manuel del Cabral, to name only some of the most celebrated figures, Nicolás Guillén (1902–1989), one of the island's great poetic and cultural figures, was a major exponent of Afro-Antillean poetry. Guillén's "La balada de los dos abuelos" (The Ballad of the Two Grandfathers, 1975) is probably the most oft-cited poem that expresses the union of white and black Cubans as a symbol of Cubanía:

> They raise their sturdy heads;
> both of equal size
> beneath the high stars;
> both of equal size,
> a Black longing, a White longing,

both of equal size,
they scream, dream, weep, sing.
They dream, weep, sing.
They weep, sing.
Sing!

On another occasion, Guillén was even more explicit: "And the spirit of Cuba is mulatto, and it is from spirit, not the skin, that we derive our definitive color. Someday it will be called 'Cuban color'" (Pérez Sarduy and Stubbs 1993: 235). Guillén's poems and statements have achieved canonical status in Cuba from literary, racial, and political points of view: He was the national poet of the island for decades and the head of the Writer's Union (UNEAC) as well.

Three different rap groups have taken a fresh (in all senses of the word) look at Guillén from three different perspectives: race, gender, and politics. The original poems are from three different periods: "Quirino," from *Sóngoro Cosongo* (1931); "La muralla," from *La paloma de vuelo popular* (1958); and "Tengo" from *Tengo* (1964). Cuarta Imagen's "La muralla" draws on Guillén's poem of the same title. In his poem, Guillén sets up an archetypal situation of a wall that has been built by all, by white hands and black hands, in order to let in the good and shut out evil. Much of the poem is structured as a dialogue, or a series of questions that are answered. There is a knock, someone asks, "Who's there?" and there comes a response: For the rose, the carnation, the dove, the laurel, myrrh, mint, the friend's heart, the nightingale, and the flower, the wall is opened; for the colonel's saber, the scorpion, the centipede, poison, the dagger, and the serpent's tooth, the wall is closed.

La muralla

Nicolás Guillén (1974), 170–71

Para hacer esta muralla,
tráigame todas las manos:
los negros, sus manos negras,
los blancos, sus blancas manos.
Ay, Ay, una muralla que vaya
desde la playa hasta el monte
desde el monte hasta la playa, bien,
allá sobre el horizonte.

—¡Tun, tun!
—¿Quién es?
—Una rosa y un clavel . . .
—¡Abre la muralla!

—¡Tun, tun!
—¿Quién es?
—El sable del coronel . . .
—¡Cierra la muralla!
—¡Tun, tun!
—¿Quién es?
—La paloma y el laurel . . .
—¡Abre la muralla!
—¡Tun, tun!
—¿Quién es?
—El alacrán y el ciempiés
—¡Cierre la muralla!
 . . .

(The Wall

To build this wall
bring me all the hands
from blacks, their black hands
from whites, their white hands
A wall stretching
from shore to summit
from summit to shore
way over on the horizon.

Knock, knock!
—Who's there?
—A rose and a carnation . . .
—Open the wall!
—Knock, knock!
—Who's there?
—The colonel's saber . . .
—Close the wall!
—Knock, knock!
—Who's there?
—The dove and the laurel . . .
—Open the wall!
—Knock, Knock!
—Who's there?
—The scorpion and the centipede
—Close the wall!)[3]

Guillén's poem envisions a utopian space, a society where good is invited in and bad is excluded. The wall runs from "el monte hasta la playa" (from the hills to the sea), forming a symbolic walled city or country. The central image is one of personal, political, racial, metaphysical, and even natural unity, with images of plants, flowers, animals, and the landscape. The poem is from the prerevolutionary period and yet seems to evoke the future society Guillén yearned for.

Cuarta Imagen's "La muralla" is a radical departure in many ways. The eight lines that begin and end Guillén's poem are reduced to four, but the four omitted are those that make reference to the unity of black and white hands (see italicized lyrics):

La Muralla

Cuarta Imagen

. . .

no tengo fama pero algo me ha tocado
tengo el público que Dios me ha mandado
como un cubano cimarrón con el machete
a ver cuál es el brete
si no presiento miedo ante látigo o el cadete

. . .

hoy como ayer
sé que me quisieran verme desaparecer
desde que volví a nacer, volví a crecer
he vuelto a rehacer
lo que yo siempre quise ser vamos a ver
si no se han dado cuenta soy cubano

. . .

quiero una muralla que vaya
desde el monte hasta la playa
desde la playa hasta el monte
allá por el horizonte.

. . .

(The Wall

I have no fame, but I do have
an audience that God gave me
like a Cuban *cimarrón* with his machete
So let's see what's going down
No fear of the lash, the soldier's wrath

. . .
Today, like in the past
I know you wanted me to disappear,
but I was born anew and grew, I'm here
remade myself
into what I want to be, let's see
in case you didn't notice I'm Cuban.
. . .
I want a wall stretching
From summit to shore
From shore to summit
There, on the horizon.)

The song, with a thick, round bass sound, makes several references to the slave past and Afro-Cuban history. Instead of black and white hands, the song mentions a *cimarrón* (runaway slave) with a machete in his hands. What follows is a fascinating synthesis of personal and collective histories that speaks to a history of both struggle and overcoming invisibility: "In case you didn't notice I'm Cuban." The reference is to being black, but the affirmation is couched within citizenship and nationality (Cuban).

Further on in the song an African identity is expressed more overtly in a reference to Siete Rayos (or Nsasi), from the *kimpugulu* or *palero* pantheon, whose equivalent in Regla de Ocha is Changó, the *orisha* of lightning and music. The singers claim their Yoruba traditions while emphasizing again their Cubanness ("soy Yoruba lucumí, como soy Yoruba de aquí de Cuba"). This is followed by perhaps the most striking lyrics in the song: "Desde Cuba suba mi llanto Yoruba / que suba el alegre llanto Yoruba / que sale de mí" (May my Yoruba weeping rise up from Cuba / may my joyful Yoruba weeping / rise out of me). What makes these lines so effective is the juxtaposition of "alegre llanto Yoruba":

Entiendan que la voz de Siete Rayos ya llegó
Y se quedó
Yoruba soy Yoruba lucumí
Como soy un Yoruba de aquí de Cuba
Desde Cuba suba mi llanto Yoruba
que suba el alegre llanto Yoruba
que sale de mí

(Understand, the voice of Nsasi arrived
And stayed
I'm Yoruba, Yoruba lucumí

And since I'm Yoruba from here, Cuba
may my Yoruba weeping rise up from Cuba
may the joyful Yoruba weeping
rise out of me.)

This combination of joy and sadness affixed to the Yoruba, within a Cuban context, is such an astoundingly rich image, further buttressed by the fact that *canto* (song or chant) is what you would normally expect to find there, not to mention that *canto* and *llanto* rhyme in Spanish. In a sense, the missing rhyme creates a double rhyme, one present, the other absent, evoking ancestral spirits. The phrase is made all the more poignant by previous lyrics in the song that claim that while time has transpired and there are no longer any black slaves, still there is a lingering "Afro-Cuban Indian effect" (*vigencia*).

Again, Cuarta Imagen has drawn on Guillén, specifically his "Son Número 6" from his book *El Son Entero* (1947). The poem begins with the *llanto* and being Yoruba, and shortly after Guillén says that if I am not Yoruba "I am congo, mandinga, carabalí" (Guillén 1974: 129), invoking the other major African influences in Cuba's diasporic history. But like "La Muralla," it is also a song about black and white unity ("negros y blancos, todo mezclado"; blacks and whites all mixed together; Guillén 1974: 130). The end of the poem reinforces the spirit of racial harmony and *mestizaje*: "De aquí no hay nadie que se separe . . . ¡que el son de todos no va a parar!" (From this moment no one separated . . . The *son* of one and all will not stop!) (Guillén 1974: 131). Cuarta Imagen's emphasis is on Yoruba and Congolese culture and religion, not the reconciliatory image of whites and blacks dancing their celebratory *son*. Cuarta Imagen does not reject the objectives of seeking that harmony, but by omission suggests that African-Cubans need to affirm their identity, culture, and needs first.

Cuban music in general and rap in particular constantly make references to Afro-Cuban culture and religion. One might ask what makes rap's references to this heritage different than those of, say, a more established salsa-timba group like Los Van Van's use of the orishas and Regla de Ocha in "Soy Todo." No doubt the Special Period (Cuba's economic decline from 1990 to 1995 after the collapse of the Soviet Union) and its aftermath saw a flourishing interest in Afro-Cuban religious practices. The ideological and economic bankruptcy of the regime made many Cubans seek out beliefs that had a long tradition on the island, be they Catholicism, Regla de Ocha, Regla de Palo, or Abakuá. *Raperos* have embraced these traditions, either as believers or as a way of reaffirming some of the deepest roots of Cuban culture. It is interesting to see how often rappers reiterate their Cubanía, as if to prove to non-*raperos* that their nationalist credentials are intact.

In many popular songs—not necessarily the Van Van example previously mentioned—references to Ocha, Palo, or Abakuá seem more like flashy, almost exotic citations of afrocubanía, but for the rappers it seems to come from within those beliefs, either as practicing members of Afro-Cuban religions, or as reaffirmation of its centrality in their own reality as African-Cubans. In addition, in some songs there is a greater emphasis in the use of Yoruba, Bantu-Kikongo, or Abakuá words and phrases, as if to affirm that insider status and challenge the listener to find out what is being said. Eleyo's "Ponle fe" is an excellent example of this, a funny and poignant song about a man whose wife leaves him so he seeks advice from a *babalao*, a *palero* and an *espiritista*. The song has passages entirely in Yoruba, as well as being sprinkled throughout with words in Congo and *espiritista* parlance, creating a rich vocal tapestry that is steeped in everyday life and Afro-Cuban lore (see Eleyo 2001).

Using these Afro-Cuban affirmations as proof of Cubanía lends *raperos* a legitimacy they need for other purposes: to engage in a critique of Cuban society without being viewed as counterrevolutionaries. While some rappers, like their U.S. counterparts, spout forth endless paeans to partying, sex, and hanging out (S.B.S.'s "Mami dame carne" comes to mind), many others are socially conscious and perform songs that deal with the revolution, racial disparities, prostitution, street life, poverty, domestic violence, obsession with money, and class differences, not to mention the lack of spiritual and ethical values.

But perhaps one should look at Cuban rap and race bearing in mind the "new cultural politics of difference" (West 1993: 3–32). These new practices are neither revolutionary (calling for an overthrow or complete dismantling of a system), nor are they "oppositional in contesting the mainstream (or *male*stream) for inclusion, nor transgressive in the avant-garde sense of shocking conventional bourgeois audiences" (West 1993: 4). Instead of favoring grand schemes of transformation, these new practices try to engage a politics steeped in everyday life or in the areas we know of as civil society, somewhat similar to classic anarchist thought. As Cornell West writes, the new cultural politics of difference "embraces the distinct articulations of talented (and usually privileged) contributors to culture who desire to align themselves with demoralized, demobilized, depoliticized, and disorganized people in order to empower and enable social action, and, if possible, to enlist collective insurgency for the expansion of freedom, democracy, and individuality" (West 1993: 4).

West's comments need to be qualified in a Cuban context. In the case of rap, the talented contributors to culture are not the privileged who want to align themselves with the demoralized. *Raperos* either were themselves those demoralized, disorganized elements of society at one point or still live among those marginalized sectors where this demoralization constantly surrounds them. They are using rap as form of social pleasure and action for the expansion of civil society. This is all the more true in light of Chuck D's comment that "Rap is black people's CNN." In Cuba, where the media is state controlled and heavily censored, rap (and Cuban rock to a lesser degree) is not only Afro-Cubans' CNN, but every Cuban's CNN.

Two other refinements need to be made to West's words. Earlier I did not mention demobilized and depoliticized: Cuba is a highly politicized and mobilized society, even if those processes are currently engineered by the state. The issue, then, is a politicization and mobilization that is not tied to the state or party ideology, even if many Cubans share the ideals expressed by these two official institutions. Cuban rappers are functioning as a countervailing voice, and the government knows this, which is why since 1999 it has "recognized" and tried to co-opt their activities and concerts.

Finally, in the final sentence we read "collective insurgency for the expansion of freedom, democracy, and individuality." To these three attributes we should add equality, an issue that comes up in many Cuban rap songs, sometimes but not always viewed through the prism of race. "Collective insurgency" seems not only a stretch within a U.S. context, but even more doubtful within a Cuban one, where it has connotations of overthrowing the regime. Whether Cuban *raperos* want to do this or not is almost impossible to ascertain, but it most certainly is not expressed in their lyrics.

A Cuban "new cultural politics of difference" would thus entail the following: an expansion of the public sphere so that social problems and issues of race can be expressed more openly and critically, a new idiom (or vernacular) for conducting politics that is neither insurrectionary nor escapist, and a redefinition of what it means to be black in Cuba. The redefinition is complex, because in part it is Afrocentric and essentialist, and at the same time it challenges homogenous, universalist, and monolithic ideas of identity and nationality. This complexity is due in part to its transnational nature, drawing on U.S. (African American), Jamaican, Puerto Rican, and African notions of what it means to be a member of the Afro-diaspora.

More important, one could see the issue as one of identity and rights. Enrique Patterson (1996: 67) has persuasively argued that Cuban blacks are less interested in issues of identity (What are we?) than in matters of citizenship (What are our rights, human and civil?) Patterson's clarification is one of emphasis, not an either-or proposition. As long as Cuban blacks are subordinated socially and denied full participation, they will be more concerned with rights than identity. In Cuba's history, the two (identity and rights) are intimately connected. Given the current regime's one-party system as well as the undeniable demographic reality of the island's nonwhite population, human and civil rights are powerful issues for Cubans, black, brown, or white.

Many Cuban rap songs refer to racism, a problem that the regime ostensibly solved after the revolution. Post-1959, the government banned all forms of public discrimination, nationalizing beaches and establishing complete public access to the schools, the workplace, and the health-care system. Under the banner of ideological and patriotic unity—and faced with the increasing hostility of the U.S. government—Cuba also dismantled Afro-Cuban clubs and mutual aid societies. Although blacks in Cuba made important social, educational, and cultural advances, persistent and more subtle forms of discrimination permeated political institutions, the media, and the tourism industry. The Special Period hit Cuba's lower classes particularly hard, affecting especially the brown and black populations who in many cases did not have family in the United States to help them out. "Polls conducted in the mid-1990s revealed that 85 percent of all Cubans felt that prejudice was rampant and that 58 percent of whites considered blacks to be less intelligent, 69 percent believed that blacks did not have the same 'values' or 'decency' as whites, and 68 percent were opposed to interracial marriage" (Fernández Robaina 2003). Almost forty years after the revolution, these are dismaying figures indeed.

These numbers are all the more remarkable given Cuba's formal commitment to ending racial discrimination, its involvement in liberation struggles in Africa (Angola, South Africa, Namibia, Mozambique, Congo), Castro's public admission that Cuba was (and is) an African-Latin nation, and its support for the New Jewel Movement in Grenada (1979–1983) under Maurice Bishop, a revolutionary experiment inspired by the Black Power movements of the 1960s and '70s. Many Cuban doctors served abroad in Africa, and many African or African-Caribbean students spent time in Cuban schools. Cuba's revolutionary internationalism led the Cuban government to create and support the Tri-Continental Congress and the Organization in Solidarity with the Peoples of Africa, Asia and Latin America, or OSPAAL (from 1966 to the 1980s), exposing Cubans to the writings of Frantz Fanon, Amilcar Cabral, Agostinho Neto, Kwame Nkrumah, and other leaders and theoreticians of African (as well as Asian and Latin American) liberation struggles. And if there is any contemporary non-Cuban figure on the island who is viewed as a hero it would be Nelson Mandela.

In the 1960s Cuba exposed its citizens to the harsh realities of U.S. racism through television and other media, in part out of solidarity with the civil rights struggle but also to reinforce the ideology among the nonwhite population that leaving Cuba for the United States was fraught with peril for them. Many Cubans still remember Santiago Alvarez's cinematic-poetic collage "Now!" (1965), a seven-minute "documentary" featuring the voice of Lena Horne that portrayed the often brutal side of desegregation struggles in the U.S. South. Cubans were provided much information about Martin Luther King Jr., Malcolm X, the Angela Davis case, and the Black Panthers. Many Panthers sought by U.S. authorities were given asylum or some type of safe haven on the island. Assata Shakur still lives in Cuba and has become friendly with Cuban rappers, offering support and advice on Afro-diasporic history and culture.

Perhaps these black realities—whether consciously manipulated or not—reinforced certain racial attitudes among Cubans and, from the government's perspective, played into its hands by making Cuban blacks think they were better off than their U.S. brethren who were being jailed, harassed, or made victims of violence and poverty. This was even more salient with regard to their African brothers and sisters, who suffered much greater physical misery under colonial or apartheid regimes. Add to this the experience of nearby Haiti, which, under the opportunistic *noirisme* philosophy of François Duvalier, created one of the most brutal regimes in Caribbean history (1957–1971). Never mind that Duvalier's glorification of a peasant past, his manipulation of vodou, his skewed interpretation of the country's racial rivalry (between mulattoes and blacks), and his racial essentialism were used to buttress a corrupt and repressive government; for Cubans (black, brown, or white) it was a reminder that an appeal to militant Afrocentricity was an agenda fraught with peril if not catastrophe (Howe 1998: 84–85). Naturally, Haiti bashing has a long Cuban (and Caribbean) pedigree that dates back to Haiti's history as the only country to be liberated by a slave revolt (1791–1804), sending shock waves through the region's planter class. Recall the slurs used decades later against Antonio Maceo, accused of wanting to turn Cuba into "another Haiti."

To be fair, most Cubans, *raperos* included, would not lay the blame for racism on the revolution: Everyone understands that racism has a long history in a country with a legacy of centuries of slavery. But the central tenet of revolutionary ideology is to create a classless society based on equality and social and economic progress, and in doing so, end racism, sexism, and exploitation. Whether expressed directly or indirectly, this infrapolitics of the dominated, these "hidden transcripts of resistance" (Scott 1990: 14, 198), are being expressed by Cuban *raperos* as part of the "new cultural politics of difference."

Guillén's "Tengo" alludes to this utopian and classless promise, but the 1999 version by Hermanos de Causa reflects impatience after forty years of alleged social transformation. Guillén refers to a *Juan sin nada* (Juan nobody, or Juan without a thing) from the past and a *Juan con todo* (Juan with everything) who has come into being thanks to the revolution. Guillén does not mention the revolution, socialism, or Fidel Castro in the poem, which makes it all the more effective. Instead, through repetition (almost always at the beginning of a line) of the word *tengo* (I have), he re-creates one of the most common tropes of the revolution, the before and after. Before the revolution, he could not talk to a bank administrator in Spanish. Because he was black, he could not go into certain bars or clubs or find work to earn enough to eat or avoid suffering from the repression of the rural guard, or go to certain beaches, usually the best ones, because they belonged to private beach or yacht clubs. The poem ends: "Tengo vamos a ver / tengo lo que tenía que tener" (I have, let me see / I have what I had to have).

If signifying involves repetition with a difference, then Hermanos de Causa's "Tengo" is signifying in overdrive (Potter 1995: 25–54). "Signifying" is an improvisational ability of rhyme, rhythm, and verbal play deeply embedded in Afro-diasporic traditions, also known as riffing, specifying, or the dozens in African American culture, or talking nonsense in the West Indies. Honed to perfection under conditions of slavery and post-emancipation adversity, verbal power substitutes for economic or political power and its critical edge, particularly against the powerful, is aimed at "the formation of a community rather than an expression of dominance" (Mason 1997: 665). Gates (1984: 285–321) developed the concept in literary theory to analyze intertextual revisions of canonical works or genres. By repetition and copying, as well as through parody and irony, an earlier work is made to serve new aims that debunk notions of authority, race, honor, and power.

Cuba's equivalent to signifying is *choteo*, an irreverent humor that mocks everything and leaves nothing sacred. Like signifying, it is imbued with a democratic spirit and tries to equalize the powerful and the powerless through humor and mockery. But *choteo* expresses a powerful disenchantment with leaders and institutions, stripping away any pretense at public legitimacy. This negative aspect of *choteo* led Jorge Mañach to write his famous *Indagación del choteo* (An Inquiry on Choteo, 1928), saying that it had eroded all faith in public life in Cuba. Unlike Mañach, then, one could say that Cuban *raperos* practice *choteo con conciencia* (*choteo* with a social conscience).

Gates inevitably links signifying to trickster figures, drawing a parallel between the Signifying Monkey and the orisha Elegguá (Eshu) of the Cuban (and Yoruba) Regla de Ocha. Elegguá opens or closes the roads (and crossroads), carrying messages to the other orishas. Ludic Elegguá likes to play fateful tricks on others. Only he knows past, present, and future without the need for divination systems: Elegguá is the ultimate signifier of time, fate, and our lives. In Cuba, he must be propitiated before all the other orishas. Through their signifying skills, Cuban *raperos* become verbal Elegguás.

In the Hermanos de Causa version of "Tengo," the only element "sampled" is the repetition of the verb *tengo*, but instead of using it as a signifier with a positive valence, the group actually refers to its opposite: *what they don't have*. In this sense, Hermanos de Causa draw on an old rhetorical strategy often employed in the *guaracha* genre. In a *guaracha* from the 1940s, Bienvenido J. Gutiérrez uses the same device to write a satirical song about how much work women do:

No hace na' la mujer

Bienvenido J. Gutiérrez

Por la mañana temprano
Compra jabón pa' lava
Hace el almuerzo enseguida
Y se pone a almidonar
No acaba bien la comida
Coge la ropa a planchar,
Las medias no están zurcidas
Las tiene que remendar
Ya está la noche prendida
Y un vestido que hay que hacer
Con mucho sueño y rendida
Pero tiene que coser
De la máquina pa'l lecho
Cerca del amanecer
Su pobre cuerpo desecho
Y no hace na' la mujer.

(That Woman Don't Do Nothing

Early in the morn
She buys soap for the wash
Makes lunch in a dash
She sprinkles the starch
She eats on the run
And begins to iron
Socks aren't mended
She's gotta have 'em darned
It's deep into the night
A dress needs to be made
She's sleepy and tired
but has to sew the attire
From sewing machine to bed
Just before the rising sun
Her weary body undone
That woman don't do nothing.)

Hermanos de Causa begin the song with references to Cuban national symbols: the flag, the island's emblem, the palm tree, and the *tocororo*, the national bird—so chosen because its blue head, white breast, and red lower body are the colors of the Cuban flag, and it has a reputation for not being able to live in captivity. But in the third verse we realize that this will not be a remake of Guillén: "Tengo aspiraciones sin tener lo que hace falta" (I got aspirations without having what I need). The song continues with references to a decaying Havana and a litany of problems: social indifference, racism, long hours of work and poor pay, consumer goods that are not affordable (because they must be bought in dollars), places that are off-limits for Cubans but open to tourists, and the absence of certain rights and freedoms, as in the verse "Tengo libertad entre un paréntesis de hierro" (I got freedom in a parenthesis of steel).

Tengo

Hermanos de Causa

Tengo una bandera, un escudo, un tocororo
También una palmera, un mapa sin tesoro
Tengo aspiraciones sin tener lo que hace falta
Tengo más o menos la medida exacta
Crónica que compacta
Polémica que impacta
Pasan los años y la situación sigue intacta
El tiempo no perdona
Pregúntale a la Habana
Que ahorita está en la lona
A nadie le importa nada
Tengo una raza oscura y discriminada
Tengo una jornada que me exige y no me da nada
Tengo tantas cosas que no puedo ni tocarlas
Tengo instalaciones que no puedo ni pisarlas
Tengo libertad entre un paréntesis de hierro
Tengo tantos derechos sin provechos que me encierro
Tengo lo que tengo sin tener lo que he tenido
Tienes que reflexionar y asimilar el contenido
Tengo una conducta fracturada por la gente
Tengo de elemento, tengo de conciente
Tengo el fundamento sin tener antecedentes
Tengo mi talento y eso es más que suficiente

(I Got

Got a flag, a coat of arms, a tocororo
Got a palm tree, a map without treasure
Got aspirations without having what I need

Got (more or less) the true measure
Chronicle that tightens
Polemics that frighten
Years go by, and things still the same
Time shows no mercy or shame
Just ask Havana, again
Against the ropes in pain
Nobody cares about jack
Discriminated against 'cause I'm black
Got a job with big demands and no pay
Got so much that I can't touch.
Got all these places I can't go in
Got freedom in a parenthesis of steel
Got so many rights I don't enjoy that I'm better off alone
Got what I have without having what I've had
Got to think, take in the content.
Got a demeanor filtered through so many folks
Got some funky elements, but I don't scare
I'm politically aware, I got the initiation
Got the foundation, got no citations,
Got my talent, and that's more than good enough.)

At first glance the song could be seen as a scathing attack on revolutionary promises undelivered and a blatant rejection of the government and its policies, but the matter is considerably more complex. The song also reaffirms a strong criticism of material values ("No confundas tener más con tener cualidades" [Don't confuse having more with being better]), consumerism ("Mientras más tienes más quieres y siempre más querrás / Mientras más tú tengas más ridículo serás" [The more you have, always the more you want / The more you have the more ridiculous you'll be]), and social indifference ("El hecho de que tengas más no te hace ser mejor que yo" [Having more doesn't mean you're better than me]), thus echoing one of the central tenets of the regime's anti-consumerist philosophy.

Other elements of the song are philosophical, psychological, and even religious:

Tengo una conducta fracturada por la gente
Tengo de elemento, tengo de conciente
Tengo fundamento sin tener antecedente

(Got a demeanor filtered through so many folks
Got some funky elements, but I don't scare,

I'm politically aware, I got the initiation
got the foundation, got no citations)

This behavior split or fractured by other people has an almost Lacanian mirror-stage ring to it, but truly it is an expression of how one's consciousness is formed by the gaze and consciousness of others (and the Big Other), its socially constructed nature. The words *elemento*, *fundamento*, *conciente*, and *antecedente* have both philosophical and streetwise connotations: *Elemento* may refer to nature's four elements but can also have a negative connotation, as in "bad element"; *sin tener antecedente* can mean new or original, but also not having a (police) record. Both *conciente* and *fundamento* have philosophical, educational, and political meanings as well, with *conciente* referring to political or social consciousness and *fundamento* speaking not only to foundations (of knowledge), but also to the quality of being a *santero*. So in three short lines Hermanos de Causa reveal their "situated knowledge": they can "drop science" from street experience, their educational training, their politico-philosophical background, and their religious dialogue with the orishas. Cuban rap's social and political context, the educational level of its creators, and the musical and linguistic ingenuity of its practitioners make it a deeply textured cultural ensemble of relations conversant with both Cuban and non-Cuban history, culture, and music.

In fact, the song shares a view of race expressed in a well-known song called "¿Quién tiró la tiza?" (Who Threw the Chalk?). In both cases race is seen through the prism of social class, and in this regard the songs share commonalities with U.S. ghetto-centric rap (Ice T, Ice Cube, N.W.A.) that has often scathingly attacked the black middle class or bourgeoisie. While this critique reveals the divisions within African American society (bourgeois blacks, buppies, baps, bohos, b-boys, and "niggas"), in Cuba it actually points to a whitening effect that occurs as a result of social class. It also highlights a locale rarely alluded to in U.S. rap: the classroom or school.

"¿Quién tiró la tiza?" features two black students, one the son of a doctor, the other of a builder or construction worker. Someone throws a piece of chalk at the teacher, and when asked who the culprit was, the students point to "el negro ese" (that black kid). "El negro ese" certainly has racist connotations, but the song further complicates the issue with class when it clearly (and ironically) suggests that the culprit could not be the doctor's son.

¿Quien tiró la tiza?

Molano MC

¿Quien tiró la tiza?
El negro ese.

No fue el hijo del doctor, no.
¿Quién tiró la tiza?
Porque el hijo del doctor, yo.
Es el mejor.

(Who Threw the Chalk?

Who threw the chalk?
It was that black kid.
Who threw the chalk?
Not the doctor's kid.
No, because the doctor's son, yo,
Is the best one.)

The song draws this class distinction by referring to the type of cologne that each student wears. The working-class kid has to use baby perfume while his upper-class counterpart can presumably afford to use European cologne, and wear Adidas footwear. In a country where consumer goods are scarce, these details loom much larger in the social imaginary than they would in the United States.

y si acaso colonia de bebito encima
En cambio los hijos de papi y mima
iban con Adidas
medias deportivas y una perfumada
nada que ver con la mía
mira, o sea, pa' quí na' más, mucho olor
solo teníamos en común el color.

(A little sprinkle of baby cologne.
But daddy and mama's boy, all primped up
With his Adidas,
And sport socks, all perfumed up
Nothing like mine
Check it out, smelling nice and fresh.
All we shared was the color of our flesh.)

So, despite the commonality of dark skin, class differences condemn the son of the laborer to suffer the blame. The issue of cologne also conjures up the racist assumptions that are related to smell.[4]

Another Guillén poem, "Quirino con su tres" also highlights the signifying nature of Cuban rap in sampling, quoting, and reworking Cuban traditions, Afro-Cuban and musical.

Quirino con su tres

Nicolás Guillén

¡Quirino
con su tres!
La bemba grande, la pasa dura,
Sueltos los pies
Y una mulata que se derrite de sabrosura. . . .
¡Quirino
con su tres!

Luna redonda que lo vigila cuando regresa
Dando traspiés
Jipi en la chola, camisa fresa. . . .
¡Quirino
con su tres!

Tibia accesoria para la cita;
La madre—negra Paula Valdés—
Suda, envejece, busca la frita. . . .
¡Quirino
con su tres!

(Quirino with His *Tres*

Quirino
with his *tres*!
Thick lips, nappy hair,
With good moves
And a mulatta melting from his charms. . . .
Quirino
with his *tres*!

Round moon looks over him
As he wobbles on home
Panama hat on his head, bright red shirt. . . .
Quirino
with his *tres*!

His black mother, Paula Valdés,
cool accessory for the scene,
She sweats, grows old, looks for grub. . . .

Quirino
with his *tres*!)

The Guillén poem is like a snapshot or a watercolor sketch. It centers on
Quirino, a *tres* (like a guitar but higher pitched) player who is popular with the
public and the ladies, and who loves to party and dress stylishly. The third and
final stanza mentions his mother, Paula Valdés, who sweats and works hard to
put food on the table. Made into a song by Emilio Grenet, it was popularized
by the great Afro-Cuban singer Mercedes Valdez, who was considered one of
the great *akpwonas* (sacred singers of Yoruba chants). Valdez was also a col-
laborator and informant of Fernando Ortiz, the multifaceted scholar who
dedicated most of his life's work to the study of Afro-Cuban culture.

Instinto, a group of three women rappers (Janet Díaz Poey, Doricep
Agramonte Ballester, and Yudith Porto Alfonso) founded in 1996 but since
disbanded, took on the heavyweights of the island's poetic, musical, and Afro-
Cuban traditions with funky and sensual aplomb.

Kirino con su tres

Instinto

Caballero ¿qué ha pasado?
El tiempo corre y no le han cantado
Kirino que han gozado
Con ese ritmo inigualado
Lo han escuchado en todo lado
En las Mercedes y hasta en Santiago
Interpretado por Merceditas
Con su pañuelo en la cabecita
¡Qué mujercita en aquellos tiempos!
Con su frescura y su movimiento
Esta cadencia que estás escuchando
Es distinto porque Instinto lo está cantando
¡Quirino
con su tres! (3x)
. . .
Y aprovecho y pido ya
Unos aplausos que sean verdá
Por Merceditas efún beyá
Que si no es por ella no canto na'.

(Kirino with His *Tres*

Guys, what's happened?

Time's gone by, and no one's sung to him
Kirino and those who enjoyed him
With that unbeatable rhythm
Heard all over,
In Mercedes and even in Santiago
Sung by Merceditas
Kerchief on her head
Some kinda woman for those times!
All so fresh, moving real fine.
This cadence that you're hearing
Is distinct because Instinct is singing it
Kirino with his *tres*!
· · ·
So let's ask for applause
Straight from the heart
For Merceditas and her art, *Efún beyá*
If not for her, I wouldn't be singing at all.)

Instinto has performed a signifying critique of several elements of the Guillén poem. They have kept the refrain ("¡Kirino con su tres!"), but the entire emphasis of the song is on Valdez. Interestingly, all physical references to Quirino are out: the big lips and the nappy hair, the ability to dance, and the mulatta who is "melting from his charms." Clearly, as an all-woman rap group Instinto is rejecting the attributes of physicality of the poem (to be fair to Guillén, his reference to these traits is made in a positive spirit), reflecting a feminist consciousness that opposes images that objectify women (sexually and racially) through a metonymic exaggeration of the body.

Instinto describes Merceditas with her "pañuelo en la cabecita" (kerchief on her head) and follows with "¡Qué mujercita en aquellos tiempos! / Con su frescura y movimiento" (Some kinda woman for those times! / All so fresh, moving real fine). Later in the song they ask the audience to applaud sincerely for Merceditas, because if not for her, they (Instinto) would not be singing. It is both a heartfelt tribute to Mercedes Valdez and a feminist revision of Quirino. Recall that the mother Paula Valdés was a "tibia accesoria" (a tepid, or cool, accessory) in the Guillén version, whereas Merceditas Valdez becomes a fountain of creativity and inspiration for Instinto. Instinto even upends (again, signifying) the use of diminutives (*cabecita, mujercita*) often used in a paternalistic or condescending fashion: "¡Qué mujercita en aquellos tiempos!" (Some kinda woman for those times!).

In the cover photo of the album *Cuba: Merceditas Valdez y los tambores batá de Jesús Pérez*, we can visually discern the comments made by Instinto. We see Merceditas Valdez dressed as a *santera*, all in white, with necklaces and a white kerchief on her head. Against the wall to her left is a beautiful statue of Ochún (la Virgen de la Caridad del Cobre), the patroness of Cuba. When Instinto claims they would not be singing were it not for Merceditas, they rhyme that line with *efún beyá*, an invocation of the *lucumí* (Yoruba) nation that has other connotations as well (the color white, which is associated with Obatalá, and the sign for death in the Yoruba divination system; Cabrera 1970). What began as a sketch of *solar* (tenement) life by Guillén becomes for Instinto a tribute, an intertextual reworking, and a statement of women's creativity as an emblem of Cuba.[5]

Conclusions: Cuba's New Age of Racial Assertions and Redefinitions

Rap has brought Cuba closer to examining the Black Atlantic/transnational connections of its music and culture. Inspired by U.S. rappers, Cubans have adopted many elements found in the music of their North American counterparts: citation (sampling of sonic, verbal, historical, and literary archives), an interrupted or discontinuous use of time, and a complex situatedness that is physical, cultural, musical, and political (Potter 1995: 3–5, 53). In their rapping and musical elaboration they embody the concepts of flow, layering, and ruptures in line (Jafa, as quoted by Rose 1994: 38). Equally significant, and also similar to the U.S. situation, despite Cuban rap's affirmation of blackness, critique of racism, and embracing of Afro-Cuban religions, its appeal crosses racial, class, and gender lines.

Still, many features of Cuban rap are unique to the island: There is an absence of what in the United States is known as gangsta rap, which points to the social circumstances of blacks in Cuba who, despite poverty and racism, do not live in the harsh and bleak ghetto environments of the United States. If gangstas are ghetto-centric warriors, perhaps the equivalent in Cuba would be the orisha warriors of Regla de Ocha: Ochosi, Ogún, Elegguá, and Changó. Indeed, the expression of Afrocentric ideas in Cuba need not hark back to the real (or imagined) glories of an African past; they are a living, palpitating presence through the practice of religion, music, and culture. Practicing *santeros,* particularly younger ones, are now more inclined to worship the orishas as African and play down the Catholic side of the religion (Fernández Robaina 2002). The growth of Rastafarianism also points to this re-Africanization of Cuban life, but within the parameters of *cubanía.*

Interestingly, in Cuban rap the *guapo,* who would be the equivalent of the rude boy from reggae or the nigga from gangsta rap, is not particularly admired. In the song "Guapo" by Obsesión the *guapo* is criticized and counterexamples of *guapería* are given: the *cimarrón* and Jimi Hendrix. Primera Base expresses similar thoughts in "En la calle" and "Malo." Another tune by Anónimo Consejo ("Guapo como Mandela") reveals similar sentiments within the context of the group's creation, its art, and its creativity, in this case upholding Nelson Mandela as the *guapo*: "Aquí llegué y no me voy / guapo como Mandela / como buen cubano / junto a mi hermano" (Here I am and I'm not leaving / *guapo* like Mandela / like a good Cuban / with my brother).

Linguistically speaking, Cuban rappers have imported English (and in some cases Yoruba) into their flow, with words often sprinkled into their lyrics untranslated. Some rappers are ingenious enough to rhyme across languages ("listen to me / ya que estoy aquí" or "niche, así nací/MC para todo el mundo aquí"). But despite the use of certain slang expressions (*qué bolá* [what's up], *asere* [friend or brother in the Abakuá variant of Efik], and so on), one cannot argue at this point that Cuban rap has a vernacular similar to that of African Americans (in contradistinction to standard English). Cuba, unlike its French, English, and Dutch Caribbean neighbors, never developed a creole or patois, although Papiamento (spoken in Curaçao, Bonaire, and Aruba) does have a few Spanish words. One could argue that Cuban Spanish has already incorporated a host of African words, but neither their use nor preponderance points to a destabilizing or counter-hegemonic expression.

The importation of certain English words has not been entirely without incident. Pacini Hernández and Garofalo (1999–2000) mention the scandal Cuban rappers Primera Base caused by using the word "nigger" in a song called "Igual que tú." Clearly meant to express racial solidarity with African Americans, the song is about Malcolm X. U.S. rappers were furious—and rightfully so—at the improper attribution of the word to someone of Malcolm's stature. Robin D. G. Kelley has described the term (written as "nigga," not nigger, another mistake made by Primera Base) as having a different meaning from the word written in standard English. In fact, it even transcends racial lines, is often used to describe anyone from the 'hood, and has come to mean any oppressed person from the ghetto (Kelley 1996: 209–11), a poignant lesson in the transnational dialogue that urges us all to be cautious in understanding how Afro-diasporic realities are seen, expressed, and represented.

Many *raperos* when performing will say "¡Pa' mis niches! ¡Pa' mis negros!" which again emphasizes a blackness that at other moments in Cuban history would have been considered heretical. It is matched by their clothing (baggy pants, baseball hats, oversized NBA jerseys, sneakers), hairstyles (dreadlocks), and body adornments, including tattoos. Through these practices they are expanding notions of Cuban blackness by questioning previous models of Afro-Cuban respectability.

More than any other segment of Cuban society, Afro-Cuban rappers are dynamically involved in redefining themselves as both people of African descent and as Cubans. They are working from the premise—conscious or not—that Cuba, historically speaking, could barely consider itself a nation if it treated such a large segment of its population (blacks and mulattos) as second-class citizens. The Cuban Revolution aimed to change that, but as Cuban *raperos* remind us, the universalist and Enlightenment dimensions (too abstract, for some) of its ideology have not been able to stamp out discrimination, racism, and social exclusivism. What is fascinating is that the revolution has also given Cuban rappers the tools (educational, cultural, ideological) with which to analyze these problems.

Not all *raperos* agree on these issues. For example, Orishas, the best-known group internationally, claim that Cuba's racial problems are virtually nonexistent (Matos 2002a). Other groups, such as S.B.S. (Sensational Boys of the Street), seem to be oblivious to social concerns, at least as expressed through their lyrics. These two groups are probably the only ones that make any serious money as rappers (although S.B.S.'s waning popularity might soon require me to qualify this statement). The Orishas live in France but travel and perform often in Cuba.

The issue of exploitation, spectacle, and appropriation of black culture as profitable enterprise is not as big an issue in Cuba as in the United States, where mainstream (white) culture has appropriated at different stages African American music of all types (blues, jazz, and the origins of rock, soul, and rap). This is not to claim that these appropriations have not happened in Cuba (see R. Moore 1997), but Afro-Cuban music, while not always seen as central to Cuban music and culture, has certainly taken on that role since the 1920s. The country's three national musical expressions—*danzón, son,* and *rumba*—are progressively more African in their forms and articulations, yet are not seen as questioning Cuban identity. On the contrary, they are offered as affirmations of *cubanía*. Rap clearly does not have the stature of the *danzón,* the *son,* or the *rumba,* at least not yet.

Cuba's redefinition of blackness is a slow, contradictory process, and it would be difficult to argue that there is a systematic, worked-out theoretical position of what *afrocubanía* means. As stated earlier, in part it involves an Afrocentric approach to certain expressions (Regla de Ocha, for example), and in part a reaffirmation of *africanía* within a context of national pride and Cubanness. In this sense we can say *afrocubanía* is both black *and* nationalist but not black nationalist in the U.S. sense that often implies separatism. It has been enriched recently by Cuban rappers' transnational curiosity and use of African American and Caribbean idioms. Perhaps Cuba's redefinition of blackness is beginning to examine the complexity expressed by Charles Mills, without denying the physical, juridical, political, and social dimensions of race: "Room has to be made for race as both real and unreal: that race can be ontological without being biological, metaphysical without being physical, existential without being essential, shaping one's being without being in one's shape" (Mills 1998: xiv). Mills' words warn of the philosophical tradition's imbrication with white supremacy, an area that Cuban thinkers and popular culture have yet to take on openly and unapologetically, except in rare instances.

Cuban rap has been vigorous in attacking racism, but for the most part has done so within the egalitarian claims of the revolution. By thoroughly embracing rap, Cuban *raperos* have sought to join the Black Atlantic dialogue. By doing so they have enlarged the notion of Cuban blackness as something that needs to be seen in an international context and have sought a non-essentialist, non-homogenous meaning of blackness. At the same time, Cuba has "nationalized" rap within its own idioms (musical, linguistic, and cultural), which is hardly surprising when you look at the origins of the *danzón*, the *son*, and the *rumba*. Cuban rap is starting to become as Cuban as Martí's mustache and Merceditas Valdez's kerchief.

Most significant, Afro-Cuban *raperos* are seriously questioning the *mulataje-mestizo* hypothesis as an organizing metaphor of Cuban culture and society. While certainly Guillén never saw the *mulataje* hypothesis as a mere whitening process, the way Guillén has been put forth as a Cuban icon, poet, and racial thinker indicates that his legacy has often been used as a cultural smoke screen to deny or avoid discussing the clear racial disparities on the island. Cuban *raperos*, in signifying on Guillén and other cultural sources, have "historicized, contextualized and pluralized" *afrocubanía* (West 1993: 3), and thereby are showing how blackness in Cuba changes and acquires new political and cultural dimensions. Their music also engages white Cubans to see whiteness as a form of forgetting (and oppression) and, by stimulating a buried historical memory, implores and demands that the island see itself as a transnationally inclusive nation with a "Cuban color" and an African heart.

Notes

1. Pertaining to government involvement, two further comments are germane. First, in September 2002 the Agencia Cubana de Rap (ACR) was formed to help train groups musically, assist them with recordings, and promote their work in the widest sense. To date, nine groups are affiliated with the state enterprise. Groups must audition to join the ACR. At the ninth Cuban rap festival (2003), many groups had never heard of the agency. With the demand for "quality" control and the presence of more than five hundred rap groups in the country, it remains to be seen whether the ACR will function as a promoter or a barrier for many groups. Second, Cuban television, an important disseminator of popular music, is still quite selective in the rap groups it presents, usually focusing on more commercial types of rap or what is called *reggaetón* (often a bad equivalent of what might be considered Jamaican dancehall at its most frivolous). Hardcore rappers don't even consider these groups as rappers. In August 2002, Elvira Rodríguez Puerto classified Cuban rap groups as follows: (1) television rappers; (2) rappers living outside of Cuba (for example, the Orishas); (3) rap groups that belong to the ACR; (4) rappers that belong to the Asociación Hermanos Saíz; and (5) street (or

underground) rappers. Hers is an interesting taxonomy for studying Cuban rap groups, but is beyond the scope of this analysis.

2. See Pacini Hernández and Garofalo (1999–2000).

3. All translations are by the author unless otherwise noted.

4. "Quién tiró la tiza?" produced a response song by Hoyo Colorao ("Tiró la tiza y qué") that basically tried to minimize the class differences, stating that both students were in the same boat because they were black.

5. Other female Cuban rap groups include Explosión Femenina, Mariana, Diamara, and Las Krudas. The last is in-your-face feminist and Afrocentric, with an extraordinary song about menstruation, "120 horas rojas cada mes" (120 Red Hours Each Month). While I have not heard the song live (only on compact disc), several local testimonies have mentioned instances of male members of the audience trying to hide when the group performs the song.

Bibliography

Cabrera, Lydia. 1970. *Anagó, Vocabulario Lucumí.* Reprint, Miami: Ediciones Universal, 1986.

———. 1988. *La lengua sagrada de los ñáñigos.* Miami: Ediciones Universal.

Castellanos, Dimas. 2002. "En torno al rap cubano y las circunstancias de su nacimiento." *Encuentro en la Red* 3, no. 460 (September 27). <www.cubaencuentro.com>.

Chuck D. 1997. *Fight the Power: Rape, Race, and Reality.* New York: Dell.

De la Fuente, Alejandro. 2001. *A Nation for All: Race Inequality and Politics in Twentieth-Century Cuba.* Chapel Hill: University of North Carolina Press.

Duany, Jorge. 2002. *The Puerto Rican Nation on the Move: Identities on the Island and in the United States.* Chapel Hill: University of North Carolina Press.

Fernández Robaina, Tomás. 1994. *El Negro en Cuba, 1902–1958.* Havana: Editorial de las Ciencias Sociales.

———. 2002. "La santería: ¿africana, cubana o afrocubana? Elementos para el debate." Unpublished manuscript.

———. 2003. "Cuba." In *African-Caribbeans: A Reference Guide*, edited by Alan West-Durán. Westport, Conn.: Greenwood Press.

Flores, Juan. 2000. *From Bomba to Hip Hop, Puerto Rican Culture and Latino Identity.* New York: Columbia University Press.

Gates, Henry Louis. 1984. "The Blackness of Blackness: A Critique of the Sign and the Signifying Monkey." In *Black Literature and Literary Theory*, edited by Henry Louis Gates. Reprint, New York: Routledge, 1992.

Gilroy, Paul. 1993. *The Black Atlantic, Modernity and Double Consciousness.* Cambridge, Mass.: Harvard University Press.

Guillén, Nicolás. 1974. *Antología mayor.* 2nd ed. Mexico City: Editorial Diogenes.

———. 1975. *Man Making Words: Selected Poems of Nicolás Guillén.* Translated by Robert Márquez and David Arthur McMurray. Havana: Editorial Arte y Literatura.

Hebdige, Dick. 1987. *Cut 'N' Mix, Culture, Identity and Caribbean Music.* New York: Routledge.

Howe, Stephen. 1998. *Afrocentrism: Mythical Pasts and Imagined Homes*. London: Verso.

Kelley, Robin D. G. 1996. *Race Rebels: Culture, Politics, and the Black Working Class*. New York: Free Press.

Krims, Adam. 2000. *Rap Music and the Poetics of Identity*. Cambridge: Cambridge University Press.

Lipsitz, George. 1994. *Dangerous Crossroads: Popular Music, Postmodernism and the Poetics of Place*. London: Verso.

López Valdés, Rafael. 1985. *Componentes africanos en el etnos cubano*. Havana: Editorial Ciencias Sociales.

Martin, Tony. 1983. *Marcus Garvey, Hero: A First Biography*. Dover, Mass.: Majority Press.

Mason, Theodore. 1997. "Signifying." In *The Oxford Companion to African American Literature*, edited by William L. Andrews, Frances S. Foster, and Trudier Harris. New York: Oxford University Press.

Matos, Denys. 2002a. "'¿Hip Hop a lo cubano?'" *Encuentro en la Red* 3, no. 450 (September 13). <www.cubaencuentro.com>.

———. 2002b. "Los ritmos de 'Emigrante.'" *Encuentro en la Red* 3, no. 416 (July 24). <www.cubaencuentro.com>.

Mills, Charles. 1998. *Blackness Visible: Essays on Philosophy and Race*. Ithaca, N.Y.: Cornell University Press.

Moore, Carlos. 1988. *Castro, the Blacks and Africa*. Los Angeles: UCLA Center for Afro-American Studies.

Moore, Robin. 1997. *Nationalizing Blackness, Afrocubanismo and Artistic Revolution in Havana, 1920–1940*. Pittsburgh, Pa.: University of Pittsburgh Press.

Okpewho, Isidore, Carole Boyce Davies, and Ali A. Mazrui, eds. 1999. *The African Diaspora: African Origins and New World Identities*. Bloomington: Indiana University Press.

Ortiz, Fernando. 1995. *Cuban Counterpoint: Tobacco and Sugar*. Durham, N.C.: Duke University Press.

Pacini Hernández, Deborah, and Reebee Garofalo. 1999–2000. "Hip Hop in Havana: Rap, Race, and National Identity in Contemporary Cuba." *Journal of Popular Music Studies* 11–12: 18–47.

Patterson, Enrique. 1996. "Cuba: discursos sobre la identidad." *Encuentro de Cultura Cubana* 2: 49–67.

Pérez-Sarduy, Pedro, and Jean Stubbs, eds. 1993. *AfroCuba: An Anthology of Cuban Writing on Race, Politics, and Culture*. Melbourne, Australia: Ocean Press.

Potter, Russell. 1995. *Spectacular Vernaculars: Hip-Hop and the Politics of Postmodernism*. Albany, N.Y.: SUNY Press.

Rivera, Raquel Z. 2003. *New York Ricans from the Hip Hop Zone*. New York: Palgrave Macmillan.

Robinson, Eugene. 2002. "The Rap Revolución: In Cuba an Insistent Musical Voice Is Pounding Home Its Points and Protests." *Washington Post*, April 14, 2002, p. G01.

Rodríguez, Arsenio. 2002. "Se abren los caminos; Cuban Hip Hop All Star." *Encuentro en la Red* 3, no. 416 (July 24). <www.cubaencuentro.com>.

Rose, Tricia. 1994. *Black Noise: Rap Music and Black Culture in Contemporary America*. Hanover, N.H.: Wesleyan University Press and University Press of New England.

Scott, James C. 1990. *Domination and the Arts of Resistance*. New Haven: Yale University Press.

Thigpen, David E. 2001. "Hidden Havana." In "Music Goes Global." Special issue, *Time*.

West, Cornel. 1993. *Keeping Faith: Philosophy and Race in America*. New York: Routledge.

West-Durán, Alan. 1997. *Tropics of History: Cuba Imagined*. Westport, Conn.: Greenwood Press.

———. 2003. *African-Caribbeans: A Reference Guide*. Westport, Conn.: Greenwood Press.

Discography

CLAN 537. 2003. "Clan 537". CIOCAN Records.

Cuban Hip Hop All Stars: Volume 1. 2001. Papaya Records. (Includes Cuarta Imagen, Hermanos de Causa, Reyes de la Calle, Explosión Suprema, Alto y Bajo, Bajo Mundo, Anónimo Consejo, Junior Clan y Grandes Ligas, Obsesión, Justicia, 100% Original, and Instinto).

Eleyó. 2001. *Sonando a Cuba*. Unicornio UN-CD9017.

Hermanos de Causa. 2003. *La causa nostra*. El Gao Productions.

Las Krudas. 2003. *Cubensi*. Self-produced.

Merceditas Valdez. N.d. "Cuba: Merceditas Valdez y los tambores batá de Jesús Pérez". A.S.P.I.C. France/Egrem X55512.

Obsesión. 2001. *Un montón de cosas*. EGREM CD-0375.

Orishas. 1998/2000. *A lo cubano*. Universal Surco 012159571–2.

———. 2002. *Emigrante*. Universal Surco 440 018 456–2.

Primera Base. 1997. *Igual que tú*. Caribe Productions CD 9242.

Punto Cero. 2001. *Punto cero*. Bis Music CD 232.

S.B.S. 1999a. *Mami, dame carne*. Universal Music LATD-40155.

———. 1999b. *Sigue al líder*. Fonovisa FPCD-9894.

———. 2000. *Guacha y guaracha*. Vale Music VLCD949.

Sin Palabras. 2000. *Orishas Dreams*. Bis Music CD 195.

Trío Hel. 2000. *Agüita de coco*. Bis Music, Artex, S.A. CD-188.

8

Re-reading Revolution

Gran Literatura and Jesús Díaz's *Las palabras perdidas*

James Buckwalter-Arias

One afternoon three young Cuban writers sit on a bench in the shade of a pine tree by Avenida de los Presidentes in Havana. One of them has recently returned from Prague, where he attended the Encuentro de Jóvenes Escritores de los Países Socialistas—a "sanctuary of socialist realism," where he was subjected to what seemed like an endless recitation of politico-literary platitudes. But his trip to Czechoslovakia was worthwhile, in large part because he met the Salvadoran writer Roque Dalton. The two Latin Americans managed to slip away from the tedious proceedings and spend some time exploring the city of Kafka while they discussed literature and shared their own writings, which happily had nothing in common with the formulaic literature promoted at the symposium. Now, sitting on a bench in Havana, the young writer informs his friends that Roque Dalton will be arriving in Cuba in a matter of weeks. The friends are ecstatic, and one of them exclaims that with the incorporation of Roque into their literary coterie, "¡Haremos de este puñetero país el centro mundial de la literatura!" (We'll turn this damned country into the center of the literary world!).

This scene, set in 1960s Havana, is from the novel *Las palabras perdidas* (The Lost Words), which Jesús Díaz published in Spain in 1992. Of course, 1960s Havana and 1990s Spain are worlds apart. In the 1960s the revolution's new and stridently nationalistic cultural project still generates great enthusiasm: The young revolution anticipates that other Latin American nations will follow its example; high-profile writers from all over the world arrive in Cuba to read their work and discuss literature in the new Casa de las Américas; art becomes much more powerful and relevant than it had been as a mere commodity in the marketplace; Cuba is turning the tide against the cultural imperialism from the north, and the caricatures of curvaceous *rumberas* and obliging musicians, mafia thugs, and sensuous prostitutes, so familiar to tourists and Hollywood audiences, are becoming a thing of the past. And this revolution, gratefully, will be *más verde que las palmas* (greener than the palm trees)—more exuberant and dynamic than the socialisms of Eastern Europe. The heady nationalism of the young writers who expect to make the island the "centro mundial de la literatura" may well be excessive, but their conviction is almost credible under the influence of the revolutionary euphoria.

By 1992, when Díaz publishes his novel about a group of young writers in 1960s Cuba, the reader is prepared from the outset for a narrative of disillusionment. The exuberance of the Güijes, as the writers-protagonists call themselves, may elicit from some readers nostalgia for the early years of the revolution, but the aspirations will be short-lived. By the 1970s, the reader knows, Cuban artists encounter the paradox of a thoroughly institutionalized revolution. Cuban letters enter their *quinquenio gris* (five gray years) and less desirable artists are, in the official lingo, *parametrizados* (parameterized)—prohibited from publishing and excluded from the island's cultural institutions. By the late 1980s and early 1990s, with the collapse of the Soviet Union and the loss of that nation's subsidies and favorable trade agreements, Cuba's cultural institutions are devastated, materially and politically. The revolution seems less likely to host the world's literary vanguard than it does to disintegrate entirely. Indeed, in the 1990s, Cuban writers unable to publish at home turn for the first time in many years to foreign publishing companies. Their writing, for better or for worse, is a commodity once again; Cuban culture begins to be reabsorbed in the international market, as the spectacular success of the *Buena Vista Social Club* documentary and compact discs dramatize. In the international imaginary Cuba becomes less a projection of the revolution and its institutional alternatives to the market than of alliances between an increasingly significant and talked-about Cuban diaspora on the one hand, and non-Cuban private enterprise on the other. In a word, Cuba has become less a centralized, insular project than a multi-nodal, transnational phenomenon.

Encuentro de la cultura cubana, the magazine that Jesús Díaz founded in 1996 about four years after breaking with the Cuban regime and taking up residence in Spain, underlines the degree to which *cubanía* is no longer solely the domain of the revolution, or even of the Miami-Havana dialectic, but also of a far-flung diaspora. Ironically, the space that is posited as the ideal locus for the *encuentro*, the space in which what Díaz has called the *cultura fracturada* (fractured culture) can begin to come together again, is the very metropolis from which Cuba gained its independence a century earlier, and which in the 1990s began to reassert its (neo)colonial interests on the island. Díaz, for his part, seems to elude the revolutionary-exile dichotomy; unlike earlier exiles, he is very much a product of the revolution (he was only seventeen years old when the rebels triumphed in 1959) and he has devoted most of his professional life to the socialist project. He finally distances himself from the regime at a historical moment—the end of the Cold War—when it may seem that socialism has definitively been "proven wrong," with Cuba finding itself more isolated than ever. The longtime revolutionary is not easily dismissed, then, as a resentful bourgeois writer seeking to exert his class privileges elsewhere.

In this essay I will focus on the way in which *Las palabras perdidas*, the novel that can be said to mark the author's break with the Cuban government, reinterprets the revolutionary experience for an international readership in the post-Soviet or post–Cold War era. Specifically, I will focus on the novel's reassertion of such categories as great art and literary genius— "mystifications" in the official discourse of the revolution—from the vantage of the Special Period, or post-Soviet years, in which Cuban culture undergoes a significant transformation. Although the novel set in 1960s Cuba looks to the past to recover "lost words" or give voice to a silenced generation, I contend that the text also represents a serious grappling with issues vital to contemporary Cuban culture, the global market, and a potentially progressive cultural politics. The protagonists imagine themselves as fundamentally apolitical, concerned above all else with *gran literatura* (great literature), and their experience might suggest that human institutions are by their very nature the implacable enemy of great art. As esoteric or lofty as their concerns may appear, however, it is also clear that their words would, in fact, *caer en el vacío* (fall into the void) if not for *some* kind of human institution. If their aesthetic philosophy seems outmoded and naive to the contemporary literary theorist, in representing their ambitions and their struggle the novel nevertheless inquires into precisely those issues that need to be addressed to begin to develop a progressive cultural politics for Cuba in the face of a new, and in many ways threatening, transnational cultural dynamic.

The Rhetoric and Politics of *Gran Literatura*

Las palabras perdidas tells the story of a group of young writers in 1960s Havana who resolve to publish in a major newspaper a literary supplement that they expect to transform the Cuban cultural scene and form the basis for what Rafael Rojas describes in his review of the novel as "una República de Letras bajo el comunismo" (A Republic of Letters under Communism; Rojas 1997: 241). They dream of a government-subsidized but autonomous publication whose only accountability is to literary greatness, which they treat as an identifiable phenomenon that transcends historically situated norms and specific institutional pressures. The explicit censorship and punitive measures they eventually encounter from government bureaucrats, then, seem to suggest that state repressive apparatuses are the primary obstacle to freedom of expression and artistic integrity. The novel written by the character el Flaco—which is textually identical to the actual Jesús Díaz novel in which el Flaco is a character—represents a vindication of a stifled generation, a triumph of freedom over totalitarianism, of memory over forgetting.

Because el Flaco's novel is textually identical to the Jesús Díaz novel—which is a commodity, of course, as well as an art object—it becomes possible to read *Las palabras perdidas* as a vindication of the free market. The "lost words" of the young writers are recovered, the reader is led to imagine, in a setting more "neutral" or "natural" than socialist Cuba, such as capitalist Spain perhaps, where the Díaz novel is published by Anagrama in 1992. Insofar as the novel appears to narrate its own journey from political repression to artistic freedom, in other words, it might be said to ratify the culture industry in which it is finally redeemed—an industry whose commodification of art is denounced by the revolution as a forfeiture of authentic, socially committed work in favor of whatever happens to be most profitable. The Díaz novel's indictment of the revolution's totalitarian cultural politics and apparent vindication of the culture industry comes, moreover, precisely at a historical moment when world events seem to discredit the socialist project and Díaz does in fact stop publishing in socialist Cuba and begins publishing in capitalist Spain.

It's not that the protagonists of *Las palabras perdidas* celebrate the capitalist culture industry; when they do make references to consumer-oriented art, it is with a characteristically modernist disdain and not, significantly, via a socialist critique. It should be stressed, however, that the protagonists' reassertion of the aesthetic autonomy the revolution disavowed and their investment in the idea of a creative realm free from institutional constraint and ethico-political imperatives, where literary genius is free to exhibit itself and where great art ultimately wins the day, comes at a historical moment when Cuban culture begins to be reabsorbed into the global market. Indeed, the protagonists' aesthetic ideology, which is deeply indebted both to romantic ideas of genius and to the modernist zeal for radical innovation, is asserted in a novel that itself can be said to mark its author's switch from publishing with the socialist state to publishing in the market, a fact that raises important questions about the relationships among *Las palabras perdidas*, aesthetic ideology, and free-market rationale.

Despite the protagonists' contempt for consumer-oriented mass culture, their aesthetic philosophy coexists peaceably, and at some level even complicitly, with market ideology. Aesthetic discourse itself, after all, developed as art objects entered the market economy toward the end of the eighteenth century:

> The emergence of the aesthetic as a theoretical category is closely bound up with the material process by which cultural production, at an early stage of bourgeois society, becomes "autonomous"—autonomous, that is, of the various social functions which it has traditionally served. Once artifacts become commodities in the market place, they exist for nothing

and nobody in particular, and can consequently be rationalized, ideologi-cally speaking, as existing entirely and gloriously for themselves. (Eagleton 1990: 8–9)

Eagleton's words seem strangely familiar in a contemporary Cuba in which art's new autonomy from the state's "social functions" and the reabsorption of the nation's culture into the international market coincide with a proliferation of aesthetic discourse in literary narrative. *Las palabras perdidas* is a profound, socially symbolic act, in Fredric Jameson's sense: Even as it marks Díaz's turn to the market and away from the state's "social functions," it levels some of its most acerbic critique at consumer-oriented literature. While true art, in this novel, presumably transcends the petty interventions of the state and the con-tingencies of the market, Díaz himself has recently opted for the latter.

When the character known as el Gordo interviews the poet José Lezama Lima, it dawns on him that "el Inmenso"—Lezama himself—"pertenecía a una especie en extinción, la de los aristócratas del espíritu, para quienes el establo de los 'best-sellers' debía apestar a estiércol" (belonged to a species on the verge of extinction, that of the aristocrats of the spirit, for whom the best-seller racks must reek of manure; Díaz 1992: 135). El Gordo muses to himself, splicing phrases from various Lezama Lima essays, that the great poet's "sufici-encia, o más exactamente, la certidumbre de que había vencido al tiempo ex-trayéndole momentos de su central contracción a través de la ciclónica fuerza genitora de su obra . . . lo situaban más allá de toda contingencia" (self-suffi-ciency, or more precisely, the certainty that he had conquered time by extract-ing moments of its central contraction by dint of the cyclonic generative force of his corpus . . . situated him beyond all contingency; p. 135).

The aesthetic discourse and market rationale that seem to go hand in hand in post-Soviet Cuba represent antitheses in the novel. One can only wonder precisely which institutional mechanisms in the real world the Great Poet is able to use to "situate himself beyond all contingency." And given the com-modity status of the Díaz novel itself, one might hypothesize that aesthetic discourse and market rationale do complement or reinforce each other after all. On the one hand, the market is sufficiently decentralized and impervious to absolute decree that its mechanisms seem almost invisible, like marionette strings, and great art and literary genius can appear to rise and act under their own power, or "a través de [su] ciclónica fuerza genitora." On the other hand, "great art" and "artistic genius" may be powerful promotional labels—not on the best-seller racks, perhaps, but certainly in the subcultures of universities and high- and middle-brow journalism.

The notion that great art and literary genius have their source not in ordi-nary individuals, language, or social experience, but rather in a sublime, tran-scendent realm emerges in the first pages of the novel, with the inspired delusions el Flaco experiences while dining with an old acquaintance in the rotating restaurant atop Ostankino Tower in Moscow. This highly unstable setting, in which the slow, almost imperceptible rotation of the tower intensifies el Flaco's panicked disorientation, serves, ironically, as a kind of anchor for the narrative. For it is in the period of at most a few hours in the rotating tower, to which we return periodically throughout the novel, that el Flaco reaches a moment of psychic crisis so intense that it can only be resolved, it seems to him, with capitulation to insanity or with salvation through writing. Capitulation to insanity is equated with silence, and salvation with articulation: el Flaco "tenía en el rostro las marcas del silencio y en la cabeza voces, gritos, preguntas a las que no sabía cómo responder" (had, written on his face, the traces of silence, and in his head voices, screams, questions, to which he did not know how to respond; p. 348).

This dilemma between speech and silence in the opening pages is the mythical moment of the novel's genesis and the narrator recognizes it as such. El Flaco asks himself: "¿Tendría valor para volver al ruedo, fe para sacrificarlo todo a aquel delirio, paciencia para sufrir un nuevo ostracismo, talento para alcanzar su objetivo? ¿Acudirían los dioses en su ayuda, si decidía luchar?" (Would he have the strength to return to the fray, faith enough to sacrifice all to that delirium, the patience to suffer yet another ostracism, talent enough to achieve his objective? Would the gods intervene on his behalf if he decided to enter the battle? p. 10). We learn in later chapters that the *lucha* (struggle or fight) el Flaco considers is the writing of *Las palabras perdidas* itself, and in contemplating his project el Flaco reveals a great deal about how he imagines literature—his strikingly modernist zeal for innovation, for example, and his romantic idea of literary genius. His vision in these moments is consistent with a perception of literature that pervades the text and which those in his literary circle share: that *gran literatura* has transcendent sources—Yoruba deities, for example, or the spirits of dead companions and literary icons.

This vision is at odds with what one critic, discussing Jesús Díaz's short stories, describes as revolutionary Cuba's "cultura nacional inspirada en el conocimiento de la dialéctica del materialismo-histórico" (national culture predicated on the knowledge of the materialist-historical dialectic; Cachán 1990–1991: 86). One can imagine a *cuadro revolucionario* like Oscar Collazos, for example, accusing el Flaco or el Rojo of "una peligrosa actitud de mistificación . . . del hecho creador" (a dangerous inclination toward the mystification . . . of the creative process) or "soberbia [vanguardista]" (vanguardist arrogance), of which he accused Mario Vargas Llosa in 1969 in a published polemic (Collazos 1969: 9–10). El Flaco says, after all, that he intends no less than to "renovar el género [de la novela]" (rejuvenate the genre of the novel; Díaz 1992: 318), and el Rojo, for his part, intends to "inventar un idioma" (invent a language; p. 35). These pretenses are reminiscent of the manifestos of the Latin American *vanguardias* of the 1910s and 1920s, where innovation was the overriding imperative, the literary demigods of the preceding generation had to be "assassinated," and the military vanguard was the metaphor of choice.

Perhaps I have sketched a cynical reading thus far, according to which the novel's narrative of state repression and the protagonists' literary ideology appear self-serving—appear to endorse, that is, the free market in which *Las palabras perdidas* actually circulates. But while this dynamic does indeed obtain, the novel is more complex than such a reading suggests. In subtle ways, the novel deconstructs both its own triumphal narrative and the principles its protagonists hold most sacred. In other words, while the novel does seem to narrate its own trajectory from repressive regime to free market, a materialist sub-narrative or counter-narrative destabilizes the implied "match" between aesthetic autonomy and market freedom. I will argue that it is precisely via this deconstructive dynamic that the novel participates most meaningfully in the debate about art and politics and begins to lay a foundation for a more sophisticated cultural theory and a more progressive cultural politics than either socialist state or capitalist market have been able to offer thus far.

By setting aesthetic and cultural ideals in the contentious interpersonal dynamic of the young artists-protagonists, the novel foregrounds the role of power struggles in constructing standards of literary excellence. In other words, literary greatness is not as transcendent and self-evident as the protagonists take it to be, and repressive state apparatuses (the horrors of which should by no means be minimized, of course) are not the only obstacle—and certainly not the first obstacle—to "great literature." Long before *El Güije Ilustrado* reaches the desk of the newspaper director, who decides to scrap the entire project and substitute a docile, politically orthodox literary supplement, the writers have already subjected the poems, short stories, and essays to a grueling process of elimination, approval, and modification—a process that is at least as much a function of the protagonists' own ambitions, rivalries, and preconceptions as it is of any stable, extrinsic aesthetic standards. We have in this group of writers, therefore, a small-scale narrative model of how cultural values are asserted, fought for, and negotiated—long before they confront the political apparatus. The reader may imagine, then, that the many *inherited* cultural values the protagonists defend or attack have themselves been formed by similar contentious processes. To this extent the artists' vision of a space for artistic integrity, beyond the pressures of political contingency, comes across as ingenuous.

El Flaco's moment of divine inspiration, his excursion into what Una had called "el territorio de los iluminados o los locos" (the realm of the enlightened or the insane; Díaz 1992: 308), is counterbalanced, as early as the second chapter, by a history of rivalries, negotiations, and compromises. El Flaco and el Rojo spend the better part of a day together discussing works of literature they have read or that they envision writing themselves. They have been rivals, we learn, since a poetry reading and critique in the university amphitheater organized by el Rojo and el Gordo when they directed the university literary magazine, *La Ladilla Ladina*. After the readings the floor was opened to debate, and "el Flaco calificó los versos del Gordo de 'triviales' y los del Rojo 'exangües, desasidos, levemente decimonónicos'" (el Flaco characterized el Gordo's poems as "trivial" and el Rojo's as "bloodless, and vaguely nineteenth century"; pp. 16–17). It is at these moments in the novel, when the writers respond to each other's poems, essays, and short stories, that the category of literature is most fundamentally elaborated and contested. Although the short stories, essays, and poems themselves, as they are incorporated into the novel, implicitly prioritize certain cultural values and literary conventions over others, it is in the interpersonal exchanges that the contentious nature of these values becomes most explicit. The balance of power shifts back and forth from one character to another and, consequently, from one cultural value to another.

Throughout the novel alliances and rivalries, affections, jealousies, and institutional power relations inform debates on realism, "conversationalism," feminism, national character, innovation, and literary influence. By scrutinizing the rhetoric of critique and praise in these exchanges we begin to get an idea of how a notion of literature posited by the group as a stable, transcendent category is in fact shaped and reshaped constantly by the same group. The comments of el Flaco regarding the poems of el Rojo and el Gordo illustrate how nebulous literary values tend to be among the Güijes, how such an imprecise characterization as *decimonónico* (nineteenth century) can be assigned, almost arbitrarily, a negative or positive value. It is certainly possible to imagine a cultural context in which *levemente decimonónico* would be a compliment, designating perhaps the subtle reappropriation of a valued literary tradition, but in the thoroughly modernist value system of the Güijes the comment is obviously derogatory.

It is long after the poetry reading and the exchange in the amphitheater when el Flaco and el Rojo spend the day together in the second chapter. El Rojo accompanies el Flaco from a bookstore in downtown Havana—which el Rojo had entered "con el temblor con que los fieles entran al templo" (trembling like the faithful as they enter the temple)—to the poor neighborhood where el Flaco lives in a cramped and deteriorating *solar* (p. 21). Together they carry sacks full of the foreign books el Flaco has bought to the Biblioteca de Alejandría (Library of Alexandria) he has managed to compile in his bedroom over time despite his limited means and in defiance of the leaking roof that threatens to destroy the entire collection. For the first time, the two discuss their literary aspirations and sensibilities in an exchange that, on the one hand, makes them vulnerable by exposing their intimate artistic identities, but on the other hand allows them to posture and define their territory. El Flaco says he intends one day to write "una novela total, o sea, una novela que incluya todos los géneros literarios, poesía, cuento, periodismo, ensayo" (a *total* novel, that is, a novel that includes *all* the literary genres—poetry, short story, journalism, essay)—a novel the reader recognizes as a description of *Las palabras perdidas* itself, which incorporates the poems, essays, and short stories of the protagonists (pp. 36–37).

But until this point, el Flaco has been writing only short stories, and he hands el Rojo a copy of his "Fidelidad." After reading it aloud, el Rojo concludes that the story is good but has a certain *aurea mediocritas*: "el cuento le parecía correcto, publicable inclusive; pero no era ni remotamente gran literatura" (The story seemed proper enough, even publishable; but a far cry from great literature; p. 42). El Rojo's comments may be read as an indictment of the whole class of literature el Flaco's story exemplifies—namely, the socialist realism now associated most strongly with the *quinquenio gris* (the five gray years), 1970–1975. The title's probable allusion to Fidel Castro with the word *fidelidad* suggests that such literature is written in deference to *el comandante*, whose statements on culture inevitably set the parameters for artists and intellectuals during the revolution.

This is the first of many times the phrase *gran literatura* is used in this novel. The existence of great literature and the ability of certain gifted individuals to recognize and produce it are the fundamental premises that ground the Güijes' project. And yet the premises are advanced here so vaguely that the reader may wonder at what point they will be articulated in more specific, less mystified terms. The *aurea mediocritas* is characteristic of the rhetoric the Güijes use to comment on one another's writing; it refers to a quality so intangible that its existence can be neither demonstrated nor disputed. But the impact of the phrase has a great deal more to do with what it connotes than what it denotes. For example, el Rojo's use of Latin gives his comment an erudite quality that is particularly striking in the context of el Flaco's neighborhood, where most residents speak a nonstandard Spanish stigmatized in much of the Spanish-speaking world. Just prior to the reading, in fact, el Flaco corrects his own mother's Spanish in the presence of his guest, telling her to say *todavía* (still) instead of *entoavía* (p. 34).

Of course, at this point in the novel we know of el Flaco's response to the poems of el Rojo and el Gordo at the university poetry reading, so we cannot rule out a revenge motive for el Rojo's comment. We also know that el Flaco's earlier critique was made in public, in the presence of Ibis, el Rojo's girlfriend at the time, who later leaves him for none other than el Flaco himself. And we know something el Flaco does not: El Rojo has remained resentful enough to seek revenge even after el Flaco and Ibis break up: "disfrutó como una doble venganza . . . y tiempo después rechazó de plano la sorpresiva propuesta del

Gordo: incorporar el Flaco a la redacción de *La Ladilla*" (he enjoyed a kind of double vengeance . . . and some time later rejected outright el Gordo's proposal to invite el Flaco to join the editorial board of *La Ladilla*; p. 19). Evidently, the Güijes exercise the limited institutional power they attain to further personal agendas long before *El Güije Ilustrado* reaches the desk of the newspaper director, the novel's central figure of institutional authority, who scraps the project.

Despite the likely personal motives for el Rojo's comments, however, as well as their ill-defined aesthetic criteria, el Flaco takes the comments to heart, abandons "Fidelidad," and writes a new story, "Flores para tu altar" (Flowers for Your Altar), with a markedly different style, characters, and cultural setting. Throughout the novel, disapproval has a profound impact on the attitudes of the Güijes and prompts an enormous amount of rewriting, regardless of how vaguely articulated the disapproval may be or how suspect its motives. To a large extent, the influence of such off-the-cuff, impressionistic remarks can be explained by the unarticulated social codes the writers accept from the outset, codes that regulate how literature should and should *not* be talked about.

Standards of literary excellence, for example, are not imagined by this group as by-products of social discourse itself, informed by the interests of the participants in that discourse; rather, they are thought of as a function of more or less stable universal values accessible only to such illumined literati as the Güijes themselves. It is not worth the effort for these writers, therefore, to deconstruct a critique when the critique comes from an authorized colleague with an acknowledged gift for judgment in these matters. To expose the seemingly arbitrary nature of a critique would be to undermine the basic principles upon which the group's identity depends, as well as the authority of the *challenger*. Individuals in this group seem to concede authority to one another, ultimately, in exchange for recognition *as* authorities; they write, critique, make concessions, rewrite, and counterattack until they can both approve and receive approval—that is, once fundamental stylistic and philosophical principles have been negotiated, and once all of their writings can be construed as adhering to those principles.

Given that the novel's materialist counter-narrative is rendered in great detail, it becomes significant that the implied triumphal narrative receives no such attention. The text leaves out the specific circumstances under which el Flaco is finally able to redeem his companions by writing a novel that incorporates their work. His work as compiler and editor—and perhaps even as merchant peddling the literary commodity—is left entirely to the reader's imagination. If *Las palabras perdidas* represents a kind of testament to the space in which the Güijes' project ultimately prevails—the space in which literature finally escapes the talons of institutional power—the narrative ends, nevertheless, with the delirious indecision of el Flaco as to whether or not he will write the novel. He is determined, on the one hand, to recover an experience through writing but has crushing doubts about being strong enough to do so, on the other. What we are left with, then, is the *evidence* of his triumph in the form of the novel itself, without the *narrative* of that triumph; we see the text gestate, but it is born in a narrative lacuna.

It is up to the reader, in other words, to imagine a possibility that the novel both raises and questions—namely, that the author (whether imagined as el Flaco or Jesús Díaz himself) can achieve at least a relative freedom from contingency, either by the brute force of his genius (like Lezama) or by writing and publishing without state interference—either in a reformed, hypothetical Cuba or, more likely, in exile. Like Díaz, el Flaco has left Cuba for an indeterminate period of time. Since his novel is textually identical with that of Díaz, the reader might imagine that he too achieves his freedom and, possibly, literary success, in exile. Because this achievement is not narrated, however, *Las palabras perdidas* can bracket the contingencies of publishing in the metropolis, as well as the question of reception in commercial, critical, and academic markets, with the peculiar varying expectations of "Third World literature."[1]

Cuban Culture and the Global Market

Confronted with the narrative lacuna in which el Flaco's novel comes into being, the reader will be tempted to substitute Díaz's own historical narrative for that void. Indeed, in the absence of an alternative narrative, the fictional interim projected by the novel itself may be indistinguishable from the author's experience in exile. Although the novel is set in 1960s Cuba, then, the lacuna draws us forward to post-Soviet Cuba and Díaz's exile in Spain, draws us ineluctably, that is, into a transnational cultural dynamic. One is inclined to postulate, of course, that rather than projecting himself into that space *más allá de toda contingencia* which his novel idealizes, Díaz has simply found a cultural and institutional setting sufficiently compatible with his agenda—developed, that is, a relationship of mutual advantage. For obvious reasons it behooves a European publisher to represent that space of artistic freedom in which a persecuted Cuban writer finally finds sanctuary. On the back of Anagrama's 1997 edition of Díaz's *Las iniciales de la tierra*, in fact, the publisher points out, "Esta primera novela de Jesús Díaz estuvo prohibida por las autoridades cubanas durante doce años" (This, Jesús Díaz's first novel, was banned by Cuban authorities for twelve years). This information is documentable, relevant to the novel, and entirely appropriate for a back cover, but it also portrays Anagrama as a kind of haven for hard-hitting, uncompromising literature while eliding the question of the publisher's own criteria; for example, what texts it chooses *not* to publish and for what reasons, or what ideological and economic considerations inform the decision to publish the Díaz novel and not some other novel or *kind* of text. Moreover, in the 1990s non-Cuban publishers—Spanish publishing houses in particular—became the best option for Cuban writers, whether they resided on the island or overseas. The cultural institutions of post-Soviet Cuba simply do not have the resources to publish as many texts as they once did, and they certainly do not have the resources to market books internationally. Publishers like Anagrama, therefore, are more than artistic or political havens: They are the main avenue available to Cuban writers seeking an international readership and financial compensation. Submitting manuscripts to foreign publishers (an act for which Reinaldo Arenas, for example, was harassed by state security in the 1970s)[2] therefore has become not only legal but also a matter of economic empowerment and professional advancement.

And yet, as we have seen, the novel that may be said to mark Díaz's shift from state cultural institutions to private publishing companies reinscribes a characteristically modernist, anti-commodification discourse. The Güijes borrow modernism's antiestablishment, antibourgeois posture, as well as a rhetoric of vanguard and revolution with its premium on innovation over tradition, youth over old age. What is idiosyncratic about the Güijes' modernist "experiment" is its attempted inscription in socialist Cuba and its implied redemption in—of all places—the free market of the metropolis. The young writers initially believe that the socialist state will assume the role of disinterested and generous patron, perhaps in a way analogous to the role José Rodríguez Feo assumed for José Lezama and the Orígenes literary group. This expectation proves to be the miscalculation that exposes the Güijes to the authorities and makes it possible for the narrative to project the ironic resolution: The true revolutionary vanguard is finally redeemed in the global marketplace. El Flaco's *lucha*, which ultimately redeems the Güijes with the novel/literary magazine *Las palabras perdidas*, may not position the writers beyond institutional contingencies, as el Flaco imagines, but rather within alternative institutions that have their own sets of contingencies. Like their modernist precursors, in other words, the Güijes misjudge or misrepresent the nature of their own cultural clout, idealizing the process whereby their own artists and artifacts may gain ascendancy.[3]

As I suggested earlier, however, the provocative, progressive valence of *Las palabras perdidas* lies neither in the modernist ethos of its protagonists nor in the novel's implied triumphal narrative, but rather in the way the Güijes' grievous miscalculations and clearly undertheorized aesthetic convictions speak to an ongoing confusion that becomes pronounced in post-Soviet Cuban discourse. In the absence of clear Cold War dichotomies, and with the intensely nationalist project of the revolution giving way to an increasingly foreign, market-generated sense of Cuba's identity and place in the world, *Las palabras perdidas* offers a rigorous narrative inquiry into precisely those relationships that both the state and the market have structured so inadequately; namely, the relationship between art and ethico-political imperatives, between entertainment and dominant ideology, between individual pleasure and collective priorities, and between aesthetic discourse and commodification.

Jesús Díaz's novel does not lay out a theoretical model or a course of action, and it offers no concrete proposals about the institutions required to foster the kind of meaningful art and cultural autonomy the author clearly desires for Cuba. Addressing the kinds of questions raised by his narrative inquiry, however, may be a prerequisite for a more sophisticated cultural theory and a more progressive cultural politics than existing socialisms and existing capitalisms have been able to generate. The novel's deconstructive dynamic and its protagonists' evident contradictions and limitations may stimulate a more probing debate, at this stage, than concrete proposals or explicit denunciations. There may be a protracted labor of the imagination, in other words, before specific institutional alternatives can be brought into the world. In an age in which the most widely circulated Cuban cultural texts are often selected, marketed, and purchased by businessmen and consumers for whom Cuba is a distant reality, *Las palabras perdidas* prefigures the debates this period will generate for years to come while leaving the burden of propositional argumentation, appropriately, with the community of readers.

Notes

1. I am thinking here not only of the "First World" market's expectations, but also, for example, of Jameson's essay "Third World Literature in the Era of Multinational Capital" (which Aijaz Ahmad refutes convincingly, I think, in his book *In Theory*) or, alternatively, the very different expectations that Doris Sommer describes as "the First World's taste for the postmodern" (Sommer 1991: 3).

2. Arenas published his second novel, *El mundo alucinante*, in France without the permission of the UNEAC. According to his own account, as well as that of Cabrera Infante, his home was subsequently searched by state security and he was isolated from official cultural institutions in Cuba. See Arenas 1992: 143 or Cabrera Infante 1993: 97.

3. See Lawrence Rainey's *Institutions of Modernism* for an excellent account of how the Anglo-American modernist work of art, despite modernism's anti-commodification ethos, "becomes a commodity of a special sort" (Rainey 1998: 3).

Bibliography

Ahmad, Aijaz. 1992. *In Theory*. New York: Verso.
Arenas, Reinaldo. 1981. *El mundo alucinante*. Barcelona: Montesinos.
———. 1992. *Antes que anochezca*. Barcelona: Tusquets.
Cabrera Infante, Guillermo. 1993. *Mea Cuba*. Barcelona: Plaza y Janés.

Cachán, Manuel. 1990–1991. "Los años duros: la revolución del discurso de la Revolución cubana." *Explicación de Textos Literarios* 19, no. 1: 84–94.

Collazos, Oscar, et al. 1969. *Literatura en la revolución y revolución en la literatura.* Mexico City: Siglo XXI.

Díaz, Jesús. 1992. *Las palabras perdidas.* Barcelona: Editorial Anagrama.

———. 1997. *Las iniciales de la tierra.* Barcelona: Editorial Anagrama.

Eagleton, Terry. 1990. *The Ideology of the Aesthetic.* Cambridge: Blackwell.

Jameson, Fredric. 1981. *The Political Unconscious: Narrative as Socially Symbolic Act.* Ithaca, N.Y.: Cornell University Press.

———. 1986. "Third World Literature in the Era of Multinational Capital." *Social Text* 15: 62–87.

Lezama Lima, José. 1977. *Obras completas.* Mexico City: Aguilar.

Rainey, Lawrence. 1998. *Institutions of Modernism: Literary Elites and Public Culture.* New Haven: Yale University Press.

Rojas, Rafael. 1997. "Bájate de esa nube." *Encuentro* 6–7: 241–43.

Sommer, Doris. 1991. *Foundational Fictions: The National Romances of Latin America.* Berkeley: University of California Press.

9

¿Venceremos o Venderemos?

The Transnationalization and Neiman Marxistization of the Icon of Che Guevara

Denise Blum

"We can in no way accept that my father should appear
on women's and men's underwear."
—Aleida Guevara, "Guevara's Daughter," 2003

Che Guevara has been called a "master of iconography" for his everlasting, transnationalized image—rivaling the photograph of Marilyn Monroe as perhaps the most replicated image worldwide. Cuban schoolchildren pledge, "Pioneers for Communism, we shall be like Che," while in other parts of the world Ernesto "Che" Guevara, the "new socialist man," has emerged as a hip advertising pitchman, selling everything from trendy T-shirts to Swatch watches and Austrian Fischer skis. His romantic image, amplified by his early death and unorthodox Communism, has allowed his appeal to *trans*cend and *trans*gress ideological lines: *trans* denoting "both moving through space or across lines, as well as changing the nature of something" (Ong 1999: 4). Using Ong's definition of transnationalism to refer to "the cultural specificities of global processes, tracing the multiplicity of the uses and conceptions of 'culture'"(Ong 1999: 4), in this chapter I interpret and analyze the visual conventions and practices at play in representations of Che, exploring the ideologies, politics, and interests that they might serve or have served. The current commodity fetishism of Che's image, at a time when socialism is scarce in the world, begs us to probe the reasons for its manipulation and popularity. Will the Cuban Communist slogan, *venceremos* (we shall overcome) remain in the future tense forever, or is the slogan, along with its country and icon, being eclipsed by *venderemos* (we shall sell)?

To understand the influence of transnationalism and the image culture of Che, I will first present a historical framework of the initial construction of

Che's image in Cuba and its successful international export in the 1960s. Second, I will introduce the icon of Che Guevara, as understood by Cubans, as a meter for the inculcation of the ideals of Cuban citizenship education. Third, I will explore the relatedness, meanings, and timeliness of the marketing of Che's image in Cuba as well as its transnationality—"or the condition of cultural interconnectedness and mobility across space—which has been intensified under late capitalism" (Ong 1999: 4). I will conclude by examining the resulting messages, on the Caribbean island and internationally, of the current globalization of the Che icon.

The Famous Photo of Che

How the photo first came into being and was marketed is in itself a foreshadowing of the liberation marketing of Che Guevara's image. The famous photo of Che, wearing his beret and looking off into the distance, was taken on March 6, 1960, at a memorial service in Cuba for the more than seventy-five dockworkers killed and several others injured in the explosion of *La Coubre*, a Belgian munitions ship in the port of Havana. U.S. counterrevolutionaries allegedly backed the explosion. Photojournalist Alberto Korda snapped the picture, which was published in the Cuban magazine *Revolución*.

In 1965 Che resigned his posts in Cuba and went to fight in the left-wing insurgency in Bolivia. In October 1967 he was executed in Vallegrande, Bolivia. The Bolivian soldiers were so afraid of him that, after Che had been shot, his hands were amputated and a wax cast of his face was sent to Argentina to prove that he was dead. Just months before Che was sent to Bolivia, Italian publisher Giangiacomo Feltrinelli asked Korda for a copy of his now-famous photo of Che. Korda gave him two copies as a gift, and shortly after Che was killed in Bolivia, capitalizing on Che's martyrdom, Feltrinelli had millions of posters of the photo printed without Korda's permission.

Mystified and mythified since his execution, Che became an instant global icon with his martyrdom. In the late 1960s, Che as the "heroic guerilla" became a symbolic representative of the Cuban Revolution. Korda's photograph was used to construct a seventeen-ton, five-story steel profile of Che on the façade of the Interior Ministry headquarters in Havana's Revolution Plaza, a frequent backdrop to Fidel's most important speeches and a virtual logo of the Cuban capital. Castro developed Che into a personality cult, and Che's image, shown along with revolutionary slogans, became a popular image on billboards. His photo was mass-distributed throughout the island and to this day is still seen framed in Cuban workplaces and homes. Around the world, poets wrote elegies, and painters and musicians commemorated him through their work. Acquiring a life of its own, the figure of Che carried over into song and onto posters. In France, Jean Paul Sartre called Che "the most complete human being of our age." In the student riots of 1968, Che's face adorned posters and banners across the campuses of Europe. Korda's image of Che, noble and defiant, with tilted beret and flowing locks, rapidly spread to T-shirts and album covers and was soon taken up by advertisers targeting youth. But Korda received no royalties; Feltrinelli had used the photo without permission and even failed to credit Korda as the photographer.

Korda's early photo canonized Che into moral sainthood. Various authors (Barthes 1981; Bergson 1990; Holly 1996; Sontag 1977; Yates 1966) discuss the location of photographs between the past and reality and agree on their role in the social and cultural processes of constructing, controlling, and directing private memories to certain ends. In these processes, photographs contribute collectively and unconsciously to the construction of a cultural history that privileges the subjective and the idea of individual articulation. The iconography of the heroic guerrilla was not necessarily the reflection of a concrete reality; its function was ideological. And that function was as much internal as international.

In Cuba, however, after a year of solemn observance, a strange silence surrounding Che lasted for fifteen years. It was only in the mid-1980s that Castro revived Che's uncompromising image as a defense against Soviet *glasnost* and *perestroika*. The Soviet Union disintegrated before the effort got very far, and the combination of that collapse and the U.S. embargo forced Castro to dollarize the economy and allow some foreign investment. Yet, as J. L. Anderson notes, Che remained standing "as the spiritual validation of what little remains of 'revolutionary' Cuba" (Anderson 1997: 376).

Cuban Schooling and Che

Che's martyrdom was soon reflected in the schools. Cuba's Pioneer student organization made a radical change in the late 1960s from being an extracurricular and selective organization to a mass student organization intimately linked with the schools. During this time, the Pioneers' slogan was changed from *¡Venceremos! ¡Siempre Listos!* to *¡Pioneros por comunismo, seremos como el Che!* As a historical marker, Che's image and certain stories about his life were now imbued in a new curriculum—from classroom textbooks to mass media.

In the now-famous text *Man and Socialism in Cuba*, Che referred to education as a fundamental aspect of human liberation. In 1965, he was the chief promoter of educational policy, advocating a "new personality training" as part of the effort to build a socialist society. Che, who embodied the revolutionary ideals in the "new socialist man" concept, stated, "We are building a new society—a just and human society in which exploitation of man by man will have no part. As a part of that, our schools need to form the New Man—one who is not motivated by greed or self-interest but by the good of all" (Guevara 1967: 36).

Che's virtues—sacrifice, hard work, anti-imperialism, honor, honesty, solidarity, patriotism—became values explicitly addressed and rehearsed in school during this stressful time of transition in the early 1960s. Civic education courses appeared for the first time in many years in 1964, resurfacing again with the fall of the Soviet bloc, when the Cuban government turned to the subject to help revive socialism. Both at the beginning of the revolution and in the early 1990s, major political and economic transitions propelled the implementation of a curriculum to solidify civic understanding and promote political solidarity with the revolution.

El amor al trabajo (love of work) is a prominent theme in the civic education textbook (Laguna Vila et al. 1997). The book contains pictures of Cuban young people portrayed as heroes in different types of work and daily life—defending the *patria* and engaged in construction, sports, education, and recreational activities. One photo shows a teenager aiming an AK-47, and other pictures depict young people active in the field experience. Another shows Che cutting cane. Under the pictures are statements such as "The defense of the socialist *patria* is the greatest honor and the supreme duty of every citizen"; "Work in socialist society is a right, a duty and a motive of honor for every citizen"; "Voluntary work, the cornerstone of our society"; and "Che: the impulse for voluntary work in Cuba." The government goal of production within the socialist system was to foster *conciencia*,[1] and Che became the model for this system.

Che also was the originator of the unique Cuban School in the Countryside program, initiated in 1971. This program placed boarding schools for students in grades ten through twelve in rural areas to enable them to do agricultural labor in the morning and attend classes in the afternoon. Basing his ideas on Marxism, Che believed that only through a combination of manual and mental labor would children receive a holistic education. These schools, now a standard on the island, attempt to be self-sufficient in food production. As students cultivate their own produce, this practicum facilitates the understanding of other textbook lessons: math, science, and the revolutionary values of service, hard work, solidarity, and honesty.

As the image and history of Che are recycled, repeated, and reproduced in the Cuban curriculum and society, the images establish a sense of place and time by revisiting the sites of social and cultural identity. For the Cuban government, the goal is to locate the displaced individual in a specific moment in history and aid in rehabilitating the national identity during the economically arduous Special Period. In developing Che into a personality cult within Cuba, Castro used the constant appearance of the icon to reinforce his goal of *conciencia*, increasing its use in times of political or economic stress.

The Resurrection and Globalization of Che

In 1997, Cuba observed "The Year of the 30th Anniversary of the Death in Combat of the Heroic Guerilla and His Comrades." In that year, on October 12, 1997, Che's remains were disinterred in Bolivia and returned to Cuba. At the opening of an art exhibit dedicated to the "image of Che," the Cuban Minister of Culture, Abel Prieto, spoke of the continued importance of Guevara's image: "Che's likeness continues to accompany progressive forces around the world with mysterious tenacity." Che's image "survives, bearing powerful ethical and revolutionary strength," Prieto added (Sundberg 1997). Despite the official celebrations honoring its fallen hero, many believe that the Cuban government was more interested in promoting Che's image than his actual ideas, many of which are in conflict with current state policies during the Special Period. The Cuban government was not alone in plundering Che's legacy, however: Everyone from Hollywood to clothing manufacturers sought an opportunity to cash in on the revolutionary's image, if not his principles.

The international, ideological, and mercantile dimensions of Che are evident in the widespread commercial exploitation of his image. Leica, the manufacturer of the camera that Korda used in 1960 to take the famous photograph of Che, used the image in its promotional material in 1999. A caption asks prospective buyers of Leica cameras: "How revolutionary do you want your picture to be?" With no copyright, Korda's photo continued to be co-opted until September 2000, when Korda finally won copyright protection for the image from a British court as part of a financial settlement with companies that had used it in an ad for Smirnoff vodka. Korda complained that the ad, for spicy vodka, trivialized the historic importance of his photograph. (Che's image was superimposed on a hammer-and-sickle motif, with a chili pepper in place of the sickle.) Tellingly, these commercial treatments of the image had little to do with Che's values and ideals.

Given that visual images frequently are adopted to communicate political trends, what might Che's growing contemporary popularity mean? Has Che become a sellout to the capitalist market economy that he fought so hard to topple? His image has been reproduced over and over again by a strange combination of people and institutions, ranging from Argentina's right-wing president Carlos Menem, who issued a Che commemorative stamp through the Cuban government, to advertising agencies selling trendy goods to Yuppies, which led a cartoonist for the left-wing Mexican daily *La Jornada* to draw an image of Che Guevara with the Nike Swoosh logo on his beret. The leftist newspaper critiques Che as becoming the ultimate corporate shill who wants to "just do it" for eager shareholders.

Conversely, Rowan (2003) explains, "Corporations attempt to exploit activist culture to promote their brands, recast the purchase of mass-produced products as an act of 'radical' self-expression and imbue companies with an 'alternative' mystique in order to secure higher profits." By associating their brand with rebellion or appealing to Baby Boomer nostalgia, corporations hope to become more appealing to various age groups. Companies hire change agents calling themselves urban anthropologists who are paid hundreds of thousands of dollars a year to discover how to make corporate brands cool (Rowan 2003). Revolution Soda has Che's famous face on the bottle, accompanied by the slogan, "Join the Revolution." Perhaps in some trendy way Marx will be back in vogue sometime in the millennium. The appropriation and co-option of revolutionary or counterculture figures is everywhere, and the corporate yoke is clamping down.

What makes the Che image so marketable? One could convincingly argue that we are drawn to Korda's image of Che because it is cool, evocative and, quite simply, sexy. The image is a marketer's dream come true primarily because Che is dead—neither can his face age, nor can his mystique be shattered—and his revolutionary ideals no longer pose a threat in the post–Cold War world.

In Madonna's CD *American Life*, she co-opts the "text," the Che beret, perhaps suggesting affiliation with the revolutionary causes that Che fought for or perhaps identifying as Che's consort, Tania, la guerrillera, later iconized by the bank-robbing, Stockholm-syndrome-suffering Patty Hearst.

The beret is effectively turned into a symbol, or a referent, denoting "revolutionary" or "rebel." Oddly, Madonna's photograph resonates with images of a beret-wearing Faye Dunaway as Bonnie in *Bonnie and Clyde*, which was released the same year (1967) as Tania's death. When the beret is positioned on the original "Tania, the *guerrillera*" or the Patty Hearst "Tania," the referent is relocated. In relocation, it exercises an iconographic function and essentially "brands" the wearer (Nash 2003).

The taboo is always fodder for commercialization, particularly when it deals with sex and violence. The photo of Che has been turned into consumer candy, devoid of any traces of Che's speeches, which hammered home the message that consumerism leads to bestialization. The beret helps Madonna package a product that promises to be an investigation of culture, gender roles, societal attitudes, fashion, and war. As the referent—the beret—is dislocated in the service of commerce and pop culture, however, it no longer remains a symbol of affiliation with a revolutionary cause. Instead, it becomes a symbol of commercially motivated metamorphosis and self-invention. *American Life* illustrates the process of packaging oneself and one's image. It also reflects the intentionality of manipulating graphics to show individuals in the process of creating identity, attempting to control the act of self-invention. The beret is reduced to a fashion statement or kitsch—not simply through its use in vodka ads, but also through the self-styling of individuals who claim to be fighting for the people as they line their pockets with the resources of the poor.

This is not to say that the Che beret cannot be revitalized and used again to symbolize affiliation with a revolutionary group. What makes or breaks the image is how individuals are perceived as they relocate the referent. When the person doing the relocating is perceived as a manipulator of icons, a creator of fashion statements and pop culture, there is an automatic self-consciousness and possible trivialization of the referent. In contrast, when individuals who then perpetrate social injustices use the icon, then the referent takes on additional power and potency.

As shorthand for several processes of cultural interpenetration and blending, transnationalism is associated with a fluidity of constructed styles and everyday practices. Only a few years ago the television show "The Simpsons" made reference to a Latin nightclub called Chez Guevara's, and anti–World Trade Organization protesters met at the Café Che Guevara in Mexico City in September 2003. A Che Guevara eatery opened in Cairo in the same year, and Egypt hopes to launch a chain of Che restaurants, raising the specter of possible Ronald McDonaldization of Che. According to the Cairo restaurant's chief manager, an advertising guru dreamed up the Che Guevara theme because of the revolutionary's international name and face recognition. Manager Yusuf Abideen commented that such a plan is "better from a commercial and marketing point of view" because it appeals to a wide cross-section of customers (Turse 2003). He maintained that beyond the black-and-red walls decorated with pictures of Che and the waitstaff clad in olive green fatigues, combat boots, and berets, the eatery tries to educate the public about Che and his ideals. Perhaps he was referring to the slightly modified excerpts from *Guerilla Warfare* on the Che-faced placemats, the gallery of photographs and portraits of Che at different stages of his life, and the opportunity for customers to write their own personal comments about him on the wall tiles (Irfan 2003). With Che's powerful ethos running counter to the capitalist system, turning him into a rebel–Ronald McDonald involves his image being "stripped of actual radical import and remanufactured utilizing a pseudo-radical chic aesthetic that preaches conformity and consumption in the guise of rebellion" (Turse 2003)— akin to Madonna's Che, Tania, and Patty Hearst–inspired creation on the cover of the *American Life* CD.

The widespread existence of such simulations of Che, in the world of consumption and elsewhere, contributes enormously to the erosion of the distinction between the real and the imaginary, between the true and the false. Every contemporary structure and event is at best a combination of the real and the imaginary. Indeed, Baudrillard (1983: 4) argues that we live in "the age of simulation," having left behind a more genuine, more authentic social world; the true and the false have disappeared in an avalanche of simulations.

Che is now a pitchman for whatever needs to be sold. The online Che store sells collectible watches at $150 each, as well as designer Che shirts, dolls, and shot glasses. And this is just one of hundreds of Che websites existing in every language, from Italian to Norwegian, including "Che quotes for motivation." With the power of technology, the Che image has been transported and reproduced at a rate that no copyright holder can keep up with. While rum-flavored Che coffee is selling briskly at the Lenin Shop in Helsinki, Brazilian supermodels are showcasing the Che bikini.

Viewed through the lens of this sort of advertising, the problems of capitalism and consumerism are those of a soulless society. Rather than suggest wage exploitation, poverty, or war, "liberation marketing" identifies the dullness of life and conformity as the main problems under capitalism. Liberation marketing urges us to change the consumer society rather than put an end to it. We are encouraged to buy products that enhance our individuality, identify us as rebels, or fulfill our desire to be on the fringe. In essence, we rebel by celebrating different consumer products (Rowan 2003). Supermodel Kate Moss wears Che T-shirts in the same manner she might wear ones of Judas Priest: Located on a supermodel or on white, upper-class urban professionals, the icon becomes the personal embodiment of radical chic—the Neiman Marxistization of Che. The irony is that this once relevant cultural icon has now become kitsch.

Once the icons of resistance become commodified, they become depoliticized; "economy has been transmuted into culture and culture into the transient and disposable world of goods" (Illouz 1997: 13). According to the change agents, rebellion is hip, and starting a revolution is encouraged as long as it is fashionable, predictable, contained by consumerism, and doesn't really change anything or promote genuine social activism.

Formerly a symbol embraced mostly by students and radicals, the image and myth of Che Guevara have seeped it seems into the ranks of the unconverted urban professional middle classes. Fleeing the cities on their annual vacations, tourists to the Caribbean island rush to buy a Che T-shirt, wear it happily during their one- or two-week stay there, and relegate it to the bottom drawer upon returning to their routine, white-collar lives. Perhaps the popularity of the image with this group represents a broadening disaffection among the middle classes with the global and domestic environment that keeps them deskbound for much of their lives—or it could just be enchantment with the trendy Che shirt. Liberation marketing exploits the widespread alienation that capitalism creates. Recognizing that there is indeed something wrong with a consumer-driven society, it uses alienation to create profit (Rowan 2003).

A leveling effect occurs when Che is ascribed to the future—showing up in an array of locations at a variety of times and places and inscribed on material and ideological goods. The irony lies in whether the deployment of his image is figured as chic, revolutionary, or white trash. This leveling effect depoliticizes the social powers and conditions that produce subjects as agents and icons, and the South American guerilla and heavy metal progenitors are made to occupy the same horizon as commodity images, or "arrested moments," divorced from their specific historical significance.

In Cuba, as in the commercial world, the new Che is softer, gentler, Christlike. "He is a redeemer figure," says art historian David Kunzle (Larmer 1997: 23), the curator of a 2004 exhibition of Che posters at the University of California at Los Angeles. Kunzle remarks, "In Havana, you no longer see images of Che with a gun" (Larmer 1997: 23). Conversely, the Churches' Advertising Network (CAN), in an effort to embolden the image of Jesus and captivate the public for Easter services in the United Kingdom, designed a poster embedding the Marxist atheist revolutionary in the face of Jesus. The bishop of Ely, the Right Reverend Stephen Sykes (BBC News 1999), noted that "the intention of the advertisement is to cause remark, and it has been successful." According to the Reverend Tom Ambrose of CAN, the aim of the poster is to make people think about Christianity and ask questions about Jesus: "We want people to realize that Jesus is not a meek, mild wimp in a white nightie, but a real, passionate and caring person" (BBC News 1999).

In these various incarnations of Che, the icon is taken out of time, making any item that is bought and sold, or simply used in advertising campaigns, inherently detached from the cultures, ideologies, and movements that produced it. As with any product, the market creates a separation between consumers and producers of those goods, even in purportedly Communist Cuba and elsewhere, where young people need not know the political ideology of the picture on their T-shirt. The globalized image mirrors imperialism, harkening back to Marx and Engels' critique of capitalism: "The need of a constantly expanding market for its products chases the bourgeoisie over the whole surface of the globe. It must nestle everywhere, establish connexions everywhere" (Marx and Engels 1978: 476). The long-awaited discovery of Guevara's bones resurrected the revolutionary icon commercially, if not politically.

Transnationalism and the Loss of Identity

Curious about the Che image and the meaning it evokes for Cubans today, I interviewed Pioneers about their identity, keeping in mind their slogan, "Pioneers for Communism, we will be like Che!" Theodore MacDonald (1985: 176) writes that the Pioneers illustrate "the degree to which doctrinaire shifts in ideological line can be mediated through the school system." Studying the Pioneers as both a meter and a generator of ideology, I offer a dialogue that transpired between Karen Wald and a group of first-grade Pioneers in the mid-1970s and compare it with my interviews in the late 1990s. The following is Wald's interview (1978: 183–84):

> "What does it mean to be a Pionero?" I asked one little girl. She blushed shyly, looking down at her toes.
> "It means to be a communist," offered one of the other children. "It means to be like Che."
> "Are you all communists?" I asked them. "Do you all want to be like Che?"
> They nodded their heads enthusiastically.
> "I'm gonna be like Tania," chimed in a little girl. I smiled.
> "Who was Tania?" I asked.
> "She fought in Bolivia with Che," several voices told me.
> "She was a guerrilla. An internationalist."

In the survey I administered to thirty-nine students about revolutionary values, I asked the same question as Wald: "What does it mean to be a Pioneer?" The responses I received in my ninth-grade survey yielded much less emphasis on revolutionary terminology. Only seven out of thirty-nine students used revolutionary terminology (two mentioned revolution, four patriotism, and one José Martí) in their answers. Most answers (43 percent) included a phrase about "being proud" or "honorable people." The more common phrases were, "It means a lot." "It's something very important." "It means to be a good student." "It means to work hard and be useful." Despite the Pioneer motto, not a single student used the words "Che" or "Communism" in defining the significance of being a Pioneer.

At Ciudad Libertad, a showcase educational compound in Havana, I was denied permission to conduct the same survey. I was allowed, however, a short audiotaped conversation alone with a group of twelve ninth-grade students who were waiting outside a school building for rehearsal. Although these students were enthusiastic to participate in my interview, they seemed to exhibit more uncertainty than enthusiasm in their answers; they all told me that to be a Pioneer was to be a Cuban student. I questioned the whole group, "No one disagrees or has anything to add?" They all seemed a bit confused, wondering if they had missed something. Then a student added, "It means to work hard and study." I probed a bit deeper, "What, then, is the difference between a Pioneer and a student in another country, say, for example, in Mexico?" The students all showed signs of supporting the answer of the vanguard student who became the spokesperson, "The difference is that in Mexico, they call their students one thing, and in Cuba we call our students Pioneers."

Perhaps one could say that my survey and oral interview were just circumstantial. But revolutionaries I spent time with, including men who had served in the Sierra Maestra and men and women who participated in the Literacy Campaign, concurred that Che Guevara was no longer talked about the way he used to be. I was frequently told, "Che had been a model for a set of different political and historical circumstances." He had spearheaded the command economy and advocated the use of moral incentives exclusively. His promotion of the "new socialist man"—one who would be exhorted to labor for society without personal gain out of a sense of moral commitment—seemed to have little relevance for the capitalist and Communist values that accompanied a mixed-market economy.

There were times I was tempted to ask, in the context of a mixed-market economy and a value crisis, "What would Che do?" But I realized from the looks these revolutionaries gave me in response to my Che questions that to them I was caught in a time warp or a nostalgic idealism, while they were ready to move on to another topic. In a society where people struggle just to have enough food, the idea of working without remuneration seems crazy. From cigar factories to *agropecuarios* (produce markets), Cuban industries have turned to material incentives. Self-owned businesses, joint ventures, and tourism are more widespread. Perhaps the word "Che," along with "Communism," has become less articulated as the aspired Communist utopia of the 1960s and '70s resulted in something vastly different than anyone had dreamed.

If the motto of the Pioneers no longer coincides with the definition apparently internalized by the students I spoke to, what, then, is the meaning of the omnipresent icon of Che on billboards, postcards, posters, T-shirts, berets, lighters, and key chains in Cuba? One revolutionary who fought in the Sierra Maestra with Che saw the pictures of my dog, Fefa, dressed as different world leaders and made a suggestion for another picture. He gave me his beret from the Sierra Maestra and a cloth wall hanging of Che so that I could dress Fefa as Che, take her picture, and send it to him. When I returned, I brought him a copy of the picture, and I placed it as the opening photograph in my small photo album of Fefa.

People's reaction to the picture of Fefa as Che was interesting. Fefa, a large, black, mixed-breed dog, sat in an olive green T-shirt with an authentic matching revolutionary beret. In the background hung the cloth wall hanging of Che. Remarkably, Fefa had the same steely stare as the image. The Cuban people I came into contact with (even officials in the Ministry of Education) seemed so amused by my dog as Che that they would borrow the photo album to show it to others. My key contact in Cuba told me that this album would be crucial to my gaining access to interviews. I followed her advice to show the photo when requesting interviews, and nearly every Cuban laughed, then warned me that I should remove the photo of Che from the album because it might cause me political problems. In the end, it was the picture of Fefa as Che that was instrumental in the Ministry of Education granting me permission to conduct long-term research in Cuban schools.

What do these events tell of the canonized revolutionary hero? Che aligned himself with the socialist view that one should not be alienated from his or her labor or commodified as one is under capitalism. Ironically, from beach towels to lighters, Che's emblazoned image has become one of the hottest-selling tourist items in Cuba. If the Pioneers' motto is, "We will be like Che," and even my dog or any tourist who purchases Che paraphernalia can be like Che, it seems only logical that the Pioneers would feel detached from a historical image that not only comes from a different time but has been transformed into a commodity by the socialist leadership that made it sacred. Has the image of Che been emptied and, with it, the meaning of the revolution?

Looking to Foucault (1990: 27), we must recognize that it is not only what is represented that is important to us, but also what is not, as those things that remain unrepresented "are an integral part of the strategies that underlie and permeate discourses." In this case, it is the invisible thread of transnationalism that transports, transgresses, and translates ideologies and histories and their associative icons into consumer discourses. However, the heightened problem in an analysis of the visual is that what is not represented and not seen cannot easily be inferred from what there is to view. History, by its own terms, is out of sight, a transient image of the already passed.

Borrowing from Baudrillard we can speculate that the commodification of Cuban life during the late 1990s has changed not only the meaning of things, but also the process by which we acquire meaning. While signs and their referents used to be more closely related to each other, commodification now mediates the relationship between sign and referent and destroys its immediacy. The sign, the image, comes unbound and can be interpreted according to a broad range of possibilities, according to the logical limits of the code that encloses it (Baudrillard 1983). The image devalues the original by concealing it, hiding it. The current images of Che have distorted the referent as they have become more removed from the historical context in which Che lived and died. As Baudrillard (1983: 9) notes, "it is dangerous to unmask images, since they dissimulate the fact that there is nothing behind them." For now, the Pioneers will continue to repeat their motto, "*Seremos como el Che.*" Yet, as time passes, Che's image, although somewhat emptied of revolutionary ideals, in its simulacra possesses a marketing value that brands the bearer as the "new commodified man."

A wealth of personal and collective meanings and perspectives about Che Guevara are being transformed, such that transnationalism presents us with "new subjectivities in the global arena" (Nonini and Ong 1997). As the image travels from one product to the next and from one continent to the next, lines and demarcations of citizenship, nationalism, ideology, and identity are *trans*gressed and *trans*formed by transnationalism. As the uses and conceptions of the Che image multiply, Appadurai and Breckenridge (1989: iii) point out, "the politics of desire and imagination are always in contest with the politics of heritage and nostalgia."

In Vallegrande, Bolivia, a major stop on tours for the curious who want to see where Che hid, fought, and finally died, enterprising villagers selling Che memorabilia profit from the boom of leftist pilgrims. Written on the wall of the Vallegrande post office, some fifty yards from where Che was allegedly executed, is a summation, perhaps adequate: "Che, alive as they never wanted you to be."

Notes

1. Che used the term *conciencia* when he formulated his ideas on moral incentives. For him, it meant more than the English translation, "consciousness" or "awareness." *Conciencia* was created through political education and participation in revolutionary activities; it involved a commitment to action (Guevara 1967). Fidel Castro has defined *conciencia* as "an attitude of struggle, dignity, principles and revolutionary morale" (Castro 1980: 59, my translation).

Bibliography

Anderson, Jon Lee. 1997. *Che Guevara: A Revolutionary Life*. New York: Grove Press.

Appadurai, Arjun, and Carol Breckenridge. 1989. "On Moving Targets." *Public Culture* 2: i–iv.

Barthes, Roland. 1981. *Camera Lucida*. Translated by Richard Howard. New York: Noonday Press.

Baudrillard, Jean. 1983. "The Precession of Simulacra." Translated by P. Foss and P. Patton. *Art & Text* (Victoria, Australia) 11: 3–47.

BBC News. 1999. "Jesus Ad Campaign 'Not Blasphemous.'" BBC Online Network. <http://news.bbc.co.uk/1/hi/uk/250752.stm>. (Accessed January 7)

Bergson, Henri. 1990 (Reissue Edition). *Matter and Memory*. Translated by Nancy Margaret Paul and W. Scott Palmer. Cambridge, MA: Zone Books.

Castro, Fidel. 1980. "Informe central al segundo congreso [del Partido Comunista de Cuba]." *Bohemia* 59 (December): 7–10.

Foucault, Michel. 1990. *The History of Sexuality.* Vol. 1: *An Introduction,* translated by Robert Hurley. New York: Vintage.

Guevara, Ernesto. 1967. *Man and Socialism in Cuba.* Translated by M. Zimmermann. Havana: Book Institute.

"Guevara's Daughter Has a Cause, in the Image of Her Father." 2003. *The Age.* <http://www.theage.com.au/articles/2003/06/27/1056683905727.html>. (Accessed October 2003)

Holly, Michael Ann. 1996. *Past Looking: Historical Imagination and the Rhetoric of the Image.* Ithaca: Cornell University Press.

Illouz, Eva. 1997. *Consuming the Romantic Utopia: Love and the Cultural Contradictions of Capitalism.* Berkeley: University of California Press.

Irfan, Hwaa. 2003. "Eating out with Che Guevara." *Islam Online.* <http://www.islamonline.net/English/artculture/2003/09/article05.shtml>. (Accessed October 2003)

Laguna Vila, D., M. L. Martínez Sierra, H. A. Mesa Hernández, E. Herrera Orúa, and J. Rodríguez Ben. 1997. *Educación cívica: 9 grado.* Havana: Editorial Pueblo y Educación.

Larmer, Brook. 1997. "Return of the Rebel." *Newsweek,* July 21, 17–23.

MacDonald, Theodore H. 1985. *Making a New People: Education in Revolutionary Cuba.* Vancouver: New Star Books.

Marx, Karl, and Friedrich Engels. 1978. "The Communist Manifesto." In *The Marx-Engels Reader,* edited by Robert C. Tucker. 2nd ed. New York: W. W. Norton.

Nash, Susan Smith. 2003. "Madonna in Che Guevara's Beret." *Xplana.* <http://www.xplana.com/articles/archives/Beret>. (Accessed October 2003)

Nonini, Donald M., and Aihwa Ong. 1997. "Chinese Transnationalism as an Alternative Modernity." In *Ungrounded Empires: The Cultural Politics of Modern Chinese Transnationalism,* edited by Aihwa Ong and Donald M. Nonini. London: Routledge.

Ong, Aihwa. 1999. *Flexible Citizenship: The Cultural Logics of Transnationality.* Durham: Duke University Press.

Rowan, Lindsay. 2003. "The Revolution Will Not Go Better with Coke." *Green Left Weekly.* <http://www.greenleft.org.au/back/2003/528/528p22.htm>. (Accessed October 2003)

Sontag, Susan. 1977. *On Photography.* New York: Farrar, Straus and Giroux.

Sundberg, Pete. 1997. "Che! Pop Hero! Martyr! Icon of the Revolution!" *The Peak.* <http://www.peak.sfu.ca/the-peak/97-3/issue6/che.html>. (Accessed October 2003)

Turse, Nick. 2003. "Heroic Guerrillas and Other Misrememberings." *The Voice of the Turtle.* <http://www.voiceoftheturtle.org/show_article.php?aid=368>. (Accessed October 2003)

Wald, Karen. 1978. *Children of Che: Childcare and Education in Cuba.* Palo Alto, Calif.: Ramparts Press.

Yates, Frances A. 1966. *The Art of Memory.* Chicago: University of Chicago Press.

10

La Cubanía in Exile

Alma DeRojas

> We have learned that you don't have to live in Cuba to be Cuban.
> Rather, being Cuban is a state of mind.
> —Vivian de la Incera, "The Thirteenth Suitcase"

In October 2000, I participated in a panel discussion about Cuban American literature of exile entitled "Creating on the Hyphen" with fiction writer Cristina García, whom I had met a few months earlier at the inaugural U.S.-Cuba Writers' Conference in Havana. After the panel, I asked Cristina to autograph my copy of her first novel, *Dreaming in Cuban*. She signed in Spanish: "Para Alma, también soñando en cubano" (For Alma, also dreaming in Cuban). Like Cristina and her novel's protagonist, Pilar, I have begun to dream in Cuban. My dreams have not always been in Cuban, however. They are the result of my desire to be Cuban, my longing to reconnect with my father's native land.

In 1961, a few days after the Bay of Pigs invasion, my father and his family fled Cuba in a ferryboat. In 1980, I was born in Philadelphia, and six years later my family moved to northeastern Pennsylvania. The only Cubans I knew there were my family. I knew no Spanish. Cuba was a mystery, a faraway island that existed only in my imagination and the occasional stories my grandparents told me. For many years, my Cuban heritage consisted of nothing more than the rice and black beans my grandmother used to cook. In the words of the Cuban American author Gustavo Pérez Firmat (1995a), I was a "cubanita descubanizada," a decubanized Cuban girl:

> Cubanita descubanizada
> quién te pudiera recubanizar.
> Quién supiera devolverte
> el ron y la palma,
> el alma y el son.

(Decubanized Cuban girl,
who could recubanize you.
Who would know how to return to you
the rum and the palm tree,
the soul and the *son*.)[1]

As I grew older, I realized how "descubanizada" I was and developed a need to "recubanize" and explore my Cuban heritage. Is recubanization possible? I believe it is. And so, in response to Pérez Firmat, I reply: The study of Cuban American literature of exile can enable *cubanos descubanizados* to recubanize. For me this process has entailed more than a study of literature, but I believe that Cuban American literature has enabled me to construct my own Cuban identity and, ultimately, to dream in Cuban. For although this literature is written primarily in English, outside of Cuba, it reflects *la cubanía*, the Cuban spirit, a term first used by the Cuban scholar Fernando Ortiz in 1940. According to Ortiz, being Cuban is not a matter of possessing a Cuban passport. To be Cuban one must possess *la cubanía*, a desire to be Cuban, which I believe is manifested in Cuban American literature of exile.

Each text expresses this spirit in a unique manner because just as there is not one way to be Cuban, there is not one way to express *la cubanía*. The reflection of *la cubanía* in literature written in English, outside of Cuba, reveals this spirit to be transnational. If being Cuban is indeed a state of mind, then it cannot be restricted by national boundaries. In this sense, Cuban national identity is transnational, for its fluidity enables *la cubanía* to transcend the physical limits of the island and to find expression in the pages of Cuban American literature. It is this literature that has enabled a Pennsylvania-born, English-speaking, freckled-faced daughter of an Irish American mother to consider herself Cuban, further evidence that the desire to be Cuban is indeed transnational.

Ortiz first used the term *cubanía* in a 1940 essay entitled "Los factores humanos de la cubanidad," in which he attempted to describe the Cuban soul, the "condición de alma" of the Cuban people (Pérez Firmat 1989: 29). For many years the accepted term to denote Cubanness was *cubanidad*, a word that dates back to the beginning of the nineteenth century (Pérez Firmat 1997: 2). Because this term refers primarily to birth or civil status, Ortiz maintained that *cubanidad* did not reflect the complexity of Cuban identity. In other words, to be born or to live in Cuba does not automatically ensure that one is Cuban. As Gustavo Pérez Firmat (1997: 3) writes, *cubanidad* is "generic rather than individual, uniform rather than idiosyncratic. In its narrowest sense, *cubanidad* designates the junction of nationality and citizenship. As such, it is a civil status embodied in birth certificates, passports and naturalization oaths, and for this reason perhaps the most fragile manifestation of our nationality." For Ortiz, being Cuban required more than the possession of a Cuban birth certificate or passport; also necessary were "la conciencia de ser cubano y la voluntad de quererlo ser" (the consciousness of being Cuban and the will to want to be Cuban; Ortiz 1973: 152).

Because he believed the term *cubanidad* did not accurately reflect this will to be Cuban, a key component of Cuban identity, Ortiz coined *la cubanía* to describe the Cuban spirit. According to him, *la cubanía* is "a self-conscious, willed *cubanidad*, a feeling of deep and pervasive identification with things Cuban" (Pérez Firmat 1989: 30). *Cubanidad* is a civil status ("condición genérica de cubano" [generic Cubanness]), while *la cubanía* ("cubanidad plena, sentida, consciente y deseada" [complete, felt, conscious, and desired Cubanness]) is an intense desire to be Cuban (Ortiz 1973: 153). According to Pérez Firmat (1997: 7), "Ortiz locates the fullest form of Cubanness in a kind of longing: to desire *cubanía* is already to possess it."

Ortiz's essays on the Cuban spirit argue that in order to be Cuban, one must want to be Cuban. Thus, the cultivation of *la cubanía* in exile is a conscious, individual choice enabled by the fact that the Cuban spirit cannot be contained to the island of Cuba. To borrow the words of Gloria Anzaldúa, being Cuban is "a state of soul"; it cannot be defined by geographical borders, for it is a matter not of residence, but of spirit. Speaking for Chicanas everywhere, Anzaldúa writes, "Deep in our hearts we believe that being Mexican has nothing to do with which country one lives in. Being Mexican is a state of soul—not one of mind, not one of citizenship" (Anzaldúa 1999: 84). In the same sense, being Cuban is not a matter of living in Cuba, but rather of possessing *cubanía*, the equivalent of Anzaldúa's Mexican state of soul.

I have loosely translated *la cubanía* as the Cuban spirit, but the full meaning of the term cannot be captured so simply. Yes, I believe it is a spirit shared by all those who identify themselves as Cuban, but the word "spirit" does not adequately reflect the key component of *la cubanía*: desire. So perhaps a better translation would be the Cuban spirit created by desire. I firmly believe this spirit does exist; however, I do not believe that it is essential, for it is constantly transformed in exile as individuals create new identities away from their homeland. Rather, I believe that *la cubanía* has five basic characteristics: It is a choice; it cannot be contained by borders; it is created by the individual; it is fluid; and most important, it is a matter of desire. These five characteristics explain the transnational nature of Cuban national identity, for they enable the spirit to transcend all boundaries.

Because *la cubanía* does not depend on place of residence and therefore cannot be taken away from those who possess the desire to be Cuban, Pérez Firmat believes that it is the expression of Cubanness most available to exiles. In his own words, "I continue to take solace and sanctuary in the Cuba of *cubanía*, a homeland one cannot leave or lose" (Pérez Firmat 1997: 11). For him, *la cubanía* is intimate, personal, spiritual, abstract, ineffable, a "willingness of the heart": "*Cubanía* forms part of one's inner life. It's not asserted but felt, it's not flaunted but desired. It's not a reflex but a choice. . . . Cubanía appears in the theater of the individual's consciousness. . . . It finds expression not in a nation . . . and not in a people . . . but in something more abstract and ineffable—in a homeland, *una patria*" (p. 7).

If Pérez Firmat is correct that *la cubanía* finds expression in a *patria* of the imagination, then the transnational nature of Cuban national identity cannot be denied. Unlike *cubanidad*, *cubanía* does not depend on the physical presence of the island. As long as individuals possess the willingness to be Cuban, the Cuba of *la cubanía* can never be lost. Cuban exiles may no longer possess a Cuban passport, but their desire to be Cuban cannot be destroyed by the effects of 1959, for *la cubanía* will survive in exile as long as it is embraced by individuals.

Although Pérez Firmat rightly asserts that *cubanía* is a choice, he would probably challenge my claim to be Cuban, based primarily on the fact that I was not born and raised on the island. Reflecting on his own children's sense of Cubanness, Pérez Firmat writes that "they are Cubans in name only, in last name. . . . Like other second-generation immigrants, they maintain a connection to their parents' homeland, but it is a bond forged by my experiences rather than their own. For my children Cuba is an enduring . . . fiction" (Pérez Firmat 1994: 5). In other words, my generation's claim to *cubanía* is not authentic because of our place of birth and upbringing. It is precisely this "myth of authenticity" that Andrea O'Reilly Herrera seeks to explode in *ReMembering Cuba: Legacy of a Diaspora*, a 2001 collection of testimonials that offers a variety of perspectives on what it means to be Cuban in exile. Despite the fact that many of the contributors either were born in the United States or left the island as infants, they claim that their feelings of nostalgia and loss are indeed genuine. Although several first-generation exiles objected to O'Reilly Herrera's decision to include members of my generation in the collection because we did not experience the trauma of exile firsthand, *ReMembering Cuba* is significant for its inclusive and fluid perspective on Cuban identity.

On a personal level, the collection is significant because it reveals to me that there are many members of my generation who share my desire to be Cuban. Although many of the second-generation contributors to *ReMembering Cuba* were raised in Miami, a surprising number were raised outside the Cuban enclave yet still affirm a sense of confidence in their Cubanness. Like me, O'Reilly Herrera was born in Philadelphia to an Irish Cuban American family. Unlike most of her siblings and cousins, she used to beg her grandparents to tell stories of life on the island, driven by "my desire to act as the guardian of our stories, our history" (O'Reilly Herrera 2001: xii). Contrary to Pérez Firmat's assertion that second-generation Cubans cannot experience authentic yearning for Cuba, O'Reilly Herrera affirms that her claim to Cubanness is indeed genuine: "I grew up longing for and dreaming about a world that no longer exists and a physical place I have never seen, except in photographs, but somehow know. As a result, I am confronted with a sense of deep personal loss" (p. 318). Driven by "an ancestral yearning for all things Cuban" (p. xi), O'Reilly Herrera reflects on the origins of her "nostalgic, vicarious desire for Cuba" (p. 319), a desire I share and seek to understand.

What explains this longing for the island? Although there is no definitive answer to this question, O'Reilly Herrera maintains that personal desire is key. In her own words, "one cannot ignore the role that desire plays in the conscious construction or acquisition of cultural identity" (p. xxvii). Certainly not all members of the second generation possess the desire to be Cuban, but those of us who feel an inexplicable longing for the island are united by "an unquenchable thirst" for all things Cuban (p. 319). In the words of O'Reilly Herrera, "we all seem to be suffering in various degrees from having been deprived of the opportunity to recall or physically know a world, a civilization that has all but been erased" (p. 319). Although I agree with her that the feelings of loss experienced by members of my generation are authentic, I also recognize that I am not an exile. I may consider myself Cuban, but I will never fully understand how it feels to lose my *patria*.

For first-generation exiles, the desire to be Cuban can never compensate for the physical absence of the homeland. The transnational nature of *cubanía* may provide exiles with a sense of comfort, but perhaps their desire to be Cuban can never be fully realized outside of Cuba. As Damián Fernández and Madeline Cámara Betancourt (2000: 3) write, Cuban national identity is "characterized by unsatisfied longing, elusive desire." In the words of Fernández, *lo cubano* is indeed "the story of desire and disenchantment," a story reflected in the political struggles for sovereignty, democracy, and the end of exile. Over time, "the unfulfilled quest for *la patria soñada por Martí* . . . increasingly assumed an intense emotional charge. . . . The desired Cuba has been and is, therefore, an elusive nation caught between ideals and deep dissatisfaction" (p. 81). National identity clearly cannot be separated from national politics. In a sense, the politics of *la cubanía* are defined by a "chasm between aspiration and realization" (p. 79). This tension between the ideal and the real gives *la cubanía* a "bittersweet" character. In the words of Fernández, "bittersweet is the taste of desire and disenchantment and of *cubanía* and *lo cubano*, time after time" (p. 98).

The bittersweet desire of *la cubanía* is evident among Cubans in exile. Many Cubans separated from their *patria* experience the desire to be Cuban daily in a world of never-ending nostalgia, "the desire to come back to an idealized past" (Belleli and Amatulli 1997: 210). The word "nostalgia" comes from the Greek and is formed from the combination of two words: *nostos* (return) and *algos* (grief). Together, the Greek words signify "sadness emerging from the desire to go back home" (p. 210). Not only do Cuban exiles desire to return to a mythical homeland of the past, but they also desire to construct a *Cuba libre* of the future. As long as this dream remains "an unrealized project, an un-achieved blend of *ser* and *querer ser*" (Pérez Firmat 1997: 8), this desire can never be completely fulfilled. In this sense, the significance of *la cubanía* in exile transcends the usual translation of the term, for the spirit reflects an unrealized desire to be Cuban.

In search of the unfulfilled goal of a *Cuba libre*, Cubans constantly trans-form their identities in exile. Their elusive desire to be Cuban reveals the dy-namic nature of identity itself, a perspective that both Ortiz and Pérez Firmat reflect in their essays. As Jorge Duany writes, "for Ortiz, national identity has no essence; it is always in the process of becoming" (Duany 1997: 13). In a sense, Ortiz was ahead of his time in his emphasis on the fluidity of identity and was one of the first scholars to recognize the transnational nature of Cuban identity. Most contemporary scholarship has embraced the idea that identity is "socially constructed, imagined, and often invented" (Duany 1997: 4). The once-prevalent view that national identity is "fixed historically and bounded by geography" has been replaced by the perspective that identity transcends all boundaries (Fernández and Cámara Betancourt 2000: 2). In this sense, "na-tional identity appears more fluid than static . . . its character more elusive and malleable than fixed and permanent" (p. 8). As Stuart Hall writes, identity is a "production" that is never complete. It "is a matter of 'becoming' as well as 'being.' It belongs to the future as much as to the past" (Hall 2000: 21–23). According to Hall, cultural identities undergo constant transformation due to the fact that identity is fluid, not static. Hall's perspective forms the basis for O'Reilly Herrera's assertion that "what it is to be Cuban or Cuban American . . . is constantly being displaced and renegotiated" (O'Reilly Herrera 2001: xxv).

Not all theorists agree with this fluid perspective on identity. Some embrace an essentialist view in which nations are concrete and well defined, culture is homogeneous, and geography is the ultimate determinant. Essentialists thus believe that Cuba is a coherent nation without internal fragmentation, except for the deep rift between those on the island and those in exile (Duany 1997: 1, 5). In the eyes of many Cubans, the nation and the diaspora are disjointed simply because of their physical separation. Those who believe that geography is the ultimate determinant of identity maintain that one must be born in Cuba to be Cuban. But what explains the desire of American-born Cubans like my-self and O'Reilly Herrera to be Cuban? Clearly, the essentialist viewpoint is too simplistic to take into account the complexity and fluidity of Cuban identity. As Duany writes in his essay on reconstructing Cubanness, *lo cubano* should be approached from a deterritorialized, transnational perspective (Duany 2000: 18, 34). The ability to transcend borders is thus one of the key characteristics of *la cubanía*. With this in mind, a transnational perspective on *la cubanía* is essential.

The very existence of a Cuban American literature of exile reveals the ability of *la cubanía* to transcend borders. Despite the many differences among Cuban American authors, the literature is united by the authors' desire to cultivate *la cubanía*. In this essay, I explore the reflection of this spirit in Cuban American literature through an analysis of the following texts: *Exiled Memories: A Cuban Childhood*, a 1990 memoir by Pablo Medina; *Next Year in Cuba: A Cubano's Coming of Age*, a 1995 memoir by Gustavo Pérez Firmat; and *Bridges to Cuba/Puentes a Cuba*, a 1995 anthology edited by Ruth Behar. Specifically, I will focus on Medina's use of sugar, Pérez Firmat's use of dreams, and Behar's use of bridges to express the Cuban spirit in exile in order to explore the economic, psychological, and cultural implications of *la cubanía* in Cuban American literature. Although not all critics may agree with my belief that the nature of the Cuban spirit can be reflected in literature, I hope my analysis of these texts will reveal that *la cubanía* can indeed be captured through words. In a similar sense, although not all critics may believe that a girl born in Pennsylvania can be Cuban, I hope that my analysis reflects not only the desire of Medina, Pérez Firmat, and Behar to be Cuban, but my own desire as well. In this light, my essay serves as a concrete example of O'Reilly Herrera's assertion that desire plays a fundamental role in the construction of my generation's Cuban identity.

Although the texts I have selected give useful insights into the Cuban spirit in exile, I realize that they provide only three perspectives. This essay does not purport to be a definitive explanation of *la cubanía*; every Cuban American author creates the Cuban spirit in a unique manner, and thus there is no single definition of it. In addition, the evocation of *la cubanía* is not limited to literature. Literature is only one form of expression, one way to express the Cuban spirit, along with music, dance, art, food, and family tradition. Literature may often present an elitist, privileged perspective, but I believe its study is essential to understanding how the spirit is developed in exile through words.

Of the many ways to express the Cuban spirit, literature has been crucial in the construction of my own identity. Although my three selected texts have been widely analyzed by critics, I chose them specifically because they reflect my personal construction of a Cuban identity. Through the words of Medina, Pérez Firmat, and Behar, I have vicariously experienced a Cuban childhood, a Miami adolescence, and the benefits of building exilic bridges to Cuba. As a college student in the tranquil countryside of central Pennsylvania who read through most of her university library's meager Cuba collection within a few months, I first found answers to my questions of identity in the pages of these three texts. In this sense, they represent the beginning of my academic exploration of Cuba, and they have served as crucial components of my journey of

Cubanization. Although I will never personally experience the trauma of exile, I hope that my attempt to vicariously understand the experience of Cuban exiles through the pages of literature reflects my personal desire to be Cuban. Using the words of O'Reilly Herrera, these texts have fulfilled (at least partially) my "nostalgic, vicarious desire" (O'Reilly Herrera 2001: 319). Transcending the boundaries of geography and politics, my selected works have both fed my imagination and fueled my undeniable passion for all things Cuban.

Because literature has played such a pivotal role in the construction of my Cuban identity, I have chosen to incorporate additional Cuban American voices in quotations interwoven throughout my essay, for these are the voices that have shaped my own identity and work, just as waves shape an island. Most of the quotes come from *ReMembering Cuba*, a fitting choice since it is this collection that first revealed to me the power of desire and the fluidity of identity. Like the borders of an island, my identity is fluid and constantly shifting, for as I continue my study of Cuban American literature, my process of recubanization continues. By including these voices, I hope to provide the reader not only with some of the voices that have enabled my recubanization, but also with additional perspectives on what it means to cultivate *la cubanía* in exile.

* * *

Despite the fact that Castro has robbed the Cuban people of their freedom and basic human rights and stolen the physical island of Cuba, he does not own the spirit of Cuba; it lives within the people and has survived and grown through the Cuban American generation. . . . There is an energy that is so sacred and so spiritual . . . it is this spiritual energy that carries us and keeps Cuba alive in our hearts.

—Gina Granto-Penque, *"On Being Cuban"*

* * *

Exiled Memories: A Cuban Childhood

Pablo Medina

Pablo Medina's 1990 memoir *Exiled Memories: A Cuban Childhood* reveals his longing to return to the Cuba of his childhood, a longing he expresses through repeated references to *azúcar*. Through sugar-coated memories, he reflects his personal sense of privileged *cubanía*. Although such memories could trap some writers in a world of nostalgia, Medina escapes the trap by examining his social conscience and exploring the economic implications of

Cuba's most important product. Through a combination of idealized child-hood memories and a more realistic vision of prerevolutionary Cuba, Medina's memoir reveals both his desire to recapture the *cubanía* of his youth and his awareness of his privileged position. This conflict between desire and aware-ness is the major source of tension in Medina's expression of *la cubanía*.

Medina decided to preserve his exiled memories after realizing that his older relatives would not live forever: "When they went, they would take with them the myths and folklore I had grown up with. That, I thought, should never be allowed to happen. And who better than I to chronicle our past for those generations who had never lived it?" (Medina 1990: x). As Angel Rama has argued, the exiled writer must become "the custodian and defender of the endangered culture" (Rama 1997: 341). Medina has become a custodian of Cuban culture through his decision to preserve his family's past and his own childhood memories. In a sense, he is preserving *la cubanía* for future genera-tions who may never return to Cuba. Thus, his text assumes the task of preserv-ing a way of life that exists in memory only. In the words of Isabel Álvarez Borland (1998: 64), "his memories become a means to ensure the survival of a collective identity."

Medina did not always envision himself as a defender of the Cuban spirit in exile, however. After years of trying to be an American, during which he be-lieved that "changing nationalities was as easy as changing clothes, speech patterns, books to read," he realized that "nationality is in the soul . . . and to change that requires much more than window dressing of one's body or tongue or mind" (Medina 1990: x). He realizes he may have repressed his sense of *cubanía* in the past, but it will always be a part of his identity. Medina accepts the fact that his previous desire for Americanization was "a quixotic attempt to become a creature I never was nor can ever be," yet he also recognizes that he is no longer "immaculately Cuban," due to years of living in the United States (p. x). Through *Exiled Memories*—"a record of my Odyssey, my return to Ithaca" (p. x)—therefore, he hopes to return to the land of his birth. In this sense, Medina's odyssey is a journey of idealized memories to a world that exists solely on the page.

* * *

The fact is that the Cuba for which I long is a figment of memory, a shadow of a shadow of a country that no longer exists.

 —Pablo Medina, *"Where Are You From? A Cuban Dilemma"*

* * *

Although he may no longer be "immaculately Cuban," Medina's odyssey asserts his *cubanía* through the very act of preserving his childhood memories, many of which are united by images of sweetness. Sugar has always been one of Cuba's main exports, and it is certainly evoked in Medina's memoir. Thus, I have chosen to refer to his sugar-coated memories as *recuerdos azucarados*, memories that reflect the sense of nostalgia that pervades the Cuban American exile community. As members of this community continue to embrace the Cuban spirit in exile, they often remember their island as a sweet paradise of endless sugarcane.

Medina's *recuerdos azucarados* reflect his desire not only to taste the sugar of his youth, but also to recapture the *cubanía* of his childhood. In a sense, this desire reveals the constructedness of his own soul. Although Medina may believe that nationality is an essential part of the soul, he has made a choice to construct his Cuban soul with sugar-coated memories, thereby revealing the nostalgia that permeates his life.

Medina's *recuerdos azucarados* begin with his description of his grandfather's sugar plantation, La Luisa, where he spent his summers. Located in Matanzas, a province where "endless fields of sugarcane . . . simmer in the sun like green fire" (Medina 1990: 5), the plantation was Medina's version of Eden, a place "of learning and experience, the crucible where humans and nature blended, where sweat gave forth fruit" (p. 7). Summer days spent at the farm began with a cup of fresh Cuban coffee, made from beans grown in the garden and sweetened with raw sugar, "a drink excelled by few" and "a nectar the gods would envy" (pp. 8–9). Such images from his childhood continue to sweeten Medina's interpretation of the past as a world in which the bitterness of exile was unknown.

* * *

But being Cuban still defines my life. Cuba is where I was born. It is where my mother ate, drank, breathed, listened to music, and felt the mist of the Malecón, cool and salty as it blew off the ocean, while she was carrying me.

—*Marta Elena Acosta Stone, "Understanding del Casal"*

* * *

The *recuerdos azucarados* continue in Medina's description of Havana, where he spent the rest of the year. His descriptions of Cuba's capital both reflect his *cubanía* and evoke the sense of nostalgia that permeates his life. "The Havana of my childhood," he writes, "is the most beautiful city I have ever known" (p. 39), and later he writes that "it was Havana that made me love all cities. It is Havana to which I compare them and always find them lacking" (p. 44). He recalls Sunday afternoons spent on the Malecón, a wide boulevard by the sea lined with stalls selling foods and drinks of all kinds: "*fritas, papas rellenas, empanadas, pasteles, pan con lechón, guarapo,* papaya juice, mango juice, and the oranges peeled and cut the way you wanted" (p. 39).

Once again, Medina's idealized childhood memories are associated with sensory details of sweetness. This *recuerdo azucarado* reveals the extent to which memories of sugar pervade the consciousness of Cuban exiles. For Medina's repeated references to sugar reflect an emotion deeper than nostalgia: They reflect the desire of exiles literally to taste the sugar of the island once more. In a sense, such details reveal the desire of Cuban exiles to taste *guarapo* (sugarcane juice) one more time along the Malecón. They long to return to a world in which one does not have to choose to cultivate *la cubanía,* a world in which the Cuban spirit is a daily reality, a spirit seen in families taking a Sunday stroll on the Malecón and tasted in the *pan con lechón, pasteles,* and papaya juice.

But to experience *la cubanía* through the taste of Cuba's sugar is not an option for those exiles who choose not to return to the island. Aware that the Cuba of their childhoods exists in memory only, many exiles prefer to preserve their idealized memories of the city before the revolution. Perhaps if they did return and taste *guarapo* along the Malecón, it would not be as sweet as they remember. Like Medina, many exiles prefer to relive their childhoods in memory only: "I harken back to my boyhood with its images of streets, buildings, statues, parks, people, and the sky blue sea that caressed and brutalized them and wonder how the city of my birth has changed since I left, whether the stories of its decline are true—if I will ever return" (p. 44).

In Medina's idealized memories, the buildings of Havana are beautiful and the coffee is as sweet as ever. Although such nostalgic memories enable him to remember the sugar of his childhood, the act of remembering can never replace the taste of sugar itself.

* * *

There was always a feeling of loss—something akin to the idea of losing Eden. It's a notion that many Cubans still hang on to, reflecting their impulse to idealize and functioning as a kind of defense mechanism that offsets reality.

—*Carlos Alberto Alvaré, "Losing Eden"*

* * *

Although many of Medina's *recuerdos azucarados* are idealized versions of the *cubanía* for which he longs, they also reveal a darker aspect of the sugar industry in prerevolutionary Cuba. Despite the idyllic depiction of La Luisa, Medina hints at a darker vision of the plantation when he describes the social hierarchy of the workers, who lived in conditions of extreme poverty. He thus avoids the trap of nostalgia by exploring the economic implications of sugar. No longer an innocent, naive child, Medina is now able to realize that "isolated, primitive, feudal La Luisa was destined for sudden death," a realization enabled by his increased social awareness (pp. 12–13).

The realistic description of the plantation reveals a disturbing aspect of *la cubanía*: the exploitation of sugar workers. Although his grandfather paid the workers well and provided them with housing, the men "worked like dogs" (p. 10). As Medina grew older, he writes, "I tried to reject men like my grandfather because they represented the exploitation of the poor and downtrodden" (p. 10). Even though his grandfather ensured that no one went hungry, poverty was ubiquitous. Workers lived in huts with dirt floors, their children often went naked, and sanitary conditions were poor, making disease and death commonplace. His grandfather may have tried to be benevolent, but the fact remains that he prospered through exploiting his workers.

Through his analysis of prerevolutionary social conditions, Medina reveals a social conscience developed in exile that has influenced his reflections on *la cubanía*. Although many Cuban exiles continue to idealize prerevolutionary Cuba, his newly developed sense of social awareness has led him to explore Cuba's social problems, uncovering an aspect of *la cubanía* that is often ignored by white, middle-class Cubans: the economic exploitation of sugar workers. This exploration reveals that contrary to the idealized memories of many Cuban Americans, prerevolutionary Cuba was not a paradise. As a young, naive, middle-class boy, he may not have comprehended the seriousness of his country's problems, but as an adult writing from the perspective of exile he is now able to understand the reasons for the revolution.

Medina's juxtaposition of idealized memories and social reality is the major source of tension in his reflections on the Cuban spirit. By confronting the causes of the revolution, he deflates his own nostalgia, again revealing that his sense of *cubanía* is constructed. His willingness to reflect on his privileged position is an indication that he has chosen to construct his own version of *la cubanía* with a sense of social awareness. This supports my belief that the Cuban spirit cannot be maintained in exile exactly as it used to be, for it is constantly transformed by experiences in the new country. As much as Medina longs to return to the Cuban spirit of his privileged childhood and to taste the island's sugar once more, he does not wish to return to the hierarchy of La Luisa. Ultimately, the preservation of memories could not satisfy Medina's desire for *azúcar*. This is the predicament of Cuban exiles everywhere: Although the Cuban spirit survives in memories, memories will never replace the taste of sugar itself.

Keeping this in mind, Medina's decision to return to Cuba in 1999 is understandable, a trip he describes in the 2002 edition of his memoir. As Rigoberto González writes in his review of the second edition of *Exiled Memories*, "the bittersweet homecoming is a moving account of the adult Medina becoming reconciled to the 'ravages of time and politics,' entering Cuba more like a foreigner and a tourist than a long-lost son" (González 2002: 2). As strong as Medina's desire to be Cuban may be, his inability to feel "at home" during his return trip reveals that his desire may never be fulfilled. That is the disturbing reality of exile, yet at least Medina can always be Cuban on the page.

* * *

For all practical, legal purposes, I am indeed an American. Yet I've just presented—defined—myself as Cuban; not even Cuban-American, but Cuban. How can I claim to be from a place I haven't seen since childhood? Because I still dream about my hometown.

—*Elías Miguel Muñóz, "Flags and Rags"*

* * *

Next Year in Cuba: A Cubano's Coming of Age in America

Gustavo Pérez Firmat

Whereas *Exiled Memories* uses sugar to convey the desire to recapture the Cuban spirit, Gustavo Pérez Firmat's *Next Year in Cuba* relies on dreams of Cuba, both collective and personal, to express *la cubanía* on the page. Despite decades of exile, Pérez Firmat believes that *la cubanía* is reflected in the Cuban American exile community's dream of returning to Cuba and in his own recurring dream of the Cuban boy he used to be. He thus reveals a major psychological conflict of Cuban Americans in exile: that between the acceptance of the United States as home and the elusive desire to return to Cuba, a conflict intensified by his description of America as a place and Cuba as a dream.

Because he is a member of the "1.5" generation (born in Cuba but raised in the United States), Pérez Firmat believes that he is able to choose his cultural habitat: He can choose either to cultivate *cubanía* or to develop his American identity. To illustrate the psychological conflict experienced by Cuban Americans of his generation, he describes two different places, each of which, he writes, "contains a part of me" (Pérez Firmat 1995b: 2).

The first place is a Durham Bulls baseball game in North Carolina, where Pérez Firmat has lived longer than he has in either Havana or Miami. Sitting next to his two children, drinking beer, he belts out the national anthem and enjoys the game, feeling "rooted, in my place" (p. 8). His decision to signify America in terms of a baseball game in North Carolina reveals how far removed from Cuba he is. When he left Cuba in 1960, he expected the move to be temporary; like most Cubans in exile, he believed that Fidel would soon fall.

Never did he imagine that thirty years later, he would still be in the United States and would know the words to the U.S. national anthem.

The feeling of being at home is only momentary, however, for then the questions of self-doubt begin: "But how is this possible? How can I feel at home in North Carolina, given my heritage? Is my feeling the result of a part I'm playing, or a part of who I am? A pose or an identity?" (p. 8). Despite his doubts, however, Pérez Firmat realizes that after three decades of life in the United States, he will never be able fully to relinquish his allegiance to America. His life is now in the United States—through his job as a professor at Duke University, his American wife from New Jersey, and his children who barely speak Spanish—but *cubanía* will always remain a vital aspect of his identity. This creates a conflict between his desire to be Cuban and his desire to be American, a conflict intensified by the fact that he can evoke Cuba only as a dream. Thus while Pérez Firmat signifies America as a place—with baseball, beer, and the national anthem—he evokes Cuba through collective and personal dreams, for, like many members of the Cuban exile community in Miami, he refuses to return to Cuba as long as Castro remains in power.

The evocation of Cuba as a dream is evident in his description of the second place that reveals his psychological conflict: a concert in Miami, just a few weeks after the baseball game in North Carolina, at which Pérez Firmat is "screaming and dreaming in Cuban" (p. 8). At the end of Willie Chirino's performance of "Nuestro día ya viene llegando," the audience erupts into shouts of "¡Cuba libre!" Because the Soviet Union has fallen just a few weeks ago, Cuban exiles in Miami believe that the end of Castro's dictatorship is near. In the words of Chirino, these exiles believe that "our day is already arriving": the day that Fidel falls. For more than thirty years they have waited, dreaming of the day when they can return to their homes, and now that dream may become a reality.

The thousands of Cubans in the audience are in a frenzy, waving Cuban flags and jamming thirty years of waiting into the two syllables of the Spanish word for free (*libre*). As Pérez Firmat writes, "for Americans, *Cuba Libre* may be no more than the name of a cocktail, but for Cuban exiles it's a dream too long deferred, the story of our lives" (p. 5). In a sense, this scene is the essence of *la cubanía* in exile, for even after thirty years of life in the United States, the love for Cuba and the desire for an elusive freedom have not diminished in the community.

Despite the passage of time and the physical separation from Cuba, *la cubanía* survives in the exile community as a collective dream of returning to the island. Some exiles thus choose to live in a cocoon of dreams in which time has stopped; instead of embracing the pleasures of bicultural identity, they dream of their prerevolutionary past and fantasize about their futures in a

Cuba libre. But although the dream of return may nourish the spiritual needs of exiles who long to maintain connections with their homeland, living in a world of past memories and future dreams prevents their appreciation of the present place, a psychological tension evident throughout Pérez Firmat's memoir. Miami's collective dream of *cubanía* may dull the pain of exile, but it is an avoidance of the possibility that the dream of a *Cuba libre* may never be fulfilled.

* * *

At the stroke of midnight, as we drank our cidra, *ate the traditional twelve grapes, and listened to the Cuban anthem on La Cubanísima, she offered the adamant toast, "el próximo año en la Habana," followed a few seconds later by a humble "si Dios quiere."*

—Maria Cristina García, "Abuí"

* * *

Pérez Firmat's deep and pervading sense of *cubanía* is evident in his reaction to the concert. Emerging from Chirino's performance, he is ready to buy a one-way ticket to Cuba. Caught up in the mood of the moment, he believes he will finally be able to recover the life he lost as a child. For a short while, he shares the collective dream of the Miami diaspora to return to Cuba; the shouts of *Cuba libre* have intensified his desire to return to his homeland. Yet although the temptation to return remains strong, he acknowledges, "no tengo regreso" (I cannot return) because returning to Cuba would be tantamount to going into exile a second time (p. 9). He realizes that a return may not be feasible because he would have to renounce his American citizenship and start over once again, yet then he wonders if "perhaps Cuba is where I finally belong, the only place where a one-and-a-halfer's fractional existence can be made whole" (p. 10). Questions race through his mind: Will returning to Cuba make him feel complete? Is it possible to return to the *cubanía* of his childhood?

He tries to convince himself that perhaps it is possible to return and recover lost *cubanía*; after all, *regreso* has been Miami's "magical, monotonous mantra" for more than three decades. Every Christmas Eve since 1960, Pérez Firmat has heard the toast "El año que viene en Cuba," the Cuban version of the Jewish promise "next year in Jerusalem." His relation of this Cuban Christmas Eve toast to the Jewish Passover promise is significant because just as Jerusalem is the focus of hopes and aspirations for Jews around the world, Cuba remains the focus of Cuban American dreams. "Next year in Cuba," however, is a promise that ultimately Pérez Firmat does not intend to keep. Although he writes that "Cuba remains my true home, the place that decisively shaped my character and my values" (p. 2), he realizes that he can no longer imagine himself living outside American culture or leaving behind the life he has built in this country.

Thus, for this author, cultivating *cubanía* is not a matter of dreaming of the day he will return to Cuba. Not only does he ultimately reject the idea of ever returning permanently to Cuba, but he also rejects the possibility of visiting Communist Cuba. Although many members of his generation have returned to Cuba, including his own brother, Pérez Firmat refuses: "I have refused to go back not just because I don't want to help Fidel out with my dollars, but primarily because I'd find it intolerable to visit places that once belonged to us, that were taken from my parents and my family" (p. 36). His brother Pepe, however, has returned three times and visited the family home, now occupied by another Cuban family. Pérez Firmat writes that he would never be able to retain his sense of composure if he did visit the house, for he regards its current occupants as "usurpers" (p. 37).

The feeling of rage that prevents him from following in his brother's footsteps creates yet another source of tension. As much as he may desire to return, Pérez Firmat realizes that his Cuban journey, the expression of his own sense of *cubanía*, can take place only in his dreams. This realization is the major source of psychological tension in his memoir, for if his journey takes place only in his dreams, then ultimately it leads nowhere.

*   *   *

All human beings are, in a sense, outcasts from a perfect place of which we have vague, ancestral memories but to which we cannot seem to return.

 —*Marta Elena Acosta Stone, "Understanding del Casal"*

*   *   *

If dreams are a window to unconscious desires, then Pérez Firmat's recurring dreams about the Cuban boy he used to be are a reflection of his deep desire to recapture the *cubanía* of his childhood. He writes about a recurring dream in which he envisions himself leaving Cuba on a ferry, slowly lurching away from the pier. When he looks back, he sees a small boy waving back at him: "I realize that this boy on the dock is me . . . the Cuban boy I was, the Cuban boy I am no longer" (p. 21). Writing about this recurring dream, Pérez Firmat realizes that he longs to reconnect with the Cuban boy he left behind and recover his lost sense of *cubanía*.

Pérez Firmat's separation from Cuba at such a crucial age in the process of identity formation has resulted in a sense of self-fragmentation. Because exiles abandon not only their possessions but also pieces of themselves, Pérez Firmat considers exiles to be amputees: "Just as people who lose limbs sometimes continue to ache or tingle in the missing calf or hand, the exile suffers the absence of the self he left behind" (p. 22). Therefore, he mourns the loss of the Cuban boy he was: "He's my phantom limb. . . . I need to bring him out of the shadows. I need to grow him back" (p. 22). For years, Pérez Firmat put Cuba out of his mind because the memories of leaving were simply too bitter to remember. "For most of the last thirty years," he writes, "I've done without my Cuban childhood. . . . I have placed an embargo on my Cuban memories" (p. 35). Now that he has reached middle age, however, he realizes the importance of reconnecting with the Cuban boy he left behind as he continues his process of self-construction. This boy represents his need to express the Cuban spirit while he constructs his Cuban American self in exile. If psychoanalytic theorists are correct that the self is "a dimension of subjectivity which is made in fantastic form, constituted through the unconscious operations of desire itself" (Elliott 1994: 6), then perhaps Pérez Firmat is constructing his self through dreams of the Cuban boy he used to be. In a sense, his *cubanía* is a metaphor for the self, constructed through desire. Although his sense of *cubanía* will continue to shift as he continues his process of identity construction, this boy will enable him to maintain his desired connection with his past.

Regaining a connection with his homeland through his dreams will thus enable Pérez Firmat to overcome the anguish of exile. As Michael Dash writes, "the end of exile, the triumph over the estranging sea, is only possible when the subject feels his or her bonds with the lost body of the native land" (Dash 1995: 332). To establish these bonds with Cuba, Pérez Firmat realizes that he does not have to return physically to the island; he simply has to lift the embargo on his Cuban memories and allow himself to dream. Yet because he adamantly refuses to return to Cuba, his Cuban journey ultimately leads nowhere, for it begins and ends in his own world of dreams. Just as memories cannot replace the taste of sugar, dreams of Cuba will never compensate for the island itself.

* * *

I live in between two worlds, like a photograph that is always developing, never finishing, always in transition or perhaps translation, between past and present, English and Spanish, Cuba and the United States, the invisible and the visible, truths and lies.

—María de los Angeles Lemus, "Stories My Mother Never Told Me"

* * *

Bridges to Cuba/Puentes a Cuba

Ruth Behar, editor

Edited by Ruth Behar, the anthology *Bridges to Cuba* deals with complex issues of cultural identity as Cuban American authors attempt to understand the cultural implications of *la cubanía* in exile. After years away from Cuba, these authors seek to understand how the Cuban spirit affects the construction of their cultural identities in exile. This quest, motivated by the desire to be Cuban, often leads Cuban American authors—including Behar and several of her contributors, among them Ester Rebeca Shapiro Rok and Eliana Rivero—to return to Cuba. All three women—Behar, Shapiro Rok, and Rivero—have crossed the bridge back to Cuba and found that the return is a crucial step in the formation of a cultural identity in exile, for it enables a deeper appreciation of *la cubanía*. Unlike Pérez Firmat, these women no longer view their identity as fragmented. Rather, they believe it is possible to weave the fragments into a fluid, coherent whole that emanates *cubanía* at all times, regardless of where they live.

* * *

Cuba is a peculiar exile. . . . We can reach it by a thirty-minute charter flight from Miami, yet never reach it at all.

—Cristina García, Dreaming in Cuba

* * *

As editor of *Bridges to Cuba*, Behar explores her own questions of cultural identity and the importance of *cubanía* in her life. Born in Cuba in 1956, Behar left the island in 1962 and is therefore a member of the second generation of exiles, those Cuban Americans who have few or no memories of the island. As a Cuban Jew growing up in the United States, she has often been questioned about the authenticity of her Cubanness: "How could I, being Jewish, claim to be Cuban? Wasn't my Cuban identity nothing more than an accident of history, another stop in a Jewish diaspora? It wasn't deep, it wasn't in my blood, the Cubanness, so who was I fooling?" (Behar 1995: 6). Despite her doubts, Behar maintained a mixture of Jewish and Cuban traditions growing up in New York: "We'd eat matzoh for a week during Passover then go with El Grupo to eat black beans, rice, fried plantains, and palomilla steak at La Rumba Restaurant" (p. 6). Because Cuba represented "nostalgia, a paradise lost" in the minds of her parents' generation, Behar was taught that "we had burnt the bridge back and were not to look behind, lest we turn into pillars of salt" (p. 6).

Once she came of age, however, Behar increasingly felt the need to look behind and build a new bridge to recover her desire to be Cuban: "Like other

Cuban Americans of the second generation who left the island as children . . . I longed to return to Cuba and see the island with my own eyes" (p. 6). Unlike many members of the first and "1.5" generations, who prefer to preserve their idealized memories, members of the second generation are often more willing to return to answer their questions of cultural identity. So Behar decided to return to the island in 1979 with a group of students and professors from Princeton. She enjoyed her trip, but after she returned to the United States conservative Cuban exiles nearly convinced her that that her desire to create a link with Cuba was foolish. As a result, she did not return to Cuba again until 1991. That trip inspired her to research the careers of other Cuban American scholars who had previously attempted to build cultural bridges to the island. In the process, she began to understand that building bridges to Cuba is a crucial aspect of the quest for cultural identity, a quest which enables the recovery of the desire to be Cuban. Since then, she has made several return trips, motivated not only by her need to validate her Jewish-Cuban identity, but also by her academic passion to build cultural bridges through such projects as this anthology.

For Behar, therefore, the cultivation of her own sense of *cubanía* in exile is achieved through her academic work. Despite her earlier doubts about the validity of her Cubanness, her work reflects her need to maintain ties with the island. Through this anthology, Behar reveals that bridges to Cuba are not only a means of reconciliation, but also of recubanization, a way to recover the key component of *cubanía*: the desire to be Cuban. After years of efforts to reject the longing she felt for the island of her birth, Behar's decision to return allowed her to embrace fully her deep desire to be Cuban.

* * *

While for years I felt that I had neatly put away pieces of my identity in different parts of the world, I now understand that I do not have to accept categories which split who I am. Instead I must construct new categories, new political and emotional spaces in which my multiple identities can be joined. Returning has been part of this healing journey.

—María de los Angeles Torres, "Beyond the Rupture: Reconciling with Our Enemies, Reconciling with Ourselves"

* * *

The decision to recross the bridge to Cuba in search of lost *cubanía* is often preceded by recurrent dreaming in Cuban, as Ester Rebeca Shapiro Rok writes in "Finding What Had Been Lost in Plain View." Shapiro Rok left Cuba in 1960 at the age of eight, a traumatic event that caused her to experience recurrent dreams of the island during her adolescence. In those dreams, she struggled to maintain her balance on a bridge. Just as she was about to cross, the ground beneath her would shift, preventing her from reaching the other side. Working as a psychologist years later, she realized that the place beckoning her on the other side was Cuba, within view but unreachable, due to her fragmented sense of identity.

Like Behar, Shapiro Rok doubted her *cubanía* due to her Jewish identity: "For many unexamined years I considered my Cuban identity an exotic appendage to my true Jewish American self" (Shapiro Rok 1995: 87). Yet despite her doubts, Shapiro Rok's childhood dreams reflect her deep and pervading sense of *cubanía*. Although she often experienced a sense of longing for Cuba as a young girl, she writes, "My private longings went underground" because "in our family psyche, leaving and losing Cuba was unremarkable in many lifetimes of diaspora" (pp. 90–91). She struggled inwardly with the conflict between her personal attachment to Cuba and her family loyalties: "After all, where do we belong as Jews if not in Eretz Yisrael, the land of Israel?" (p. 91).

Despite her family's objections, in 1990 Shapiro Rok decided to cross the bridge back to Cuba in order to answer her questions of identity and to satisfy her longing for the island. This trip confirmed her own sense of *cubanía* and allowed her to begin to understand the multiple strands of her Cuban Jewish Eastern European American identity. Thus began "a slow and profoundly meaningful process of weaving one whole life out of the fractured fragments of immigration" (p. 92), a process that began with dreams of bridges. Yet what finally allowed Shapiro Rok to weave the fragments of her multiple identities into a coherent whole was not dreaming of bridges, but building them by actually returning to the island. In the process, she has not only accepted her multiple identities but also satisfied her intense longing to be Cuban.

Returning to Cuba allowed Shapiro Rok to find "what had been lost in plain view": her personal sense of *cubanía*. As her decision to embrace her Cubanness shows, the cultivation of this spirit in exile is a choice. Shapiro Rok may have doubted her Cubanness for years due to her Jewish identity, but her decision to build bridges has enabled her to express the Cuban spirit in exile. While she never made it to the other side of the precarious, swinging bridge in her adolescent dreams, in reality she has crossed the bridge, regained her balance, and most important, cultivated her spirit.

*   *   *

The exile's return does not bring closure to the conflicts of identity, but it does heal the pain of fragmentation. For me, writing about leaving Cuba, assimilating to U.S. culture and forging my own place within it, and returning to Cuba has been, and continues to be, a difficult process. "No es fácil," the Cubans from Cuba would say. Thomas Wolfe had it right:

"You can't go home again." But perhaps trying to do so, even on the blank space of a computer screen, is good enough.

—Gabriella Ibieta, *"Fragmented Memories: An Exile's Return"*

* * *

While Behar focuses on building bridges and Shapiro Rok on weaving the fragments of identity, Eliana Rivero looks at borders in her essay "'*Fronterisleña*,' Border Islander" to examine issues of *la cubanía* in exile. She begins the essay by remembering a day in the summer of 1979, just after she had gotten back from her first return trip to Cuba, as she gazed out her window in Arizona across the border to Mexico: "Here I was, Cuban to the souls [*sic*] of my feet, with a couple of bottles of Havana Club rum in my cupboard and some black beans bubbling on the stove, looking at the northernmost reaches of Latin America from a border town in which I felt out of sorts, at the margins of life. . . . I was literally looking at life from *la margen* (the bank, the shore; Rivero 1995: 339).

Rivero uses the feminine form of "margin" in Spanish to suggest the ebb and flow of tides, as opposed to *los márgenes*, the border of words on a page. *Las márgenes*, however, are loose and imprecise, the line where land meets water, an image Rivero uses to evoke the space of her original identity, the coastline of Cuba. Her desire to assimilate, however, made her reject this coastline for many years prior to her return.

Eighteen years after leaving the island at the age of nineteen, Rivero returned to Cuba in 1979. The trip had a profound effect on her construction of self; it was "a journey to my roots, which I had suppressed for a long time" (p. 341). During the 1960s, Rivero underwent a process of "decubanization" in moving from Miami to Arizona, and she felt that a return to Cuba was necessary to reclaim her Cuban identity: "Over the last decade I have fully traveled the road back to 'recubanization' . . . a full-fledged affirmation . . . of Cubanness" (p. 343).

Rivero's recubanization has enabled her to celebrate life on *las márgenes*. The anxiety she experienced on her first return from Cuba—of being a Cuban woman in the United States, living in a border town—has been replaced by a sense of wholeness. Rivero may be Cuban by origin and culture, but she has lived outside of Cuba most of her life. She therefore considers herself "a hybrid, a *puente* [bridge], a being of two places at once, but also of one place which is dual and fluid and rich" (p. 343). This sense of wholeness despite exile is possible because, she realizes, "soy lo que soy donde estoy" (I am what I am wherever I am; p. 343). In the words of Gloria Anzaldúa, Rivero has become a "moldeadora de su alma" (a shaper of her soul): "Según la concepción que tiene de sí misma, así será" (According to the conception she has of herself, such will she be; Anzaldúa 1999: 105). Rivero's self-conception reflects not only her acceptance of her hybridity, but also her deep desire to be Cuban no matter where she lives. By choosing to embrace the Cuban spirit, Rivero has reshaped her own soul, a process that began when she decided to return to the island.

Rivero's ability to redefine her cultural identity reflects my belief that identity is a matter of desire; it is a creation of the self that constantly evolves. Just like *las márgenes* of an island, identity is fluid. This fluidity enables the cultural cultivation of *la cubanía* in exile. Away from the island, Cuban exiles must choose to express the spirit of their homeland as they redefine themselves, for they are in charge of the "production" of their cultural identities (Hall 2000). The effect of the fluidity of identity on the cultivation of *cubanía* in exile is evident in Rivero's ability to redefine herself. Although the separation from Cuba is painful, she realizes that the ability to redefine her cultural identity is a privilege. Through her words, Rivero has overcome the dislocation of exile. By embracing the positive aspects of bicultural identity, she has achieved a sense of wholeness. She accepts the "porous borders" of her islander identity and realizes that they are made "more penetrable by the sand particles . . . of the desert where I live" (Rivero 1995: 343–44). No matter where Rivero lives, even in the desert of Arizona, she realizes that she will always be Cuban in spirit. She is truly a "border islander," for her borders are loose and imprecise and reflect the ebb and flow of tides, the coastline of her soul. Unlike *los márgenes* of politics, *las márgenes* of identity are fluid, allowing *la cubanía* to float across all political and geographical borders.

Alma Cubana/Cuban Soul

As Behar, Shapiro Rok, and Rivero demonstrate, bridges to Cuba are a means of recubanization, for they enable the recovery of the desire to be Cuban. Although Rivero believes that one can be Cuban wherever one is, she recognizes that a return to the island may be a necessary step for some Cuban Americans to express *la cubanía* after years of exile. Returning to Cuba has enabled these women to weave the fragments of their identities into a coherent whole, in contrast to those exiles who possess fragmented senses of identity. Perhaps if they followed in the footsteps of those Cuban Americans who chose to return, these exiles would be able to reconcile their Cuban childhoods and American adulthoods, as have Behar, Shapiro Rok, and Rivero. Unlike those exiles trapped in a world of nostalgia and bitterness, these three women are not content to dream of "next year in Cuba." Instead of dreaming of the day Fidel dies, they have chosen to return and build bridges, beginning a healing process that enables them to create the Cuban spirit within themselves.

Yet bridge building does not necessarily end the desire to dream in Cuban.

In a sense, all Cuban Americans who choose to express *la cubanía* in exile, regardless of whether they have returned or not, continue to dream of the island. For it is these dreams that enable authors to reflect *la cubanía* on the page. If indeed the desire to be Cuban can never be fully realized, then "dreaming in Cuban" will continue to inspire Cuban American literature of exile.

Of the many ways to express *la cubanía* in exile, I believe that literature is one of the most essential, for it is not only a way to preserve memories and collective dreams, but also a type of cultural bridge. In a sense, Cuban American literature of exile can be a bridge between Cubans on and off the island, as *Bridges to Cuba* demonstrates. In addition, this literature can serve as a bridge between generations of Cuban Americans. Although I never personally experienced separation from my homeland, reading Cuban American literature has enabled me to understand the traumatic experience of exile. These works have revealed to me the personal consequences of 1959 on a deeper, more emotional level than any history text could offer.

More important, these texts have enabled me to dream in Cuban. I am now able to dream of the sugarcane in Matanzas, *Nochebuena* (Christmas Eve) in Havana, and Sundays on the Malecón. My dreams, however, are the result of more than reading Cuban American literature, for that is only one aspect of the process of my recubanization. Although I am able to experience a vicarious Cuban childhood and Miami adolescence through the words of Medina and Pérez Firmat, their words cannot convey to me the taste of *guarapo*, the smell of tobacco, and the sounds of a cha-cha-chá. Words, like dreams, cannot substitute for the place itself.

Returning to the poem by Pérez Firmat, "Cubanita descubanizada," I would like to expand my answer to the question he poses. In addition to the study of Cuban American literature of exile, I believe that my "return" to Cuba was a necessary step in my recubanization. The real awakening of my Cuban spirit did not occur until I decided to create my own bridge to Cuba, thereby experiencing the reality of what had been a mythical homeland. I needed to move beyond my family's black-and-white photos to see the island in color, with my own eyes. No longer did I want to rely solely on my family's memories; I needed to make my own. So in the summer of 1999, I traveled to Cuba to take a class on Cuban culture and history at the University of Havana, becoming the first in my family to see the island in almost forty years.

Most of my family, including fifty-four of my grandfather's fifty-five first cousins, left Cuba after the revolution. During my trip I had a chance to meet the one who remained, Bebito. As he sat in his rocking chair by the window, I spent hours listening to his stories about the DeRojas family. Before leaving, I recorded a video message from Bebito for my grandfather: "A pesar de todo lo que nos separa, te quiero" (Despite all that separates us, I love you). Through conveying his message to my grandfather, I became a bridge for my family, divided by four decades of exile. A few months after I left, Bebito died at the age of ninety. I think of him often—his smile, his laugh, his stories—memories enabled by my journey.

Bebito's words reveal an important aspect of *la cubanía*: No matter where Cubans live, no matter what ideology they believe in, they are united by a desire to be Cuban, a desire that transcends all political and physical boundaries. Being Cuban is not a matter of living in Cuba, as my own recubanization reveals. Although I am an American citizen, I am Cuban in spirit. In this light, my own sense of identity is clearly transnational, for it is based on the fluidity of desire. Due to the fact that my father was born in Cuba, I have always been Cuban by blood. Yet I believe that desire, not blood, is the most important factor in *la cubanía*. I possess this desire, and so I consider myself Cuban both by blood and in spirit. I recognize, however, that my desire to be Cuban will never be fully realized as long as some people believe that one must be born on the island in order to be Cuban.

Therefore, my journey of recubanization is never-ending as I strive to convince others of my Cubanness. Like *las márgenes* of an island, my Cuban spirit is fluid and constantly shifting as I construct my ever-changing identity in exile. Like all Cuban Americans who desire to cultivate *cubanía*, I am the shaper of my own Cuban soul, *mi alma cubana*.

Like Behar, Shapiro Rok, and Rivero, I have chosen to shape my soul by returning to the island. In a sense, my own journey reflects the journey of Pilar Puente in Cristina García's *Dreaming in Cuban*. A Cuban American who returns to the island at the age of twenty-one, Pilar experiences the reawakening of her own *cubanía* in Cuba: "I've started dreaming in Spanish, which has never happened before. I wake up feeling different, like something inside me is changing, something chemical and irreversible. There's a magic here working its way through my veins" (García 1992: 235).

The magic in Pilar's veins is *cubanía*, a spirit awakened by her decision to recross the bridge to Cuba. In fact, Pilar's last name, Puente, means "bridge" in Spanish. Like Pilar, I have built a bridge between the island of my roots and the country of my birth, and doing so has enabled me to feel the magic in my own veins. This magic has in turn inspired me to express my journey through words. Six months after returning from my first trip, I traveled to Cuba once again for the inaugural U.S.-Cuba Writers' Conference, where I had the opportunity to meet Cristina García. This conference marked the beginning of my dream one day to publish a book of nonfiction essays in which I combine my family's memories of prerevolutionary Cuba with my own experiences in Communist Cuba.

I often think about the significance of my name, Alma, which means "soul" in Spanish. With every word I write, I try to express *mi alma cubana*, and although it may be difficult to capture a soul in words, this is my passion. I truly believe that my soul is Cuban, a creation of myself enabled by my desire to explore my heritage, my longing to "return" to the island, and my choice to cultivate *la cubanía* in exile. In my essays I seek to capture this spirit awakened through the power of words, dreams, and bridges. Through the process of recubanization, I have begun to dream in Cuban, and with my dreams, I will build bridges of words between the spirit and the page.

Notes

1. Translations by author.

Bibliography

Álvarez Borland, Isabel. 1998. *Cuban-American Literature of Exile: From Person to Persona*. Charlottesville: University Press of Virginia.

Anzaldúa, Gloria. 1999. *Borderlands/La Frontera: The New Mestiza*. 2nd ed. San Francisco: Aunt Lute Books.

Behar, Ruth, ed. 1995. *Bridges to Cuba/Puentes a Cuba*. Ann Arbor: University of Michigan Press.

Belleli, Guglielmo, and Mirella Amatulli. 1997. "Nostalgia, Immigration, and Collective Memory." In *Collective Memory of Political Events*, edited by James W. Pennebaker et al., 209–20. Mahwah, N.J.: Lawrence Erlbaum Associates.

Dash, Michael. 1995. "In Search of the Lost Body: Redefining the Subject in Caribbean Literature." In *The Post-Colonial Studies Reader,* edited by Bill Ashcroft, Gareth Griffiths, and Helen Tiffin, 332–35. New York: Routledge.

Duany, Jorge. 1997. *From the Cuban Ajiaco to the Cuban-American Hyphen*. Cuban Studies Association Occasional Papers Series 2, no. 8 (October 15). Miami: Cuban Studies Association.

———. 2000. "Reconstructing Cubanness: Changing Discourses of National Identity on the Island and in the Diaspora during the Twentieth Century." In *Cuba, the Elusive Nation: Interpretations of National Identity,* edited by Damián J. Fernández and Madeline Cámara Betancourt, 17–42. Gainesville: University Press of Florida.

Elliott, Anthony. 1994. *Psychoanalytic Theory: An Introduction*. Cambridge: Blackwell.

Fernández, Damián J. 2000. "Cuba and *lo Cubano*, or the Story of Desire and Disenchantment." In *Cuba, the Elusive Nation: Interpretations of National Identity*, edited by Damián J. Fernández and Madeline Cámara Betancourt, 79–99. Gainesville: University Press of Florida.

Fernández, Damián J., and Madeline Cámara Betancourt. 2000. "Interpretations of National Identity." In *Cuba, the Elusive Nation: Interpretations of National Identity*, edited by Damián J. Fernández and Madeline Cámara Betancourt, 1–13. Gainesville: University Press of Florida.

García, Cristina. 1992. *Dreaming in Cuban*. New York: Ballantine.

González, Rigoberto. 2002. "Pablo Medina's Classic Tale of Cuba's Past, Present Reissued." *El Paso Times* (3 November). <http://www.borderlandnews.com/stories/living/20021103-39140>. (Accessed September 2, 2004)

Hall, Stuart. 2000. "Cultural Identity and Diaspora." In *Diaspora and Visual Culture: Representing Africans and Jews*, edited by Nicholas Mirzoeff, 21–33. New York: Routledge.

Medina, Pablo. 1990. *Exiled Memories: A Cuban Childhood*. Austin: University of Texas Press.

O'Reilly Herrera, Andrea, ed. 2001. *ReMembering Cuba: Legacy of a Diaspora*. Austin: University of Texas Press.

Ortiz, Fernando. 1973. "Los factores humanos de la cubanidad." In *Orbita de Fernando Ortiz*, edited by Julio Le Riverend, 149–57. Havana: UNEAC. Reprint, 1940.

Pérez Firmat, Gustavo. 1989. *The Cuban Condition: Translation and Identity in Modern Cuban Literature*. New York: Cambridge University Press.

———. 1994. *Life on the Hyphen: The Cuban-American Way*. Austin: University of Texas Press.

———. 1995a. *Bilingual Blues: Poems 1981–1994*. Tempe, Ariz.: Bilingual Press/Editorial Bilingüe.

———. 1995b. *Next Year in Cuba: A Cubano's Coming of Age in America*. New York: Doubleday.

———. 1997. *A Willingness of the Heart: Cubanidad, Cubaneo, Cubanía*. Cuban Studies Association Occasional Paper Series 2, no. 7 (October 1). Miami: Cuban Studies Association.

Rama, Angel. 1997. "Literature and Exile." In *The Oxford Book of Latin American Essays*, edited by Ilan Stavans, 335–42. New York: Oxford University Press.

Rivero, Eliana. 1995. "'Fronterisleña,' Border Islander." In *Bridges to Cuba/Puentes a Cuba*, edited by Ruth Behar, 339–44. Ann Arbor: University of Michigan Press.

Shapiro Rok, Esther. 1995. "Finding What Had Been Lost in Plain View." In *Bridges to Cuba/Puentes a Cuba*, edited by Ruth Behar, 85–95. Ann Arbor: University of Michigan Press.

Contributors

Sarah A. Blue earned her Ph.D. in geography at the University of California, Los Angeles. Her article "State Policy, Economic Crisis, Gender and Family Ties: Determinants of Family Remittances to Cuba" was published in *Economic Geography* (January 2004).

Denise Blum is assistant professor at California State University at Fresno in the department of curriculum and instruction. She has coedited a special issue of *International Journal of Qualitative Studies in Education* (2001) entitled *Cuba: Revolution, Culture and Education*.

James Buckwalter-Arias is assistant professor in the modern languages department at Hanover College in Indiana. He is working on a book-length manuscript on post-Soviet Cuban literary narrative.

Alma DeRojas earned a master of arts degree in Latin American and Caribbean Studies at Florida International University (FIU). Currently she works as a coordinator for the Cuban Research Institute at FIU.

Jorge Duany is professor of anthropology at the University of Puerto Rico. His latest book is *The Puerto Rican Nation on the Move: Identities on the Island and in the United States* (2002).

Damián J. Fernández is director of the Cuban Research Institute and professor of international relations at Florida International University. He is the author of *Cuba and the Politics of Passion* (2000) and the coeditor of *Cuba, the Elusive Nation* (UPF, 2000).

Gisela Fosado works at the American Museum of Natural History in New York City with the Margaret Mead Film and Video Festival. She is currently editing a documentary examining sex tourism in Cuba.

Katrin Hansing is director of the South-South Collaboration Ties between Cuba and Africa research unit at the University of Bayreuth in Germany. Previously she was a postdoctoral fellow at the Immigration and Ethnicity Institute at Florida International University in Miami.

Lázaro Lima is assistant professor of Spanish and Latino studies at Bryn Mawr College. His published and forthcoming articles have or will appear in *The Wallace Stevens Journal*, *Dactylus*, *Journal of Early American Studies*, *Pedagogy*, and in the edited collection *American History through Literature* (2005).

Sarah J. Mahler is an associate professor of anthropology at Florida International University in Miami. Among her publications are *American Dreaming: Immigrant Life on the Margins* (1995) and "Transnational Migration: Bringing Gender In" in *International Migration Review* (2003), coauthored with Patricia Pessar.

Susan Thomas is an assistant professor of music and women's studies at the University of Georgia. Her recent research looks at contemporary Cuban music making as a transnational process, and focuses on musical communities in Havana, Madrid, and New York City.

Alan West-Durán has published two books of essays: *Tropics of History: Cuba Imagined* (1997) and *African-Caribbeans: A Reference Guide* (2003). He was the editor-in-chief of *Latino and Latina Writers* (2004) and has published two books of poems: *Dar nombres a la lluvia/Finding Voices in the Rain* (1995) and *El tejido de Asterión o las máscaras del logos* (2000).

Index

Abakuá, 130
Abjectification, 95
Academics. *See* Research
Aesthetic ideology, 154–55
Affective engagement with past, 98n.9
Affective life of locas, 91
Africa: diaspora, 121–22; liberation struggles in, 133
African American society, 133–34, 139
African cultures, 124
African music styles, 105, 108, 129–30
Afrocuba de Matanzas, 110
Afrocubanía, 146, 147
Afro-Cubanist movement, 106, 123, 125
Afro-Cuban music: dance, 115; jazz, 105, 123; rap, 124, 129–30
Afro-Cuban religions: majority of Cubans, 47; in music, 129–30, 144; relative purity of, 51; ritual economy, 2; *santeros,* 143, 144; Special Period, 130
Afro-Cubans: clubs and mutual aid societies, 133; in formal and informal economies, 73; history, 121–22; massacre (1912), 122; triangular culture, 123
Agencia Cubana de Rap (ACR), 147n.1
Agency, 53; by level of formality, 54; meso level, 55; structural analysis, 53–54
AIDS, 90, 98n.10
Airlifts (1965–1973), 26
Alfonso, Gerardo, 118
Allende, Salvador, 48
Ambiguity, 62–63, 75; tourists comfortable with, 70–71
Americanization, 187
American Life (Madonna), 170–71
America as a place, 192
Anagrama publishers, 161–62
Anthropology: private worlds and, 80–81; sex tourism and, 69–70
Anti-Communism: disidentifying, 87; evangelists, 50; first migrant cohort, 26
Apollo Theater, 121
Arenas, Reinaldo, 93, 162, 98n.11, 163n.2
Art, commodification of, 154

Art Bembé (2003), 118
Artistic genius, 155
Asia, 73
Athanai, 116, 118
Atheist state, 47, 49
Aurea mediocritas, 159
Authenticity, myth of, 182
Autobiographical act, 80
Aztlán, 86, 99n.15

"La Balada de los dos abuelos" (1975), 125–26
Balseros. See Rafter (*balsero*) experience
Barbería, Luis, 107, 117
Bay of Pigs invasion, 47
Bed-and-breakfasts, 31
Before Night Falls (2000), 98n.11
Behar, Ruth, 185, 196–200
Beret as symbol, 170–71
Bicultural identity, 192, 200
Black Atlantic, 121–22, 123, 144, 147
Black market commission system, 74–75
Black nationalism, 122
Blackness: invisibility, 129; redefining, 125, 145–46
Black Panthers, 133–34
Bolivia, 166, 177
Borders: importance, 45; *margen,* 199; transcending, 184–85
Bridge of Hope Cuba-Florida Covenant, 54
Bridges, cultural, 201
Bridges to Cuba/Puentes a Cuba (Behar, ed.), 185, 196–200
Buena Vista Social Club, 108, 117, 152
Buena Vista Socialization, 69
Bufos, 108–9
Bugarrón, 85, 94, 98–99n.13
Bush, George W.: axis of evil notion, 42; remittances restricted, 39n.7

Café Che Guevara, 171
Camacho, Juanito, 116
Camaján, use of term, 76n.5
Camarioca boatlift of 1965, 26

Capitalism, development of, 44
Capitalist culture industry, 154
Carcassés, Robertico, 118
Caridad del Cobre. *See* Virgin of Caridad del
  Cobre
Casa de las Américas, 151
Case studies, 25
Castillo, Nilo, 117
Castro, Fidel: allusion to, 159; on *conciencia*,
  177n.1; demise predicted, 191, 192; dissi-
  dents imprisoned, 42; visit to Chile, 48
Catholic Church, 47; financial aid, 50, 51; po-
  litical/religious ties, 56; social agenda of, 48
Censorship, 153
Cervantes, Ignacio, 106, 108
"Chan-Chan," 117
Changó, 129
Che image: in Cuba, 166, 167, 173;
  deconstructing, 176–77; famous photo,
  166–67; as iconic, 165, 166–67; ideological
  function, 167; leveling effect, 173; meaning
  of icon, 175; Neiman Marxistization of,
  172; redefinition, xvii–xviii; simulations,
  171–72. *See also* Guevara, Ernesto "Che"
Che restaurant chain, 171
Chez Guevara's, 171
Chicanos/Chicanas, 86, 181, 99n.15
Chile, 48
Chirino, Willie, 192
Choteo: politics of, 89; signifying, 135
Churches' Advertising Network (CAN), 173
CIA (Central Intelligence Agency), 38n.2
Cimarrón, 129, 144
Citizenship: abject, 85; dual, 13; stateless, 94
Civic education courses, 168
Civic spaces, religion and, 43
Civil rights movement, 133
Civil society: international relations, 43; rap
  music, 131
Clinton, Bill, 98n.10
Clinton administration immigration policy,
  99n.17
Cold War: détente, 26–27; fixed animosities,
  57; reincarnations, 42
Collazos, Oscar, 156
Collective memory, 189
Colonial era, 46
Commodification of Cuban life, 176
Commodity fetishism, 165

Communication: with relatives, 34; religion-
  based, 57
Community workers, queer, 88
Conciencia, 168, 177n.1
Consejo, Antonio, 144
Constructivism, xvi
Consumerism: Che's image, 169–73; criticized,
  138; family visits, 27; scarcities, 140
Contradanza, 105–6, 108
Correo de Cuba, 14
Cosmopolitanism in music, 105–7
Counterpublics, 88
"Cuando salí de la Habana nadie me
  despedí," 113
"Cuando salí de la Habana" (Ochoa), 110–14
Cuarta Imagen, 126, 128–29, 130
*Cuba: Merceditas Valdez y los tambores batá
  de Jesús Pérez*, 143–44
Cuba boom, 69
Cuba libre as unfulfilled goal, 184
Cuban Adjustment Act (1966), 2, 12, 18, 26;
  protections, 39n.5
Cuban Americans, 16; anti-emigré stance, 18;
  policies toward, 13, 14. *See also* Exiles
Cubanía: afrocubanía, 146, 147; being Cuban,
  202; bittersweet desire, 183; black-white
  union as symbol, 125–26; bridges to Cuba,
  197; capturing in words, 185; as collective
  dream, 192–93; cubanita descubanizada,
  179–80; as desire to be Cuban, 181–84,
  202; diaspora links to, 152; dreams, 191;
  in exile, 181–82, 192; five characteristics,
  181; fluidity of desire, 202; hegemony of
  feeling, 83–84; literature of exile, 180; as
  metaphor for self, 195; origins of term,
  180–81; Ortiz use of term, 180–81; politics
  of, 183; preserving, 187; rappers, 130;
  recurring dream, 194; return to childhood,
  193, 195; second-generation claims to,
  182–83, 185; social awareness and, 190;
  spirit cultivated, 198; taste of sugar, 189;
  transcending borders, 185
Cubanidad: abject, 94, 99n.14; in the academy, 95; after death, 94; as civil status,
  181; critical reflections on, 87; displaced
  geographies of, 86; as hip, 84; musical
  styles, 107, 118–19; as nostalgic commodity, 87; Ortiz on, 180–81; Pérez Firmat on,
  180; performances of nationalism, 83; po-

tential, 82; in the public sphere, 87; queer, 79–80, 88–91; raft as metaphor, 97n.4; South Beach, 84; transnational, 84
Cubanization, of churches, 48
Cuban Refugee Program, 26
Cuban Research Institute conference (2003), xiii–xiv, 2–3
Cuban Revolution, religion, 47
Cuban School in the Countryside program, 168
Cuban Union of Writers and Artists: Guillén heading, 126; symposium, 14
Cultural identity. *See* Identity
Cultural imperialism, 151
Cultural institutions, 152
Cultural memory, 80
Cultural studies, xiv
Culture, custodian of, 187
Czechoslovakia, 151

Dalton, Roque, 151
Danza, 105, 106
Death rites, 93–94
De la Nuez, Iván, 87–88
Del Risco, Enrique, 104, 115
Del Valle, Pepe, 116, 117
Department of Puerto Rican Community Affairs, 15
Desire, to be Cuban, 186
Development aid vs. remittances, 30
Diaspora, African, 121–22, 132
Diaspora: *balsero* experience, 81; collective dream, 193; geography and, 184–85; politics changing, 117; recovering *lo cubano,* 17
Diaspora relations: conferences, 14; normalizing, 14
Díaz, Jesús, 151, 152
Direct investment, 9
Discrimination, 133, 146
D'León, Oscar, 115
Doble Filo, 121
Dollar economy, 28, 31
Dollar income, 31t, 31
Dollar stores, 28–29, 38n.3
Dominican Republic: boat people, 2; cities settled, 5, 6t, 7; dual citizenship, 13, 15; electoral representation compared, 12–13; ethnic enclave, 8–9; history compared, 1;

movement of immigrants, 2; remittances compared, 10t, 11; self-perceptions, 16; surplus labor, 14; voting rights, 15
Drag, 88, 89, 91, 97n.1
Dreaming in Cuban (García), 179, 202
Dreams: bridge building and, 200–201; literature of exile, 201; nature of, 194
Dual citizenship, 13
Dual economy, 38–39n.4
Dub poets, 124
Duvalier, François, 134

Eastern Europe, 72, 151, 152
ECHO-Cuba, 54
Economic crisis: emigration and, 28, 29; religion and evangelism, 46; remittance policy, 37. *See also* Special Period in Time of Peace
Economic dependence on U.S., 17–18
Economic development, sugar elites, xv
Economic mobility, love/sex and, 63
Economic power, sex tourists, 72
Education: Che Guevara, 167–69; Cuban School in the Countryside program, 168; Protestants, 47
Eisenhower, Dwight, 26
Electoral representation compared, 12–13
Elegguá, 135
Elián González custody case, 42, 81
Emigration, clergy and laity, 47
Emigration policies. *See* State policy, Cuban; State policy, U.S.
Emigrés, musical links, 116
Employment: earnings vs. remittances, 31t; peso sector, 28
Encuentro de Jóvenes Escritores de los Países Socialistas, 151
Encuentro de la cultura cubana magazine, 152
End of the Cold War: confusion over art, 162–63; exiled writers, 153; for exiles, 192; religious restrictions, 49
Entry visas, 13
Equality: economic, 64–65; rap music, 132
Estado del tiempo (1994), 99–100n.17
Ethnic drag, 91
European Union, 42
Evangelism, 46, 49, 50; ECHO-Cuba, 54
Exceptionalism, Cuban: as burden, 2, 18; challenged, 3; isolation myth, xiii; migration, 1

Exchange booths (CADECAs), 28
Exiled Memories: A Cuban Childhood
(Medina), 185, 186–91
Exile identity, presumed origins, 84–85
Exiles: 1.5 generation, 191; as amputees,
195; as bugarrones, 85; compassion for
relatives, 29, 34–36; *cubanía*, 181–82; desire to taste the sugar, 189; Díaz as, 152–
53; dreams of return, 192–94, 195; first-
generation, 16, 183; Generación Ñ,
86–87; idealized memories, 189; identity
in exile, 184; international portrayal, 57;
links to Cuba, 29; marginalization of
queer *cubanidad*, 80; melancholia, 82; narratives of self-abnegation, 86; negative stereotypes, 16; New Year's toast, 193; popular attitudes in Cuba, 16; psychological
conflict, 191; rafter experience, 81; religious, 47–48; return of, 190–91, 192–94,
198–99, 200; second-generation, 16, 196,
197; (self-)analysis, xviii; as self-definition,
2. *See also* Cuban Americans; Locas al
Rescate

Family connections, 34; immediate vs. ex-
tended, 36f, 36–37, 38
Family reconciliation, 26–27
Farmers' markets, 28
Feeling, hegemony of, 83–84
Feeling, vocabulary of, 79
Feltrinelli, Giangiacomo, 166, 167
Female passivity, 73
Fiction, Cuban rafters in, 81
Fidel y la religión (1985), 48
Flamenco tradition, 114
Flamingo Park, 87
Foam parties, 90
Food rations, 28
Foreign policy, frameworks examined, 43–44
Foucault, Michel, 79, 97n.2, 176
Fowler, Julio, 117
Freedom, practices of, 79, 86, 89, 97n.2
Free market system, 154, 157; globalized Che
image, 171–73; liberation marketing, 172–
73; rationale, 155
French Caribbean, 105–6

Gangsta rap, 144
García, Cristina, 179, 202
Garvey, Marcus, 122

Gay sex tourism, 61–75
Generación de los topos, 116
Generación Ñ, 86–87
Ghost rafts, 93–96
Ghost stories, 83, 98n.9
Gift giving, 64–65
Gitano (gypsy) music, 114
Global market, literature, 154, 161–63; pro-
cesses, 44–45
Global musical culture, 106
God, 57
Gottschalk, Louis Moreau, 106
Great art, 153, 155
Great literature, 153; arbitrary critiques, 159–
60; freedom from contingency, 161; imag-
ining, 156; obstacles, 157–58; rhetoric and
politics of, 153–61; standards, 160
Grenada, 133
Guantánamo Bay, 28
Guapo figure, 144–45
Guaracha music, 135–36
Guevara, Ernesto "Che," as icon, 165; as
model, 175; moral incentives, 175, 177n.1;
moral sainthood, 167; personality cult,
166, 169. *See also* Che image
Güijes, 152, 159, 160, 162
Guillén, Nicolás, 123, 125–30, 147
Gusanos (worms), 15–16, 85, 98n.12
Gutiérrez, Bienvenido J., 135–36

Habana Abierta, 114, 115, 117
Habanera genre, 105, 106
Haiti: boat people, 2; militant Afrocentricity,
134; music, 105–6
Haiti bashing, 134
Hard currency income, 28
Hauntings, 83, 92–95; queer, 96
Havana, described, 188–89
Hearst, Patty, 170
Heidegger, Martin, 100n.18
Hendrix, Jimi, 144
Hermanos al Rescate, 79, 81, 99n.17
Hermanos de Causa, 134–39
Hip-hop music, 107, 110
Hip-Hop Unity Concert, 121
History, music history, 105
HIV, South Beach, 90
Household-level survey of migrants, 24–25,
39n.13
Hughes, Langston, 123

Humor, disarming, 89
Hybrid essentialism, 125
Hybridity, 199–200

Identification and Employment Bureau, 15
Identitarian projects, 88
Identity: Afro-Cubanist movement, 123;
   author's, 185–86; bicultural, 192; blackness and rights, 132; contemporary sense,
   184; as displaced geography, 86; essentialist view, 184; in exile, 184; as fluid, 184,
   200; new categories, xvi, xvii; redefining,
   200; righting past political slights, 82
Illegal immigrants, 28, 39n.5
Images of Cuba, isolation myth, xiii
Immigrants, Cuban: electoral representation
   compared, 12–13; occupations, 7–8, 9; re-
   lief and services for, 38n.2; second-generation, 182; three periods, 25–30; timing
   compared, 4, 5t; urban, 5, 6t, 7
Immigration: by migration period, 33–34, 34t;
   common denominators, 3; similarities with
   other groups, 2; timing compared, 4, 5t;
   volume of Hispanic Caribbean, 3–4, 4t
Income levels, 32t, 32
Influences on Cuban culture, overview, xiv
Informal sector: employment, 19n.10; income,
   31t, 31
Las Iniciales de la tierra (1997), 161
Instinto (group), 142–44
Intellectuals, ideological change, xviii
Interactivo (group), 118
Interdisciplinarity, xvi
Interés, relaciones de, 63–66, 72, 75
Internationalism in music, 108–9
International relations: framework bias, 43–
   44; nonstate actors, 43; state-centric, xiv,
   xvi; transnational relations vs., 45
Internet access, xiii, xiv
Internment camps, 92, 100n.21
Interviews, 25
Intrahistories, 83
Isolation, just vs. unjust policies, 42
Isolation myth, xiii; musical ties, 117; over-
   view, xvii; religious festivals, 51; religious
   ties, 42–43, 57

Jamaican dancehall music, 147n.1
Jamaican musicians, 124
Java (bag of toiletries), 39n.9

Jesus Christ, 173
Jewish Cubans, 196
Jiménez, José Manuel (Lico), 109
John Paul II (Pope), 30
La Jornada, 169–70

"Kirino con su tres" (Instinto), 142–44
Korda, Alberto, 166, 167, 169

Labor markets, 7–9
Lachatañere, Rómulo, 123
Lady of Charity. See Virgin of Caridad del
   Cobre
Lam, Wilfredo, 123
Larramendi, Boris, 117
Latin, use of, 159
Latin American Bishops' Conference
   (Medellín, Colombia), 48
Latin jazz, 123
Latin Tinge, 106
Lecuona, Ernesto, 109
Left wing: disarming, 89; public identities, 87
Legal status, 1; compared, 3–4, 12
Leica camera company, 169
Lezama Lima, José, 155
Liberation marketing, 172–73
Liberation theology, 6t
Literary genius, 153, 154, 155–56, 157
Literary ideology, 157
Literary values, 158
Literature: desire to be Cuban, 186; of exile,
   179, 185, 201; Puerto Rican, 99n.14; spirit,
   185; Third World, 161. See also Las
   palabras perdidas
Locas al Rescate, 79–96; Mar Tini, 88–90; so-
   cial praxis, 95; takeovers as parodies, 81
Lo cubano: bittersweet, 183; in diaspora, 17;
   transcending borders, 184
Loss, feeling of, 189
Love, 63
Luchar, 61, 64; defined, 75–76n.1

Machado, Gerardo, 122–23
Machismo, 65
Madonna, 170
Madrid, 114, 115, 117, 118. See also Spain
Mafia, 81
Malcolm X, 145
Malecón, 188, 189
Mañach, Jorge, 100n.18, 135

Mandela, Nelson, 144–45
Margen, borders, 199–200
Mariel boatlift: abject citizenship, 85–86; backlash, 27; community engagement, 95; disidentified, 84; gays, 85; Locas al Rescate, 79; Marielitos defined, 97n.3; public opinion, 16, 17; tentative transnationalism, 27
Martí, José, 123
Mass-market appeal (music), 117
Material incentives, 175
Materialist-historical dialectic, 156
Material values criticized, 138
Mécanica (swindle), 66–69, 74, 75n.4
Medicine sent to Cuba: by family members, 34; church support, 49; *paqueticos* program, 49–50
Medina, José Luis, 115–16, 117
Medina, Pablo, 185, 186–91
Menem, Carlos, 169
Menéndez, Paul, 118
Mestizaje, 130, 147
Methodists, 54–55
Mexican, state of being, 181
Mexico, 109
Miami: Caridad hermitage, 92; Catholic radio program, 49; collective dream, 193; displaced geographies of *cubanidad,* 86; economic success, 7–8; gay influx, 85; island priests and pastors, 50–51; as post-Communist city, 88; religious exiles, 47–48; as space of memory, 86
Migration: depoliticized, 29; exceptionalism, 1, 17; first period (1959–1979), 26–27, 33, 34t; home country context, 25; legal status, 1; links to home country, 24; literature, xiv–xv; longer patterns, 17–18; nation-state and, 24; overview, xvii; public discourses, 15–17; second period (1980–1989), 27–28; sexual, 100n.17; stereotypes, 16–17; third period (1990–present), 28–30; transnational perspective on, 45; young Cuban women, 62
Migration cohorts: amount of remittances, 35t; most recent compared, 1–2; relationships with relatives, 35f; religious motivation, 56
Migration Division of the Department of Labor, 15
Ministry of Culture, 125, 169
Ministry of Education, 175–76

Miscegenation, 125–26
Modernity, critiques of, 82–83, 98n.9
Montaner, Rita, 109
Morocco, 72
Moscow, 156
Moss, Kate, 172
Movimiento magazine, 125
Mulataje, 125–26, 147
Mulatta, sex tourism, 73
"La Muralla" (Guillén), 126–29
Music: as artistic contraband, 104; collaborations, 118; cultural appropriation, 146; *ida y vuelta,* 108; notated, 106; signifying in, 135, 143; social change and, xvii; transnational experience of, 109–19. *See also* Afro-Cuban music; *Individual musical genres*; Musicians; Rap music
Musical comedians, 108–9
Music history, 105, 106
Music making, as multicultural enterprise, 104
Musicians: exit visas, 116; expatriate, 117; relocated to other countries, 116–17; success abroad, 109
Music industry, 118
Musicologists, 104
Music publications, 107

Narratives of self-abnegation, 86
National identity: desire and, 183; national politics and, 183; Special Period, 168–69; transnational, 180
Nationalism, writers, 152
Nationality, 187, 188
Nation-state: deterritorialized, 24; migration and, 24; role of, 24; shifts in state policy, 37; transnational nation-state, 19n.3
Naturalization, 13
Neiman Marxistization of Che, 172
New cultural politics of difference, 131, 132, 134
New socialist man, 167–68, 173
New York, 118
Next Year in Cuba: A Cubano's Coming of Age (Pérez Firmat), 185, 191–95
"Nigga," use of term, 145
"No hace na' la mujer" (Gutiérrez), 136
Nonstate actors, international relations, 43
Normative maps, xv
Norm diffusion, xvi

North American music, 105
Nostalgia, 183–84, 186, 188, 190, 196
"Now!" (1965), 133
Nueva trova movement, 115, 116

Obesesión, 110, 121, 144
Ochoa, Kelvis, 110–14, 116, 117, 118
Ochún, 144
1.5 generation, 191
Online Che store, 172
Online music journals, 115
Open-door policy, 17
Operation Bootstrap, 14
O'Reilly Herrera, Andrea, 182–83
Organization in Solidarity with the Peoples of
    Africa, Asia and Latin America (OSPAAL),
    133
Orígenes literary group, 162
Orishas (group), 110, 117, 146
Ortega y Gassett, José, 100n.18
Ortiz, Fernando, 105, 108, 142, 180
Otherness, 62, 69, 73; identitarian slippage,
    85
Outmigration, 14

Paez, Fito, 115
Las Palabras perdidas (1992), 151;
    deconstructing, 157; on revolutionary expe-
    rience, 152; rhetoric and politics, 153–61
Panama, 28
Papiamento, 145
Paz, Octavio, 99n.13
Peñas, 114, 115, 116
Pentecostal congregations, 50
Pepito Pérez myth, 100–101n.22
Pérez Firmat, Gustavo, 179, 180, 181–82,
    185, 191–95
Permanent residency, 26
Personal experience, 83
Photographs, role of, 167
Pilgrimages, 52–53
Pingueros, 61, 63, 66, 69, 75n.1; strategies,
    71–72, 74
Pioneer student organization, 167, 173–75
Plantation, 188, 189–90
Political exiles: migrant cohort, 26; remit-
    tances, 33, 34; visits and remittances, 37
Political oppression, sexual personhood, 85
Political purposes, Catholic Church, 56
Political representation, 12–13

Postmodern approaches, xiv
Prenuptial agreements, 65
Prieto, Abel, 169
Primera Base, 144, 145
Productivity bonuses, 31
Progressive cultural politics, 153
Prostitution, 62, 63
Protestants, 47, 48–49, 50–51
Publishing, contingencies of, 161
Puerto Rico: cities settled, 5, 6t, 7; DJs, 124;
    electoral representation compared, 12–13;
    ethnic enclave, 8; history compared, 1; legal
    status, 3–4; migrant citizens, 15; movement
    of immigrants, 2; remittances compared,
    10t, 11; self-perceptions, 16; surplus labor,
    14; timing of immigration, 4; as
    transnational colonial state, 15; volume of
    immigration, 3–4
Puerto Rico Office of Information, 15
Purchasing power, 29

Queer, use of term, 97n.1
Queer haunting, 96
Queer spaces, 96
"¿Quién tiró la tiza?" (Molano MC), 139–40,
    148n.4
"Quirino con su tres" (Guillén), 140–42
"Quirino" (Guillén), 126

Race, redefining blackness, 146
Racial hierarchy, women tourists, 73
Racism: prostitution, 63; "¿Quién tiró la
    tiza?," 139–40; rap music, 132–35, 147;
    sex tourism, 73
Radical chic, 172
Rafter (*balsero*) experience, 81–82; abject citi-
    zenship, 85–86; community engagement,
    95; economic crisis and, 29; as emblematic,
    79; ghost rafts, 93–96; Locas al Rescate,
    79; repatriated Cubans, 2
Rap music, 107; Afro-Cuban roots, 124, 129–
    30; attire, 145; as countervailing voice,
    132; critique of Cuban society, 131; ele-
    ments adopted, 144; features unique to,
    144; festivals, 124–25; gangsta, 144;
    ghetto-centric, 139, 144; racism, 132–35;
    redefining process, 145–36; Rodríguez tax-
    onomy, 147–48n.1; situated knowledge,
    139; U.S. pioneers, 124; women in, 142,
    148n.5

Recubanization process, 179–80, 186, 197, 199, 201, 203
Recuerdos azucarados, 188–89
Regla de Ocha, 129, 130, 144, 146
Regla de Palo, 130
Relaciones de interés, 63–66, 72, 75
Religious faith, use of transnational as term, 45–46
Religious fervor, 46
Religious freedom/tolerance, 47, 49
Religious leadership, 48, 50, 56
Religious networks, overview, xvii
Religious opening, 29–30
Religious organizations, 43
Religious ties: analytical categories, 53; Catholic Church, 56; intentions and, 53, 55–56; isolation myth and, 42–43; overview, xvii; sister church relations, 54–55
Religious tourists, 46, 50–51
Religious visas, 50
ReMembering Cuba: Legacy of a Diaspora (O'Reilly Herrera), 86, 182–83
Remittances, 30–32; amount compared, 10t; by immediate vs. extended relatives, 36f, 36–37; by migration period, 33–34, 34t, 35t; compared, 9–12; context of, xvi; cost of, 11; early migrants, 33, 34t; economic crisis, 28, 65; household importance, 31t, 31; humanitarian concern for relatives, 29, 34–36; impact on household income, 31–32, 32t; importance, 32; increase, 30; overview, xvi; political exiles, 33, 34; political reasons not to send, 24; restrictions by U.S., 39n.7; social, xvi; uses for, 11, 12; visits and, 36
Research: *cubanidad* in the academy, 95; depoliticized, 87; theorizing compared, 87; tourism parallels in, 70
Resistance, hidden transcripts of, 134
Restaurants, 31
Reuniones para Conocerse Mejor, 51
Revolución magazine, 166
Revolutionary internationalism, 133
Revolution Soda, 170
Right wing: Cuban exiles, 81; disarming, 89
Rincón de San Lázaro (Cuba), 52
Rincón (Hialeah), 52
Rivero, Eliana, 199
Rock en español, 115
Rodríguez Feo, José, 162

The Roots, 121
Rueda de casino dancing, 108, 110
Ruíz Espadero, Nicolás, 108
Russia, 108
Russian cartoons, 113

Safe-sex education, 95
Safety valve, 2, 14
Salas, Esteban, 105
Salsa boom, 110, 115
Sargasso Sea, 94–95, 101n.23
Sartre, Jean Paul, 167
Saumell, Manuel, 106, 108
S.B.S. (Sensational Boys of the Street), 146
Secondary labor market, 8
Self, ethic of care of, 79, 97n.2
Self-construction, 195
Self-disclosure, 80
Self-employment, 19n.10; incidence, 19n.10; income, 31t, 31
Self-fragmentation, 194–95, 198, 200
Self-made entrepreneur, 7
Self-making, ethics of, 80
Service sector, 7
Settlement patterns compared, 4–5, 6t
Sex tourism: ambiguity, 70–71; anthropology and, 69–70; Asia, 62, 73; commercial aspects, 62–63, 75; cruising exchanges, 67–68; deception, 73–74; defined, 76n.2; differences, 72–73; liminal states, 72; long-term relationships, 67; relationships, 61
Sex tourists: ambiguity, 62–63; economic power, 72
Sexual migration, 100n.17
Sexual servants, 72–73
Sex workers, 61–62
Shakur, Assata, 134
Shapiro Rok, Ester Rebeca, 196, 197–98
Shared culture, 64–65
Sharing, 64
Siete (2003), 116
Siete Rayos (Nsasi), 129
Signifying, in music, 135, 143
Simons, Moisés, 109
"The Simpsons," 171
Singer-songwriters, 110, 114
Situated knowledge, 139
Slang expressions, 145
Slavery, 121, 122, 123, 124, 129
Social conscience, 190

Social and cultural messages, xvi
Social inequality, 19n.11
Socialist realism, 159
Socialist society, 167–68
Social praxis, 95
Social remittances, xvi
Social science methodologies, 82–83
Son, early ensembles, 105
"Son Número 6" (Guillén), 130
Soul, 202–3
South Beach: *cubanidad*, 84; gay influx, 85; HIV, 90; nightclubs, 86–87
Soviet Union, end of: Che's image, 167; Cuban state policy changes, 28
Spain: colonialism in Cuba, 46; exiles in, 151, 152; publishing houses, 161–62. *See also* Madrid
Spanish-Cuban American War, 4, 122
Spanish language, African and English words, 145
Special Period in Time of Peace: Afro-Cuban religious practices, 130; cultural transformation, 153; daily life, 16; impact on lower classes, 133; impact on relationships, 65; migration and remittances, 14; national identity, 168–69; rafters and, 99n.17; religious impact, 49. *See also* Economic crisis
Speech and silence, dilemma between, 156
Spiritual energy, 186
State-centric studies, xiv
State policy, Cuban: civil institutions, 44; conciliatory, 27–28; Cuban American policy, 13, 14; effect of, 25; emigration, 13–14, 18, 32, 37–38; Mariel immigration, 27; queers and *gusanos*, 85; remittances, 37; "social functions," 155
State policy, U.S.: isolation myth, xiii; Mariel immigration, 27; rafters, 99n.17; remittances, 30; stages of emigration policy, 17
Sugar: economic development, xv; plantations and privilege, 185, 186, 188–89
Surplus labor, 14

Tania, 170
Teatro vernáculo, 106
Television, rap groups on, 147n.1
Temporary residence abroad, 14
"Tengo" (Guillén), 126, 134–35
"Tengo" (Hermanos de Causa), 136–39
Ten Years' War, 4, 122

Thailand, 62
Third World literature, 161
Timba music, 108, 110
Tini, Mar, 88–91, 92, 95
Toast for New Year, 193
Tocororo (national bird), 136–37
Torrens, David, 118
Tourism: Afro-Cuban religions, 51; gay sex tourism, 61–75; income distribution, 65; parallels with researchers, 70; religious, 46, 50–51; South Beach, 84, 85; women tourists, 72, 73
Transculturation, 105, 108, 124
Transmigrants, 45
Transnational analytical framework, 44–46
Transnational communities, Hispanic Caribbean, 3–7
Transnationalism: agent and receiving, 15; as condition of social life, xv; defined, 165, 97n.1; global processes vs., 44–45; history of, xv; literature, xiv–xv; migration issues, 17–18; overuse of term, 44; role of nation-state, 24
Transnational migration, 45
Transnational nation-state, defined, 19n.3
Transnational relations, 45
Travel restrictions: eased, 30; entry visas, 13; musicians' visas, 116; religious visas, 50; reversed, 39n.6
Travel visas, for clergy, 50
TRD (tiendas recuperadoras de divisa), 38n.3
Trickster figures, 135
Tri-Continental Congress, 133
Two Cubas, 43

Unidades Militares de Ayuda a la Producción, 100n.21
Universal Negro Improvement Association (UNIA), 122–23
Urban settlement, 5, 6t, 7
Urkiza, Pavel, 118
Urrutia, Gustavo, 123
U.S.-Cuba Writers' Conference (Havana), 179, 202
U.S. occupation of Cuba, 47
U.S. Treasury Department, 30

Valdés, Paula, 141, 142, 143
Valdez, Mercedes, 142–44
Vanguards, literary, 156–57

Los Van Van, 117, 130
Varela, Carlos, 114, 115, 116
Vargas Llosa, Mario, 156
Venceremos slogan, 165
Victim-centered discourse, 62–63
Villa, Ignacio (Bola de Nieve), 109
Virgin of Caridad del Cobre, 51–52, 90, 91–93, 144
Visa lottery (*bombo*), 16, 56
Visits: annual rates, 30; circular migrants, 13; compared, 9; discouraged, 24; remittances and, 36
Voyeurs, 69

Wage levels, 28–29
Warsaw Ballroom, 90–91, 92
West, Cornell, 131
Wet foot–dry foot policy, 17, 18, 97–98n.8

Weyler, Valeriano, 100n.21
White, José, 109
Whitening, 125, 139, 147
White supremacy and philosophy, 146–47
Women rap artists, 142, 148n.5
Women tourists, 72, 73
Workers: industrial, 7, 8t; plantation, 189–90; service, 7; urban working class, 9; in U.S. labor markets, 7–9

Yearning, 85, 94, 96; second-generation, 183
Yoruba Cultural Center, 51
Yucas (young urban Cuban Americans), 84, 86
Yusa, 118

Zamora, Pedro, 98n.10
Zarzuela, 105, 106